Library of
Davidson College

Policy-Planning Organizations

Policy-Planning Organizations
Elite Agendas and America's Rightward Turn

JOSEPH G. PESCHEK

TEMPLE UNIVERSITY PRESS   Philadelphia

Temple University Press, Philadelphia 19122
Copyright © 1987 by Temple University. All rights reserved
Published 1987
Printed in the United States of America

The paper used in this publication meets the minimum requirements of American National Standard for Information Sciences—Permanence of Paper for Printed Library Materials, ANSI Z39.48-1984

Library of Congress Cataloging-in-Publication Data

Peschek, Joseph G.
  Policy-planning organizations.

  Bibliography: p.
  Includes index.
  1. Policy sciences—Research—United States.
2. Conservatism—United States. 3. United States—
Politics and government—1945–   I. Title.
H97.P47. 1987   324   86-23120
ISBN 0-87722-468-4 (alk. paper)

Contents

	Preface	vii
1	Policy-Planning Organizations and American Politics	1
	Perspectives on Policy-Planning Organizations	
	Corporate Liberalism and Elite Conflict	
	The Brookings Institution	
	The Trilateral Commission	
	The American Enterprise Institute	
	The Heritage Foundation	
	The Institute for Contemporary Studies	
2	America's Postwar Policy Regime	39
	International Aspects of U.S. Power	
	Domestic Foundations of Economic Growth	
	Impasse: The Political Context	
	Processes of Elite Mobilization	
3	International Economics, National Politics	69
	International Dimensions of the U.S. Economy	
	Origins of Trilateralism	
	Global Interdependence and Trilateral Managerialism	
	Monetary and Trade Issues	
	North-South Relations	
	Energy Policy	
	The World of the 1980s	
4	Foreign Policy: From Détente to Cold War	107
	Intra-elite Conflict and the Breakdown of Consensus	
	Détente, Interdependence, and American Foreign Policy	

CONTENTS

The Conservative Attack on Détente
Trilateral Managerialism in Crisis: The Carter Years
"From Weakness to Strength": AEI, ICS, and Heritage

5   Economic Stagnation and Domestic Policy Conflict   165
Turning Point: The 1970s
Keynesian Liberalism in Retreat: The Brookings Institution
Toward State Capitalism? The Trilateral Commission
The Free-Market Critique of Planning
"Free the Fortune 500!": The American Enterprise Institute
Toward Reaganomics: ICS and Heritage Foundation
Conflict in the 1980s

6   Politics, Ideology, and the Erosion of Liberalism   203
Social and Political Sources of Crisis
Huntington: The Democratic Distemper
Technocratic Liberalism
Systemic and Social Crisis
The Public Philosophy of the AEI
A Conservative Agenda for the 1980s
Democracy and the Limits of Policy-Planning

Notes   243

Index   281

Preface

THIS BOOK ANALYZES the rightward turn in American politics during the last decade by exploring how leading policy-planning organizations help to reshape policy agendas in a period of broad political and economic change. The activity of policy organizations is set in the context of a declining postwar political economy and an extensive political mobilization of elites that emerged in response to that decline in the 1970s. Five important policy groups provide a focus for understanding elite policy debates: the American Enterprise Institute, the Brookings Institution, the Heritage Foundation, the Institute for Contemporary Studies, and the Trilateral Commission.

Early chapters give basic information on the five organizations, set forth an argument about their role in the policy-formation process, and detail the breakdown of the institutional arrangements, ideologies, and policies that had guided the postwar political economy. With this background, I proceed to analyze evolving perspectives and policy debates in the substantive areas of the international economy, foreign policy and national security, domestic economics, and political institutions and democratic practices. Throughout the book the analysis of policy-planners is related to real-world developments from the early 1970s through the mid-1980s.

I began this project while a graduate student at the University of Massachusetts in Amherst, where the advice and support of Kenneth M. Dolbeare, Gerard Braunthal, and Dan Clawson were most important. They have continued to be helpful to me. The comments of Michael Schwartz and an anonymous reviewer were detailed beyond the call of duty and have resulted in a number of improvements. Of course I alone am responsible for what is written in this book. Michael Ames and the staff of Temple University Press have been encouraging and patient, for which I am grateful. Finally, I would like to thank my parents, Walter and Magdalin Peschek, and my sister, Mary Collier, for their assistance and support.

1

Policy-Planning Organizations and American Politics

IN THE EARLY 1970S a series of domestic and international developments unsettled the U.S. political economy, calling into question the durability of the "American Century" that had seemed so possible after World War II. During 1973 there were a number of indications that a turning point in the postwar era had been reached. A peace agreement to end U.S. involvement in Vietnam was signed, and a debate over détente and America's post-Vietnam military posture began to take shape. A set of international monetary jolts early in the year led to the second devaluation of the dollar in fourteen months. The problem of reducing inflation without creating massive unemployment proved stubbornly intractable. The long-impending energy crisis hit home, exacerbated by the October war in the Middle East. Furthermore, the Watergate affair created a political crisis for the Nixon administration and pointed to the loss of governability and authority that would be much discussed in the mid-1970s by neoconservative intellectuals.

There has been no waning of challenges to the American system in the years since. As this troubling trajectory of crises moved through the 1970s and into the 1980s, political struggles around locating the causes of problems and defining the appropriate policy options took shape. At stake was the future direction of American politics and its impact on the global position of the United States, the health of the domestic economy, and the distribution of burdens and benefits flowing from policy choices. At the level of American elites, the economic–political conjuncture of the 1970s and 1980s gave rise to widespread political mobilization, helping to effect a rightward shift that was most visibly manifest in the two presidential election victories of Ronald Reagan. While the politicization of business leaders and other elite actors was expressed through a variety of agencies and strategies, an important role was played by an expanding network of public policy institutions.

This book explores neglected terrain within American politics. It examines private policy-planning organizations not only as objective producers of research and recommendations, but also as active agents linked to power blocs and policy currents, reflecting and in turn shaping ideological shifts and political regroupings in a time of momentous economic transformations.

After looking at the relationship between an elite policy network and the policymaking process, we shall focus on five policy-planning organizations that have been particularly important in recent years: the American Enterprise Institute, the Brookings Institution, the Heritage Foundation, the Institute for Contemporary Studies, and the Trilateral Commission. All five groups either began or significantly expanded their operations in the convulsive early 1970s. In that period the conservative American Enterprise Institute was beginning its rapid growth and expansion of influence, while the long established moderates at the Brookings Institution were bringing out important new studies on international economic issues and foreign policy. In 1973 a conservative group called the Heritage

Foundation established itself in Washington, D.C., a year after a counterpart on the right, the Institute for Contemporary Studies, was launched in San Francisco. The year 1973 was also the inaugural year of the Trilateral Commission, which was to some degree the vanguard elite policy organization of the mid-1970s.

Encompassing sometimes conflicting views on a broad array of issues, these groups are representative of elite positions that range from moderate liberalism to New Right conservatism, as they evolved and vied for influence over the last fifteen years. As such, they are a lens through which we can follow the working out of ideology and policy by social groups contending for dominance in a critical period of political change. But policy-planning organizations do not merely reflect already existing elite positions. They are sites where consensus is forged, orientations are clarified, and proposals for action are prepared and publicized. My account of the policy network will be a dynamic one, analyzing changes in both the institutional structure and the ideological underpinnings of the policy-planning process in light of pressing economic and political conditions. For that reason, Chapter 2 gives a broad overview of the U.S. political economy since World War II, highlighting the economic and political terrain on which policy-planners work. This interplay among the recasting of policy institutions, the forging of political ideology and analysis, and the currents of contemporary history will be a theme throughout the book.

This book is a systematic analysis of the efforts of leading policy-planning organizations to analyze and propose solutions to the crisis of the American political economy, on both domestic and international levels, from 1973 through the mid-1980s. After the context-setting of Chapter 2, four substantive chapters examine the analysis and recommendations of these policy-planners, and their close allies and co-thinkers, on critical areas of policy: international economics, foreign policy, the domestic economy, and political institutions, processes, and ideology. Postwar developments in these four spheres were important constitutive elements of the American social order. The argument here is that by the early 1970s these political and economic arrangements and institutions were subject to increasing pressures. The strains intensified throughout the 1970s and persisted in the 1980s, despite the efforts of the Reagan administration to revitalize the economic system and global position of the United States. These developments pose the problems and dilemmas with which key policy-planning organizations grappled in the period under review. The analysis in this book is based on a scrutiny of the publications of these organizations that best represent their understanding of the problems manifest from 1973 through the mid-eighties, of the sources of these problems in the breakdown of the post-1945 liberal capitalist order, and the changes in basic priorities and policies necessary to stabilize the political economy.

While the five organizations I focus on are undeniably important, they are not necessarily uniquely influential or the key players in the policy process on all major issues. Rather, they are representative of a larger elite policy network that includes many policy organizations and other actors striving for similar ends. On economic issues there are several key business groups, such as the Committee for Economic Development, the Conference Board, the Business Council, and the Business Roundtable. The foreign-policy debate is shaped by the pivotal Council on Foreign Relations and a number of other groups that will be noted in Chapter 4. These institutions sometimes interlock with one another and with the five policy groups under study. There is no "conspiracy" at work. We are simply looking at the institutionalized efforts of dominant and aspiring elites to shape policy and buttress a social order subject to multiple counterpressures. Because the focus will be on elite policy actors, organizations such as the Institute for Policy Studies that offer radical alternatives to the higher circles of the center and the right will not be discussed.

The American Enterprise Institute (AEI), the Brookings Institution, the Heritage Foundation, the Institute for Contemporary Studies (ICS), and the Trilateral Commission all address a wide range of domestic and international issues from a standpoint of professed objectivity and nonpartisanship (though the Heritage Foundation is strident in its conservatism), but all have extensive ties to corporate and financial funding and other sources of power. I have selected five groups that often reveal a center–right fissure on major issues, because I see discord among the elites as an essential political fact of the period under review. These disagreements are related to opinion groupings among business and political elites and to broader political coalitions that have historical moorings in past conflicts. But the divisions among policy-planning organizations cannot be tidily mapped to discrete economic sectors or class fractions.

The political role of policy-planning organizations is finally receiving some attention. By 1981, commentators were noting the influence of a number of policy-research institutions on Ronald Reagan's transition team and executive-level appointments. Consistently cited as likely to have an impact on Reagan's policies were the American Enterprise Institute, the Heritage Foundation, the Hoover Institution, the Institute for

Contemporary Studies, and the Center for Strategic and International Studies in Washington, D.C.[1] Many high-level members of the new administration, including the President himself, were affiliated with one or more of these organizations, as well as with the hawkish Committee on the Present Danger.[2] While estimates of political influence are somewhat subjective, it is worth citing the Reagan White House official quoted by journalist Gregg Easterbrook: "Without AEI, Reagan would never have been elected. AEI made conservatism intellectually respectable."[3]

For those whose political attention span reaches a few years back, the influence of policy-planning organizations on a new administration that was promising a break with the past was not unfamiliar. After the 1976 election, the potent presence of the Brookings Institution, the Trilateral Commission, and foreign-policy advisers from the Carnegie Endowment's journal *Foreign Policy* was noted as President Jimmy Carter put together his government.[4] In neither Reagan's nor Carter's case did these observations give rise to much analysis of the significance of these institutional ties. Although journalists are writing about policy-planning organizations more frequently, there has been a paucity of careful examination of the range of ideas produced with practical intent by the research institutions. This book is meant to help fill the gap on the subject.

In this chapter a framework of analysis is developed in three steps: First, by relating policy-planning organizations to social and economic power in the United States and outlining their political function; second, by tracing the origins and history of these institutions to the changing nature of the modern political economy, focusing on the relationship between capitalism and the state; third, by accounting for the differences in political and ideological orientation among policy-planners through the concept of "policy currents" that help mediate class interests and state policy. Finally, basic information about the history, structure, and activities of the American Enterprise Institute, the Brookings Institution, the Heritage Foundation, the Institute for Contemporary Studies, and the Trilateral Commission is presented.

Perspectives on Policy-Planning Organizations

Within the discipline of political science, respect for the research conducted by "think tanks" is acknowledged, of course, but there has been little actual study of these organizations as actors whose work has significance within the larger political system. One of the few political scientists who has studied the structure and functioning of policy-planning organizations, Thomas Dye, reports that many of his colleagues did not think his research was an appropriate concern of political science.[5]

The acceptance of a split between "private" and "public" uses of power may help to account for this dismissive attitude. Political scientists who examine policy only as the outcome either of intergovernmental processes or of overt interest group pressure from outside the government will miss the significance of policy-planning groups in the political process, for it is at the more subtle levels of identifying and defining problems, shaping public understanding of issues, and constructing a political agenda that their impact is felt.[6]

In the popular accounts we do have, policy-planning organizations are often depicted as public-spirited institutions, innocent of political aims despite revelation of a few blemishes. Such is the case with Leonard and Mark Silk's *The American Establishment*, which discusses Harvard University, the *New York Times*, the Ford Foundation, the Brookings Institution, the Council on Foreign Relations, and the Committee for Economic Development, with briefer sections on the Trilateral Commission and the American Enterprise Institute.[7]

According to the Silks, the modern American Establishment, which includes policy-planning organizations as a central component, represents a "Third Force" that is connected to but distinct from business and government. Simply put, "Where the aim of business is profit, and the aim of politics is power, the aim of the Establishment is disinterest and public morality, which is why, in our conception, it so resembles a state church."[8] Although the Silks worry about the occasional deflection of the Establishment from its dedication to truth, liberty, and the public interest, they see the Third Force as a necessary ingredient in our national life—and one that has performed rather well. Their view accords with David Rockefeller's simple description of the Trilateral Commission as "a group of concerned citizens interested in fostering greater understanding and cooperation among international allies."[9]

A more probing concept of the American Establishment is developed by Philip Burch, who defines it as "the institutionalized leadership structure of the country outside the government." According to Burch, "this key complex has clearly been dominated by many, but not all, of the nation's top economic interests" and is organizationally centered in such groups as the Business Council, the Committee for Economic Development, the Council on Foreign Relations, and, since the early 1970s, the Business Roundtable and the Trilateral Commission. These groups have close ties with one another and play a key role in the national policymaking process.[10] They do so not by pursuing the immediate profit potential of individual enterprises, but by defining the systemic interests of business in contexts where compromise and long-term planning may be called for.

Elaborating on this position, we could argue that the conditions of existence of modern capitalism are not secured by economic processes alone, that the reproduction of capitalist social relations also involves political, social, and cultural organization, which helps create conditions within which growth and profits are realized and potentially disruptive social conflicts are managed. Not simply capitalist transmitters, the institutions described by the Silks develop the ideology and long-range plans that convert problems of the political economy into manageable objects of public policy. In this way these groups help maintain a general set of economic and social arrangements, inside of which class relationships form a core. From this perspective, we can look at the professionals and intellectuals who staff and write for independent policy-planning organizations as engaged in production of policy, ideology, and plans that "transcends particularistic private sector or bureaucratic interests," as Irvine Alpert and Ann Markusen point out.[11]

The political role of policy-planning organizations has been further detailed and clarified by conservative political scientist Thomas Dye and by G. William Domhoff, a radical sociologist.[12] Dye and Domhoff make two important moves in analyzing policy-planning groups. They examine such groups in relation to the major sources of economic and social power in the United States, and they develop a general model of their role in the policymaking process.

For Dye, all societies are governed by elites, and democracy is a "romantic fiction."[13] His concern is to identify the members of America's elite and to show how they perpetuate their rule. The elite, argues Dye, are those who occupy the leadership positions in key economic, social, and political institutions, such as corporations, banks, investment houses, law firms, the mass media, foundations, the military, and the three branches of government. Using criteria of institutional importance, Dye identifies 7,314 elite positions and looks into the social backgrounds of the people who hold them. His findings confirm studies showing that top institutional leaders are atypical Americans in that they are recruited from "the well-educated, prestigiously employed, older, affluent, urban, white, Anglo-Saxon, upper- and upper-middle-class male populations of the nation."[14] While there is some upward social mobility into elite circles, those who rise come largely from middle- or upper-middle-class families. Very few children of working-class families move up into the leadership of key institutions.

In addressing the question of how institutional leaders make public policy, Dye develops an oligarchical model of national policymaking that links private corporate and financial power to public decisionmaking.[15] His model shows corporate and personal wealth providing seed money to foundations, universities, and policy-planning groups to conduct research, study, planning, and formulation of national policy. In the process, policy consensus on key issues is built and channeled to the media, to certain government advisory committees, and eventually to the government itself for adoption and implementation. The institutions involved at every stage in the process are governed by corporate leaders and the wealthiest. For our purposes, Dye's main conclusion is that "policy-planning groups are the central coordinating points in the entire policy-making process."[16] He identifies the key groups that generate "action recommendations" on a wide range of policy issues as the Council on Foreign Relations, the Committee for Economic Development, the Brookings Institution, and, more recently, the Business Roundtable.

Most pluralist political science, such as the early work of Charles Lindblom, looks only at the "proximate policy makers": the President, Congress, federal agencies, congressional committees, White House staff, and interest groups. But for Dye these people and groups are involved only with the means, rather than the ends, of public policy—the "details of implementation." His point is that "the agenda for policy consideration has been set by other elites before the 'proximate policy makers' become involved in the policy-making process."[17] The most important agenda-shapers are the policy-planning groups.

Domhoff's approach is similar. He and Dye use the same formal diagram of the policy network, which Domhoff first developed in 1970. Having located a social and economic upper class that is highly class-conscious, Domhoff shows how it dominates the United States politically through four general processes: the special-interest process, the policy-formation process, the candidate-selection process, and the ideology-shaping process. The policy-formation process is "the means by which general policies of interest to the ruling class as a whole are developed and implemented."[18] At the center of this process are policy-planning groups, which Domhoff calls "consensus-seeking organizations of the power elite" and "training grounds in which new leaders for government service are informally selected."[19] His "Big Four" of the policy network consists of the Council on Foreign Relations, the Committee for Economic Development, the Conference Board, and the Business Council, aided by other satellites and think tanks, notably the Brookings Institution.

In his account of the policy-formation process, Domhoff traces the history of the most important research organizations, explaining how they shaped policy directions in the past. Drawing on the scholarship of James Weinstein and David Eakins, he argues that the National Civic Federation (NCF) was the forerunner of today's policy-planning organization, as well as the source of much of the most important social and economic legislation implemented between 1900 and 1918.[20] The NCF was a prototype of the Council on Foreign Relations, the Brookings Institution, the Trilateral Commission, and similar groups in at least two ways. First, its basic directions were set by leaders of big business and bankers, together with allied educators, social scientists, lawyers, politicians, and a few coopted labor leaders. Second, its basic goals were to rationalize the economy through state action in accord with corporate and banking interests and to channel class conflict into manageable grievances—away from radicalism and socialism.

In another important study, Laurence H. Shoup and William Minter detailed the influence that the Council on Foreign Relations (CFR) has had on U.S. foreign policy for over half a century.[21] Formed after World War I, with strong support from New York–based financial interests, the CFR came into its own as a political force during World War II, when its War and Peace Studies Project, working with the State Department, prepared plans for such postwar institutions as the International

Monetary Fund, the World Bank, and the United Nations. After the war, the CFR continued to be a source of both policy proposals and appointees to top U.S. foreign-policy positions.

With regard to domestic economic policy, historians such as David Eakins, Robert Collins, and Kim McQuaid investigated the significant impact of the Business (Advisory) Council, the Committee for Economic Development (CED), and the Business Roundtable since the 1930s.[22] The corporate executives of the CED, for example, were crucial in redirecting the Employment Act of 1946 to probusiness aims. More recently, the Business Roundtable, representing the leadership of two hundred large corporations, helped to defeat prolabor legislation, while bending tax and regulatory policies toward corporate interests. In short, there is a great deal of evidence that major policy organizations, directly or indirectly tied to corporate financial interests, have helped to translate broad class concerns into state policy in twentieth-century America.

Corporate Liberalism and Elite Conflict

Underlying the scholarship of Weinstein, Eakins, and others that Domhoff draws on is what has come to be known as the "corporate liberal" interpretation of U.S. history. In this view, more sophisticated corporate leaders and their allies came to believe that the reform of capitalism, and its relationship to government, was necessary after 1900. Marking a change from the laissez-faire liberalism of the nineteenth century, liberal reform now aimed at stabilizing the business system through a more active state, so that profits could be made on a predictable basis by the major corporations. Moderate social policies were sponsored to blunt the impact of middle-class progressive and radical socialist movements. An ideology of social responsibility stressed the mutual interest of all groups and sectors in a soundly functioning liberal capitalist order no longer ridden by class antagonism.

According to this reading, policy-planning organizations, which made their first appearance in the Progressive Era, were instruments of corporate liberal reform. While maintaining an ideological facade of technical objectivity, they provided the research and expertise on which to base a rationalizing policy. In fact, they tacitly accepted the ends of corporate capitalism and functioned to head off radical reform, while facilitating systemic adjustments to emerging problems. Under the mantle of a transformed liberalism, the corporate capitalist class restructured both institutions and ideology so as to secure their dominance in an increasingly politicized economy. Among the corporate liberal policy organizations formed between 1916 and 1950 were the National Industrial Conference Board, the National Bureau of Economic Research, the Brookings Institution, the Twentieth Century Fund, the National Planning Association, the Committee for Economic Development, and the American Assembly.[23]

The theory of corporate liberalism grants central importance to the relationship between classes and the state, as does Marxian political theory. Most contemporary Marxist work on the state is much more sophisticated than the crude version mentioned by Leonard and Mark Silk, in which "big business *is* the American Establishment."[24] Following Antonio Gramsci, many Marxists see class rule as a complex process in which economic, political, cultural, and juridical actors and institutions are welded into a hegemonic bloc for specific historical periods. Intellectuals and professionals help establish and maintain the ideological leadership of the ruling bloc by representing its ideas as in the general interest of society. But hegemony is never absolute in the Gramscian conception. Counterpressures potentially disruptive of class rule are always present, along with elements of opposing blocs, and systemic contradictions can never be fully controlled by the ruling class. Though not Marxist, the work of Dye and Domhoff helps explain how class power is translated into political rule through the mediating role of corporate liberal policy-planning organizations.

While the theory of corporate liberalism is useful in challenging mainstream views of liberal reform and the role of policy-research groups, it has been criticized for overstating the capacity of enlightened capitalists to reform the system in their own interests during periods of crisis. If all policies and social institutions are seen as functional to the process of capital accumulation because they have been constructed by a cohesive capitalist class, argues Fred Block, we lose the ability to explain actual historical outcomes.[25] Theda Skocpol contends that the corporate liberal theory is unable to account for the actual process of New Deal policy and that it seriously underplays the specific weight and autonomy of state institutions and political parties in structuring the outcomes of class conflict and political struggle.[26] While corporate liberals may attempt to gain support for system-rationalizing policies, there is no guarantee that their designs will be implemented. Some adherents of corporate liberalism theory expected vanguard capitalists to install a form of national economic planning in the

1970s, yet policy has gone in the opposite direction, emphasizing markets and privatization.

In a spirited reply to criticism of the corporate liberalism framework, Domhoff denies that the theory is "functionalist," in the sense of granting reform capitalists the power to override social contradictions and co-opt protest so as to achieve systemic equilibrium. Furthermore, expansion of the state, according to Domhoff, is likely only in periods of massive pressure from below, such as the 1930s and 1960s. In less turbulent times, the reform thrust abates as routines are reestablished under the auspices of more conservative capitalists and their political supporters. The corporate liberals represent only one social grouping attempting to influence public policy.[27]

These differences among corporate elites parallel divergent political outlooks among policy-planning groups. In the context of a general drift to the right, rivalry between centrist and conservative positions among policy-planners renewed in intensity and importance in the 1970s, and that rivalry is a major theme of this book. Leading policy organizations do not display an ideological consensus on the major issues. While there is not serious opposition on every issue, there are significant rifts that find expression in contending policy-planning organizations, with no contemporary National Civic Federation around to exercise firm leadership in crisis management.

There are many theories of ruling-class divisions, some of which are discussed by Dye and Domhoff. Two frameworks should be helpful in interpreting the discord among policy-planners. The first of these is Michael Klare's analysis of an elite-level conflict between "Traders" and "Prussians" over foreign policy.[28] The "Traders" are aligned with multinational capital and see the major threat to U.S. hegemony as divisions within the capitalist world and economic nationalism in the Third World. The Traders advocate greater collaboration among the advanced capitalist powers, concessions on North–South trade, and the pursuit of détente with the Soviet Union. They are closely associated with the Trilateral Commission and the Atlanticist wing of the foreign-policy establishment.

Standing in opposition and gaining strength are the "Prussians," a bloc of military officers, intelligence operatives, Cold War intellectuals, arms producers, and some domestic capitalists. They see Third World turmoil and the growing assertiveness of the Soviet Union as the main challenges to U.S. hegemony, and they advocate a strong military buildup of conventional and nuclear forces. Their organization is the Committee on the Present Danger.

Klare notes that these groupings are not sociologically precise and that many political leaders drift between the two poles.[29] His thesis does provide a useful, nonreductionistic way of understanding conflicting political tendencies. It is similar to the second framework for interpreting the disagreements among policy-planners: Paul Joseph's notion of "policy currents."[30]

Joseph defines policy currents as "alternative conceptions, found among the capitalist class, state managers, and other defenders of the capitalist order, for exercising U.S. power within the limits imposed by different oppositional forces."[31] Power can be economic, political, or military in nature. The policy currents reflect different strategies for achieving the common aim of maintaining capitalist relations at home and asserting U.S. power while opposing socialism abroad. Not simply an emanation of economic interests, a policy current articulates common positions that can be found among the capitalist class, leading state officials, journalists, academics, and personnel of important foundations and think tanks.[32] Policy currents, Joseph argues, express long-standing political tendencies within the ruling coalition that derive from the challenge of oppositional forces and the history of different types of policy responses to problems. Joseph uses this approach to develop an original analysis of the politics of the Vietnam War.

We shall be looking at the extent to which the five organizations that are the focus of this book can be placed in distinct policy currents. My hypothesis is that there are discernible center and rightist strategies on a range of policy issues, though on some matters there is considerable agreement. The spectrum of positions I will examine does not exhaust the realm of alternative policy choices, but we can approach the work of the following five policy-planning organizations as an entry point into the struggle to define the future of American politics.

The Brookings Institution

The Brookings Institution, whose origins lie within the emerging corporate liberalism and elite reform thrust of the Progressive Era, is the oldest of the five organizations. It was founded in 1927 through a merger of three groups organized by a Saint Louis businessman, Robert S. Brookings. Combining a devotion to national service with his belief in a rationalized economy, Brookings became a consultant to the Commission on Economy and Efficiency upon President William Howard

Taft's request and later served on the War Industries Board, where he became chairman of the Price Fixing Committee. Previously he had been one of the original trustees of the Carnegie Endowment for International Peace.[33]

In 1916 Robert Brookings helped establish the Institute for Government Research (IGR) to promote efficiency in government organization and administration. In the early years, the board of trustees included prominent business leaders, bankers, educators, and political figures, such as Herbert Hoover, Felix Frankfurter, Elihu Root, Mrs. E. H. Harriman, and Charles W. Eliot of Harvard. The presence of Rockefeller Foundation men and money in the young IGR led to suspicions that it was a Rockefeller front-group. Brookings himself, at the age of seventy, embarked on a two-month fund-raising tour in 1920 that raised $324,550 for the IGR from ninety-two corporations and twelve individuals. The major accomplishment of the institute during this period was devising a proposal for an integrated federal budget that was passed by Congress in 1921 as the Budget and Accounting Act, creating the Bureau of the Budget and granting the executive branch more control over government finances.

In 1922, with a long-term grant from the Carnegie Corporation, Brookings set up the Institute of Economics to do for economic policy what the Institute for Government Research had been doing for public administration. Under the leadership of Harold G. Moulton, a University of Chicago economist, the new institute conducted research in the areas of international economic reconstruction, international commercial policies, agriculture, and labor and industry. Its staff frequently consulted with congressional and executive officials, as well as with private industry. The studies of international economics received close attention from the Dawes Committee, then considering the problem of postwar German reparations.

The third group was the Robert Brookings Graduate School of Economics and Government, incorporated in the District of Columbia in 1924. Intended as a training school in public service for graduate students, this third Brookings venture was short-lived. It merged with the IGR and the Institute of Economics in 1927 to form the Brookings Institution, as it is called to this day.

Robert Brookings, who died in 1932, was a typical Progressive Era corporate reformer. He accepted a positive state acting to smooth out the business cycle while instituting reforms to abate class conflict and incorporate workers into the capitalist system. At times he described his set of ideas as economic democracy, a "third way" between laissez-faire capitalism and socialism or communism. Leonard and Mark Silk capture this dimension of his ideology neatly: "Brookings was troubled by the power exercised by great corporations over workers, and believed the situation would be improved by making every man a species of capitalist, through profit-sharing, and by including labor representatives on boards of directors."[34]

It is somewhat surprising, then, that the Brookings Institution was not initially supportive of Franklin D. Roosevelt's New Deal, even though Roosevelt requested assistance from the Institution in preparing his first economic program in 1933. As Franklin Roosevelt abandoned his balanced-budget campaign rhetoric, opposition developed from Harold Moulton, the Brookings Institution's first president and a man considerably more conservative than Robert Brookings. As World War II approached, the strains began to ease. Moulton was appointed to the War Resources Board in 1939, and around the same time a number of prominent New Deal supporters were added to the Brookings board of trustees. By the early 1950s the Brookings Institution was liberal enough to be the target of several inconsequential McCarthyite attacks. In truth, the Brookings alliance of business and professionals espousing free trade and administered reform represented the dominant ideas of the post-1945 American political economy.

In the 1950s and 1960s the Brookings Institution consolidated its position as the leading private research group on domestic policy. Robert Calkins replaced Moulton as president in 1952 and moved Brookings away from its image as "a sanctuary for conservatives and a spokesman for major industry groups."[35] Calkins expanded the staff, created new research projects on government finance, and solidified the Institution's own finances by obtaining $14 million from the Ford Foundation. These trends were continued by Calkins' successor, Kermit Gordon, who was president from 1967 until his death in 1976. Gordon's credentials included a stint with the Ford Foundation, membership on John F. Kennedy's Council of Economic Advisers, and service as Lyndon Johnson's budget director. Gordon recruited academic luminaries like Arthur Okun, Henry Owen, George Perry, Gilbert Steiner, and Doak Barnett, set in motion the annual *Setting National Priorities* budget review, began a defense analysis project in 1969, and in general made the Brookings Institution a Democratic government-in-exile during the Nixon–Ford years.

In 1976 Republican Bruce MacLaury became president of the Brookings Institution. An economist and banker with experience in the Federal Reserve System, the Treasury Department, and the Organization for Economic Cooperation and Development, MacLaury is also a member of the Council on Foreign

Relations and the executive committee of the Trilateral Commission. The same sort of elite connections are evident with the last two chairmen of the Brookings board of trustees—Douglas Dillon and Robert Roosa. Roosa, who also worked in the Treasury Department and the Federal Reserve System, is a director of several top corporations, a partner in the private banking firm of Brown Brothers Harriman and Co., and a member of the Council on Foreign Relations and the Trilateral Commission. Most Brookings Institution trustees are experienced in business, government, academia, and the private policy groups that bring them together.[36] Many of Brookings' fifty senior fellows and research associates have found positions in both Democratic and Republican administrations. For example, Charles Schultze and Henry Owen served as chairman of the Council of Economic Advisers and as coordinator of the U.S. team at the economic summits, respectively, under President Jimmy Carter. Other Brookings leaders have advised Walter Mondale on economic issues.

The Brookings Institution has a reputation for high-quality research in economics, social policy, and national defense issues. Its outlook has been marked by a confidence in the use of social-science techniques to improve public policy. Its budget of over $10 million annually enables the Institution to maintain a large staff, publish many studies, and engage in a good deal of testimony at Capitol Hill hearings. As its leaders' institutional affiliations suggest, the Brookings Institution has been associated with the liberal internationalist wing of the American ruling class. But the conservative challenges of the 1970s are reflected in recent Brookings activity. New concern with such issues as monetary policy, capital formation, deregulation, and Soviet policy is perhaps a reaction to changes in the political agenda brought about by the right. With the impact of the economic crisis on the mainstream of liberal democratic capitalist thought, a once-confident Brookings liberalism has been in retreat.

The Trilateral Commission

Of the five policy-planning organizations under consideration, perhaps the Trilateral Commission has received the most commentary. In the 1980 campaign, the Trilateral ties of Jimmy Carter, George Bush, and John Anderson came under attack from some of Ronald Reagan's supporters, and the seminal role of David Rockefeller has often been noted. While such personal connections are important, they take on greater significance when understood in the context of the Trilateral Commission's overriding project: management of a global political economy undergoing multiple and deepening crises. Because the developments that gave rise to the Trilateralist thrust are analyzed in some detail in Chapter 3, only the salient facts about the Commission's first decade of activity will be noted here.[37]

The Trilateral Commission is a private policy-discussion group of around three hundred influential citizens from the advanced capitalist world of Western Europe, Japan, and North America. The largest numbers of members are from business and banking, with others drawn from government, academia, the media, and labor. Within the corporate section, the represented firms tend to be internationally oriented rather than domestically enclosed, while many of the world's largest banks, with global operations, have directors who are Trilateral Commission members. Among the U.S. corporations that have been represented are Bechtel, Boeing, Cargill, Coca Cola, Deere, Ford, General Electric, Hewlett-Packard, Texas Instruments, and Weyerhauser. In addition, the Commission has had strong ties to leading organs of opinion formation: major newspapers and magazines, corporate law firms, and internationalist research groups and foundations. The American politicians and academics selected for membership were consistently "technically-oriented systems thinkers intelligently responsive to research and recommendation in a global framework."[38] With several labor leaders included, the Commission encompasses all the main elements of the postwar ruling coalition, regrouped and concentrated to tackle the threatened disintegration of the system they presided over.

The formal founding of the Trilateral Commission came in 1973, following more than a year of organizing efforts by David Rockefeller, Zbigniew Brzezinski, and other corporate, political, and academic leaders affiliated with the Brookings Institution and the Council on Foreign Relations (which Rockefeller also chaired).[39] Speaking at such gatherings of the elite as the European Bilderberg meeting, Rockefeller floated the idea of a new international policy organization with important pacesetters in the Trilateral regions. Initial funding came from Rockefeller interests, but money soon flowed in from interested individuals, corporations, and foundations. A membership was assembled, by invitation only, and the Trilateral Commission came to life in mid-1973 with Brzezinski as its director and "major intellectual dynamo," as a Commission brochure put it.

According to the Trilateral Commission, the early 1970s were "a time of considerable discord among the United States and its democratic industrialized allies in Western Europe and Japan."[40] The U.S. economy was declining relative to those of its allies, the international monetary system was in disarray, and the incipient energy crisis was looming on the horizon. Moreover, the existing political institutions seemed inadequate, as governments lost the support of their citizens, and leaders retreated into narrow, self-serving policies. From a Trilateralist perspective, the most grave instance of political shortsightedness was the Nixon administration's nationalistic, bullying approach to the international economic crisis of 1971. By his unilateral import surcharges and suspension of the convertibility of gold into dollars, Nixon seemed to threaten the international cooperation that had promoted free trade and economic liberalization in the previous twenty-five years. It was in this context that Rockefeller and other multinationalists began to organize a group that would promote a coordinated capitalist strategy for managing global problems.

The full Commission meets annually in one of the three regions. In the interim, an executive committee of about thirty members attends to the ongoing activity of the Commission and each region has its own Trilateral headquarters. A bulletin of the North American branch, called *Trialogue,* reports on developments within the Commission and provides a forum for debate and discussion of current problems and policies.

Task force reports form a major topic of discussion at Commission meetings and are a central component of the Trilateralist reach for influence. These reports, prepared by rapporteurs from each of the three regions in consultation with

Commission members and others, address crucial world problems and make policy recommendations. By 1986 the Commission had published thirty reports.

The height of influence for the Trilateral Commission came during the Carter administration, when more than twenty-two Commission members served in executive branch positions at or above the rank of assistant secretary. Carter himself was an early member, crediting his experience in the Trilateral Commission with shaping his international outlook.[41] During the 1976 presidential campaign, Carter's foreign-policy advisers were mostly Trilateral Commission members, and Brzezinski reportedly wrote all Carter's foreign-policy speeches.[42] A number of Carter policies bore a Trilateral imprint. An emphasis on international economic consultation, a conciliatory approach in South Africa and Central America, and the attempt to implement a comprehensive energy program all fit in with Trilateral Commission objectives. But Carter's track record on these and other issues was mixed, creating increasing frustration for the President as his one-term administration wore on. Coordination of policy with the allies was difficult to achieve amid the renewed economic downturn that struck the advanced capitalist sectors. Within the United States, a conservative coalition of "Prussian" foreign-policy hard-liners and economic protectionists grew in opposition to Carter's policies, with strong support in Congress, the Pentagon, parts of the intelligentsia and media, and among certain declining industrial sectors and defense-based firms.

In the 1980s the Trilateral Commission remains an important source of discussion and ideas within the foreign policy establishment. High-level Reagan administration officials have addressed the group on several occasions, while Trilateralists have served on a number of prestigious commissions and study groups on Central America and arms control. But hard-line organizations of the resurgent right now compete with a center that has itself become more conservative, enjoying the support of the forces that swept Ronald Reagan into the presidency.

The American Enterprise Institute

During the 1970s the American Enterprise Institute (AEI) grew rapidly in influence, challenging the Brookings Institution for the title of Washington's leading think tank. When Ronald Reagan became President, a number of AEI associates took up important posts within the administration. More than thirty AEI scholars and officials have served in senior Reagan administration positions, including Jeane Kirkpatrick, ambassador to the United Nations; Murray Weidenbaum, chairman of the Council of Economic Advisers; James C. Miller III, director of the Office of Management and Budget; Lawrence Korb, assistant secretary of Defense; Norman Ture, under secretary of the Treasury; Roger Fontaine, National Security Council; Rudolph Penner, director of the Congressional Budget Office; Barber B. Conable Jr., president of the World Bank; foreign policy troubleshooter Philip Habib; and Michael Novak, special representative to the U.N. Human Rights Commission in Geneva. Several of these appointees have since left government, but the ties between the Reagan administration and the AEI remain strong, if not without conservative rivals.

Previously on the fringes of national political discussion, the AEI has been able to wield clout only in the last decade. In

1943 the American Enterprise Association, as it was then called, was founded by Lewis H. Brown, president of the Johns-Manville Corporation, to promote freemarket economics in the face of a rising tide of liberal Keynesianism.[43] In 1954, when William J. Baroody Sr. became executive vice-president of the AEA, the annual budget was only $80,000 and there were four full-time employees. Baroody, who came from the U.S. Chamber of Commerce, became president of the renamed American Enterprise Institute in 1962 and remained in that position until 1978. After advising the ill-fated Goldwater campaign in 1964, the AEI began to grow and break out of its ultraconservative cast, attracting new scholars and sources of funding while initiating many policy-research programs from a responsibly conservative, probusiness perspective.

Over the years the corporate ties of the AEI have changed considerably. Until the 1960s, according to Philip Burch, "Its board of trustees was made up largely of rightist corporate officials, many of whom were strictly second-tier figures."[44] In the past decade a number of more moderate, high-level corporate executives came on board. As of 1980, for example, the board of trustees included such big-business leaders as Willard C. Butcher of Chase Manhattan Bank, Robert Hatfield of the Continental Group, H. J. Haynes of Standard Oil of California, David Packard of Hewlett-Packard, W. F. Rockwell Jr. of Rockwell International, Mark Shepard Jr. of Texas Instruments, and Walter Wriston of Citicorp. Defense contractors, banks, and drug companies are well represented.

Perhaps more significant was the three-year campaign launched by the AEI in 1978 to raise $60 million for an endowment, mainly from large corporations. The special development committee that oversaw this project included Walter

Wriston, Willard Butcher, Reginald Jones (chairman of General Electric), Thomas Murphy (former chairman of General Motors), conservative professors Paul McCracken and Irving Kristol, and, serving as honorary chair, Gerald Ford. Jones, Murphy, and Wriston are all leaders of the powerful, secretive Business Roundtable, which has itself helped funnel corporate funds to the AEI.[45] William J. Baroody Jr., who became president of the AEI when his father retired, stated that corporate contributions mushroomed in the late 1970s. In 1977 about two hundred corporations accounted for 25 percent of the $5 million annual budget. By 1981 six hundred corporations were contributing 40 percent of the budget, now well over $10 million a year.[46] The response of business to the AEI was explained by Irving Kristol in this way: "AEI's views on economic policy appeal to the business community. It has been the citadel of free-market economics as the demand for AEI's kind of thinking began to expand. The business community suddenly woke up to the fact that it had enemies. Initially, it never took Ralph Nader seriously, but now business leadership has become much more sophisticated and aggressive."[47]

The AEI devotes over 20 percent of its budget to an elaborate outreach program to promote its ideas on regulation, taxation, foreign policy, and other issues. They prepare radio and television programs for six hundred stations and send out opinion/editorial pieces by associated scholars to newspapers around the nation. Key members of the executive branch, Congress, the media, and the academy are made aware of the latest findings. Special seminars for business executives are provided. University libraries may join a program where they receive all AEI publications free of charge. In short, the AEI takes the "war of ideas" seriously and wages it systematically, with enviable resources. It has been of great importance in the growing respectability of conservative ideas since the mid-1970s.

This ideological struggle for the soul of public policy has been assisted by the intellectual firepower the AEI has drawn in. Included are free-market economists like Arthur Burns, Paul McCracken, Rudolph Penner, Herbert Stein, and Murray Weidenbaum, legal scholars Bruce Fein, Robert Bork, and Antonin Scalia, and such neoconservative intellectuals as Irving Kristol, Robert Nisbet, Ben Wattenberg, and James Q. Wilson, to name but a few. More than eighty other scholars at universities throughout the United States maintain an adjunct relationship with the AEI, which has many joint projects and personal interlocks with the Hoover Institution at Stanford.

In the 1970s there was an impressive expansion in the number and variety of AEI publications. There are four periodicals: *AEI Economist*, *AEI Foreign Policy and Defense Review*, *Public Opinion*, and *Regulation*. Countless studies of widely varying lengths on a large number of policy issues were produced. Reprints of seminars and policy forums, usually including a liberal voice or two, were made available. Though conservative, the AEI is not so predictably hardline as the Heritage Foundation. It is drawn more to the Republicanism of George Bush and Gerald Ford than to that of Jesse Helms or Paul Laxalt. It is interesting to note that a sprinkling of AEI directors and scholars—including David Abshire, Arthur Burns, D. Gale Johnson, Paul McCracken, and David Packard—are present or former members of the Trilateral Commission. The style and image of the AEI are of nondogmatic, inclusive conservatism, overlapping with the internationalist wing of the foreign-policy elite.

Many observers believe that the AEI has equaled or surpassed the long-dominant Brookings Institution on domestic policy. Herbert Stein, formerly of Brookings and now at the AEI, pictured the relationship of these two institutions in recent years when he said, "It's probably true that both are moving to the middle, but the middle is moving to the right."[48] But in the mid-1980s the AEI seemed to reach its peak of influence, before encountering obstacles. Other policy groups were more aggressive in responding to current policy issues, while some conservative contributors believed that the AEI was drifting too far toward the center. As budget problems grew, charges of bad management led to the resignation of William Baroody Jr., as president in 1986 and his replacement on an interim basis by the economist Paul McCracken.[49] Still, the AEI commands the financial, intellectual, and reputational resources to remain a central actor in the policy-formation process.

The Heritage Foundation

By the mid-1980s the Heritage Foundation had become, in the view of many observers, the most influential think tank in Washington.[50] Its studies and analyses were regularly reported in the press, its Capitol Hill contacts were excellent, and thirty-nine former Heritage staff members had been appointed to middle-level administration posts. President Reagan gave an address on foreign policy at the Heritage Foundation a week after the April 1986 bombing of Libya. With an annual budget of well over $10 million, a modern headquarters near Capitol Hill, and a large staff of committed young conservatives, the Heritage Foundation deploys growing resources in the struggle for the soul of the Reagan administration.

The Heritage Foundation was formed in 1973 by two strategists of the New Right—Edwin Feulner Jr. and Paul Weyrich—with $250,000 in seed money from Joseph Coors, the Colorado brewer who is a longtime supporter of right-wing projects. Another major conservative donor, Richard Mellon Scaife of the Pittsburgh Mellon fortune, soon provided even more funding, and in the 1980s Heritage received support from such rightward-flowing sources as the Olin Foundation, the Noble Foundation, the J. Howard Pew Freedom Trust, New York businessman and political candidate Lewis Lehrman, the Reader's Digest Association, and many large corporations, including some from South Korea and Taiwan. There is little evidence, however, that corporate donors represent a distinct "cowboy" sector of the business community.[51] A unique aspect of Heritage Foundation funding is the proportion received in small donations from individuals, amounting to about one-third of revenues.

Heritage came to public attention in 1980, during the Reagan transition period, when it released a massive blueprint for a conservative administration called *Mandate for Leadership*, which had been prepared before Reagan became the Republican nominee. Presidential aide Edwin Meese personally received the study, with its recommendations for reshaping every aspect of government and policy in a conservative direction. Heritage later claimed that more than 60 percent of its proposals had been adopted by the administration. In 1984 the Heritage Foundation followed up with *Mandate for Leadership II*, intended to continue the conservative revolution in Reagan's second term. Both studies have been widely circulated in Washington and are frequently cited and discussed in the media.

More than two hundred policy papers are produced annually at Heritage. Many are short and contain clear policy recommendations designed to be consumed by congressional aides and executive-level officials who have little time for reading scholarly analyses. They are often written by young staff members who have been recruited to the Heritage Foundation, despite its modest salaries, and who are ideologically committed to conservative approaches. Heritage studies are hand delivered to members of Congress and officials in the executive branch. In 1983 Reagan told the Foundation: "Your frequent publications, timely research, policy papers, seminars and conferences account for your enormous influence on Capitol Hill and—believe me I know—at the White House."[52]

In Washington the Heritage Foundation serves as a meeting place for conservatives, with daily lectures, debates, and briefings. Corporate representatives meet with government decision-makers through the Washington Policy Roundtable, while the Third Generation Lecture Series brings together young conservatives to discuss media relations and combating liberalism on campus, among other topics. A resource bank of scholars and policy experts around the nation has been compiled to provide the media and congressional hearings with conservative commentary. Heritage also sends material to hundreds of newspapers across the country, much of which ends up in editorials or news stories. In addition to books, monographs, and policy papers, the Heritage Foundation publishes a quarterly journal, *Policy Review*, and several newsletters.

Many domestic and foreign policies of the Reagan administration, from enterprise zones to Star Wars, coincide with Heritage Foundation proposals, and perhaps not without cause.

Heritage is now a bridge for right-wing policy currents to enter policy debate. It is also a common ground for the New Right, hard-line anticommunists, free-market advocates, and neoconservatives, as suggested by a board of trustees that includes former U.S. Information Agency head Frank Shakespeare (chair), Joseph Coors, Midge Decter of the Committee for the Free World, Lewis Lehrman, and former Secretary of the Treasury William Simon, all of whom are closely tied to other conservative organizations. The steady rise in the political influence of the Heritage Foundation since its founding in 1973 is a significant index of the changing course of American politics.

The Institute for Contemporary Studies

Joining the American Enterprise Institute and the Heritage Foundation in creating intellectual thunder on the right is the lesser-known, San Francisco–based Institute for Contemporary Studies (ICS). Its rise to prominence coincided with the presidential victory of Ronald Reagan, but the links extend further back. The Institute was formed in 1972 by a group of men who had worked for Governor Ronald Reagan in the California state administration.[53] Serving as the ICS president for many years was H. Monroe Browne, a cattle rancher who had been appointed by Reagan to the state Occupational Health and Safety Administration Appeal Board. Browne was later named ambassador to New Zealand by President Reagan. Longtime ICS executive director A. Lawrence Chickering worked for Reagan at the state Office of Economic Opportunity. Edwin Meese

III, a close associate of Reagan's in his California years, was in on the founding discussions and served on the board of directors. Also a director before becoming secretary of Defense was Casper Weinberger.

Representing corporate and financial backing on the board of directors were men like Vincent W. Jones of Coldwell Banker, Leif Olsen, a Citibank executive and former chairman of the ICS board of directors, and Donald H. Rumsfeld, president and chief executive officer of G. D. Searle and Company, a former secretary of Defense and a personal representative of President Reagan in the Middle East. A partial list of corporate contributors in 1980 (amounts not known) included AT&T, Chase Manhattan Bank, Exxon, Ford, General Electric, IBM, Mobil, Shell, Texaco, and U.S. Steel. While these giants are not openly identified with the right, the conservative ties of the ICS are more clearly revealed by the support received from such right-leaning funding sources as the John M. Olin Foundation, the Sarah Scaife Foundation, and the Smith Richardson Foundation.

The Institute for Contemporary Studies sees itself as an alternative to the liberal policy organizations, such as the Brookings Institution. "We didn't feel that the existing framework or network of established think tanks gave the complete story," explained H. Monroe Browne.[54] In 1975 the first ICS book was published. *No Time to Confuse* was an attack on a previous study by the Ford Foundation that had recommended more government involvement in energy issues. As the 1970s moved on, the pro–free market, anti–"big government" ideology of the Institute meshed with the larger political drift to the right and the discrediting of liberal, Keynesian economic-policy positions. Stanford's Michael J. Boskin, who edited a major ICS volume on the economy, was an early apostle of the supply-side creed. While not as vociferous as the Heritage Foundation, the ICS does not hesitate to identify itself as conservative, on the right, and allied with Ronald Reagan, contrasting in this respect with the somewhat more circumspect American Enterprise Institute.

The ICS makes do with a leaner budget and a much smaller staff than the AEI, Brookings, or Heritage. As an activist, high-profile organization, the ICS promotes its views through congressional briefings, press conferences, a news service, a speakers bureau, and radio slots. Regular roundtable discussions at the Institute bring together business, government, and academic leaders, who debate contemporary policy issues. But the main outreach avenue is the publication of well-promoted, multiauthor books on subjects ranging from the budget, industrial policy, and national security to education, the media, immigration, and social security. Priding itself on its rapid response to current public debates, the ICS has been able to commission studies and have them edited and published within three to six months. Also produced is the quarterly *Journal of Contemporary Studies*, previously called *Taxing and Spending*. In 1985 the ICS co-published Edward Luttwak's *The Pentagon and the Art of War*, perhaps the most influential text in the bipartisan "military reform" movement.

The policy analysts and intellectuals who work with the ICS or contribute to its publications overlap heavily with the AEI, the Hoover Institution, and the Georgetown Center for Strategic and International Studies. Its academic advisory board in 1986 consisted of Peter Berger, Michael Boskin, Robert Hall, Seymour Martin Lipset, Arnold Meltsner, Paul Seabury, Aaron Wildavsky, and Richard Zeckhauser—most of whom are also affiliated with at least one of the other conservative policy centers. A reading of the ICS newsletter shows broad involvement of the network of neoconservatives, free-market economists, and foreign-policy hard-liners in ICS seminars, studies, and conferences. With the Reagan administration installed in 1981, the ICS saw its role as directly influencing its friends in government while continuing to mold opinion in the public sphere. While it is difficult to judge the specific impact of an organization like the ICS, it does seem that on major topics of economic policy, defense, and deregulation the efforts of the Institute and its policy-planning co-thinkers have paid off, altering the general framework of policy debate and influencing the specific policy decisions of the Reagan administration.

2
America's Postwar Policy Regime

WHAT ACCOUNTS FOR THE EXPANSION and politicization of the elite policy network in the 1970s and 1980s? We have seen how policy-planning organizations operate in the American political order, given historical examples, and profiled five of the current leading players. But we need to understand the dynamics of the policy-planning process, establishing the economic and political context that has both reshaped the policy network and given rise to the problems that policy-planners were grappling with in the 1970s and 1980s. This will provide the background for Chapters 3 through 6, which will explore the reactions of policy elites to challenges in four key areas of policy. The five policy organizations already described serve as entry points into the political debate.

The multiple pressures afflicting the liberal capitalist order in the United States since the early 1970s are not disparate occurrences lacking a common source. They are signs of an underlying process of transformation in the post-1945 political economy. The last decade-and-a-half has been an extended period of challenge and crisis in American liberal democratic capitalism—to borrow a term for a historically specific set of social, political, and economic arrangements.[1] The international and domestic components of this system will be described throughout this book, but at this point an overview of leading elements of this interconnected regime will help us construct a framework for interpreting what policy-planning organizations have been up to.

We need to uncover the defining features or contours of America's postwar "policy regime," which Edward S. Greenberg defines in terms of "intertwined sets of problems, constraints, political coalitions, and public policy packages existing in temporary equilibrium." Underlying the rise and decline of policy regimes are stages in the development of the U.S. political economy, which is understood as a form of capitalist democracy.[2] I will examine this social order by outlining several factors that bear crucially on the course of the policy-planning process in recent years. First, there are those institutionalized features of the postwar capitalist system that made possible its rapid economic growth and relative stability but that came undone in the 1970s, with attendant social and political dislocations.[3] Second, I will identify certain linkages between elite and mass political structures and patterns of public policy in postwar America, including the role of parties, labor unions, and social reform movements. Finally, we will look at how elite mobilization in the 1970s changed the balance of power in the political process, in part by reshaping the policy-planning network, and thereby propelled the rightward reconstruction of policy and ideology.

International Aspects of U.S. Power

International politics and economics played a strong role in shaping postwar America. Hence, the decline in the international position of the United States in the 1970s was bound to have far-reaching social and political implications. Emerging from World War II with an intact society, a pent-up economy, and both the political will and the capability to assert dominance in world affairs, the United States became the hegemonic state in the international system. With the dollar as the key international currency, foreign investment by U.S. corporations expanded swiftly, while American exports dominated leading industries on a global basis. A vigorous economy, in turn, made possible a worldwide military system spanning foreign bases, treaty arrangements, "internal security" assistance programs, arms sales, and counterinsurgency activities to ensure the social and political preconditions for capitalist accumulation on a world scale.

By 1973 the economic and strategic sides of U.S. hegemony were both under pressure: The dollar could not sustain its position and was twice devalued, American goods were increasingly losing out to competition from Japanese and European imports, and large parts of the Third World sought independence from U.S. economic and military control, symbolized by the Vietnam War and the militance of the Organization of Petroleum Exporting Countries (OPEC). In short, international developments were vital to policy-planners grappling with the crisis of American politics in the 1970s. Let us look into the rise and decline of U.S. hegemony more closely.

Facilitating the international expansion of the U.S. economy were a number of policies and institutions established in the mid-1940s, often referred to collectively as the Bretton Woods system. In planning for postwar international economic stability, policymakers were influenced by the negative lessons of nationalism in the 1930s, which in their view had led to destructive economic protectionism, fueling the Great Depression and catalyzing political forces leading to World War II. In the words of AEI economist Thomas D. Willett, "Bretton Woods represented a deliberate decision by the participating countries to reestablish a liberal international economic order based on a strengthened framework for international cooperation as opposed to a reversion to a system of economic nationalism and heavy state control of international transactions."[4] On the specifics of postwar economic policy, there were disagreements within and between the State Department and the Treasury Department, between the United States and Great Britain, and between Congress and interest groups. But by and large, a liberal perspective favoring a more open world trading system shaped the key decisions concerning reconstruction of the international economy and America's leading position within it.[5] As we have seen, the institutional framework to support international economic expansion had been prepared in detail during the war by the most important policy-planning organization of the day, the Council on Foreign Relations.

Expansion of world trade and investment required a stable international monetary order. At the 1944 Bretton Woods Conference in New Hampshire, representatives of forty-four nations met to consider the design of such a new order. While the proposal of John Maynard Keynes for an international central bank was not adopted, the International Monetary Fund (IMF) and the International Bank for Reconstruction and Development (known as the World Bank) were set up to help member nations overcome temporary trade deficits and to make loans to help finance the postwar recovery. But these bodies, with their modest resources, could not by themselves stimulate a European economic rebound. By 1947, "the United States stepped in to fill the gap left by Bretton Woods" and developed "a new international monetary system, the dollar standard, based on unilateral American management."[6]

The long-term outcome of the new monetary system was that the U.S. dollar became the principal world reserve currency, the medium of most international transactions, and a kind of surrogate for gold. Since dollars were highly valued by foreigners, the United States was regularly able to run balance-of-payments deficits, sending more dollars abroad than it was taking in, without fear of demands for redemption in gold at the fixed rate of $35 an ounce. Private foreign investment, public credit, imports, and overseas military expenditures fed the outflow of currency, yet the United States was not pressured to devalue. The nature and limits of this system are summarized by a Trilateral Commission report thus:

> The U.S. dollar emerged after World War II as an international currency that provided liquidity, elasticity, and financial stability to the international monetary system. But confidence in the dollar, and in the system itself, depended inter alia on a well managed American economy, and that precondition ceased to be met in the late 1960s.[7]

Alongside monetary reforms, the lowering of tariff barriers removed obstacles to the expansion of international trade and finance and the further development of a liberal world capitalist order. Under the General Agreement on Tariffs and Trade of 1947, the United States and its trading partners steadily lowered tariffs on imports, although the European Economic Community (EEC), with U.S. assent, continued to maintain some obstacles to U.S. goods. In the talks of the early 1960s, the Kennedy Round, tariff reductions of 50 percent were negotiated. Stimulated by these measures, the volume of world trade grew at an annual average of 10 percent in the postwar period, nearly double the growth rate of the world economy itself.[8]

Contributing to the very existence of strong U.S. trading partners was the Marshall Plan, which injected $13 billion of capital into Western Europe from 1948 to 1951. This helped to finance the recovery of the war-torn economies, provided markets for U.S. exports, and allied Western European governments to the United States, forestalling possible shifts to the left. It was the unique position of economic and political strength with which the United States emerged from World War II that enabled it to gain hegemony in the world system. As the Trilateral Commission put it: "One power had overwhelming might and influence, and others were closely associated with it."[9] Both our capitalist allies in Europe and our socialist ally, soon to be enemy, in the Soviet Union were lifting themselves out of the smoke and rubble in 1945 and were in no position to challenge American leadership. There was domestic opposition to the Marshall Plan and other measures, but it was overcome by the Truman administration, which tied the liberalization of the international economy to the need for American leadership in the global struggle against Soviet communism.[10] A seminal statement of this "containment" doctrine was published in the July 1947 issue of the Council on Foreign Relations journal *Foreign Affairs*, the famous "Mr. X" article by George F. Kennan, who later regretted the political uses it was put to.

The politics and economics of American hegemony had a vital military–strategic underpinning which derived from conceptions of national security that were worked out in elite policy circles during the 1940s. In a wide-ranging survey, Melvyn P. Leffler demonstrates that American defense officials and other policymakers developed a truly global conception of U.S. security interests even before the onset of the Cold War. Included within the domain of American reach were

> a strategic sphere of influence within the Western Hemisphere, domination of the Atlantic and Pacific Oceans, an extensive system of outlying bases to enlarge the strategic frontier and project American power, an even more extensive system of transit rights to facilitate the conversion of commercial air bases to military use, access to the resources and markets of most of Eurasia, denial of those resources to a prospective enemy, and the maintenance of nuclear superiority.[11]

While conventional accounts of the dynamics of the Cold War often emphasize the United States responding to a Soviet threat, defense analysts and intelligence officials of the time viewed Soviet military power as gravely weakened by the war and as only one aspect of a set of challenges to an American-defined liberal capitalist world order. As Leffler puts it, "American assessments of the Soviet threat were less a consequence of expanding Soviet military capabilities and of Soviet diplomatic demands than a result of growing apprehension about the vulnerability of American strategic and economic interests in a world of unprecedented turmoil and upheaval."[12]

Domestic reluctance to commit massive resources to military spending lingered in the late 1940s, until the Korean War made possible an increase in the defense budget from $14 billion to $34 billion. As a share of the gross national product, defense spending doubled to more than 10 percent in 1951 and remained near this figure throughout the 1950s and 1960s, providing, in Gabriel Kolko's view, "that critical break-even point of economic stimulus which made much of the rest of the economy viable and far less perturbed by a crisis of demand."[13] This stepped-up defense effort had been advocated even before the outbreak of the Korean War in the now famous "National Security Council 68" planning document of 1950. Painting a chilling portrait of an implacable Soviet threat, that document went on to make a quasi-Keynesian argument for the demand-sustaining effects of military spending on Western economics. For example: "The distinction between aid in support of foreign military effort abroad and aid for economic recovery is largely artificial."[14] In this way, policy-planners linked the domestic objective of state-stimulated economic growth and the imperatives of securing global hegemony for the United States.

During the 1960s problems emerged that put severe pressure on the reign of the American Century that Henry Luce stridently foresaw in 1941. Japan and Western Europe, and West Germany in particular, recovered from the war, attained high levels of economic growth, and became strong competitors with the United States in the world market. Negative trade balances began to appear in several U.S. manufacturing industries, as well as in the unprocessed goods sector (food, fuel, raw materials), leading to protectionist pressures.[15] At the same time, given the renewed economic vigor of Europe, the EEC's relatively protectionist stance toward the United States seemed no longer warranted to American policymakers and capitalists.

On the monetary side, the unique role of the dollar began to come undone. The high value of the dollar in the postwar era had in effect subsidized multinational corporations and international banking interests while making imports of foreign goods cheaper, with the consequences for domestic industry just described. Meanwhile, the Vietnam War was producing inflation within the United States as well as huge balance-of-payments deficits, creating fear of a "dollar glut" that would distort international financial markets. Foreigners no longer had confidence in the dollar-based system, yet any attempt to recast the terms of international arrangements seemed certain to threaten various interests.[16] In response to these portentious developments,

> international financiers agreed that reform was needed, that no national currency could completely dominate the system, and that national currencies should be pegged to their relative and interdependent strengths in a fluid manner. By 1970 serious discussion was underway to accomplish these and other changes while continuing to move toward freer trade relations.[17]

Within an international system characterized by growing interdependence and mounting economic problems, a nationalistic, go-it-alone policy by the United States was exactly the wrong medicine from the standpoint of international financiers and America's capitalist allies. But in 1971 a nationalistic turn in American international economic policy is just what occurred, culminating in the "Nixon Shocks" of August 15, which dissolved progress toward unified reform. In violation of the Articles of Agreement of the International Monetary Fund, Nixon suspended the conversion of dollars into gold, hoping to achieve an effective devaluation of the dollar and to improve the trade and payments balances of the United States. With respect to trade policy, Nixon disregarded obligations under the General Agreement on Tariffs and Trade and imposed a 10 percent surcharge on most imports coming into the United States. In some respects the new policy was successful. By early 1972, Japan and the EEC had agreed to loosen trade restrictions on U.S. imports, and Japan and other Asian nations had agreed to slow the growth of their textile sales in the United States.[18] But these events caused grave concern in multinational circles and, as Chapter 3 will show, gave impetus to the formation of the Trilateral Commission.

As we shall see in the next two chapters, the international economic disorder and foreign-policy challenges that pressed in on the United States in the early 1970s did not abate. Loss of international competitiveness continued, and monetary structures remained precarious, as with the staggering accumulation of Third World debt, approaching $1 trillion in the mid-1980s. At the same time, American precepts of national security were shaken by a string of Third World revolutions, the rise of the Soviet Union to rough strategic parity, and technological "refinements" in the nuclear arms race. There were plenty of "dysfunctions" to spur on the activity of policy-planning organizations. More were provided by the breakdown of the accords of the domestic political economy.

Domestic Foundations of Economic Growth

From roughly 1945 to 1970, the United States and other advanced capitalist countries experienced an unprecedented period of sustained economic growth. But only a few years after the New Economics enthusiasm of the 1960s, simultaneous inflation and high unemployment, termed "stagflation," wracked the economy, a shaky debt structure threatened corporate and financial interests with bankruptcy, and the growing gaps between government revenues and expenditures led to concern about a "fiscal crisis of the state." With Keynesian liberalism in retreat, some elites called for neocorporatist planning to hold the political economy together, while free-marketers desiring a reduction in government size and scope began a remarkable political and intellectual comeback.

During the 1970s, economics became a more salient public issue, widely debated in national politics. The politicization of economic policy was itself a sign that established policy approaches were being called into question by stagflation. As long as the economy produced growth and relative prosperity in the postwar era, a tacit consensus sustained policies in which the relationship between economics and politics was not made explicit in public debate.

Compared with the dark years of the 1930s, the record of the American economy after World War II was one of great success, setting standards against which the crisis of the 1970s can be measured. During the 1960s, the growth rate of real gross national product per capita reached 3.3 percent, only to fall to 2.2 percent in the 1970s. Price inflation averaged only 2.2 percent annually in the 1950s and 2.6 percent in the 1960s, but rose to a yearly rate of 7.5 percent in the 1970s, reaching double-digit levels at times. While high compared to other advanced capitalist countries, U.S. unemployment rates of 4.5 percent of the 1950s and 4.8 percent for the 1960s compared favorably with the 1970s average of 6.2 percent, a figure that continued to creep upward to more than 10 percent in 1982.[19] Underlying these achievements in the boom period from 1947 to 1968 were a 107 percent increase in the real net value of structures and equipment in manufacturing, a more than doubling of output per worker, and a 70 percent increase in real personal income per capita in the United States.[20]

Recent explanations of this postwar cycle of growth and crises by radical political economists draw on the concept of an "institutional structure" of capitalist accumulation, "a set of social/economic/political institutions that provide a certain stability and thereby generate prosperity for a capitalist system."[21] The argument is that the crisis of the 1930s was overcome by a historically specific restructuring of the social system of accumulation, in which the state played a larger role through demand management and other policies that helped make possible the prosperity of the 1950s and 1960s. But over time, internal contradictions sprang from the initially successful institutional structure, leading to the economic crisis of the 1970s and 1980s and the need for further restructuring.

This framework points to the inseparable social and political aspects of economic policy, a perspective that will be useful in evaluating economic statements of the five policy organizations, where such connections are often not made explicit. We can direct our attention to how, in a period of crisis, economic policy proposals point toward a broader process of restructuring in which the social order as a whole is implicated.

On the domestic side of the postwar order, three elements may be singled out for attention: the role of the state in steering the economy, the relationship between capital and labor, and government programs of income security and social and economic regulation. These components, or "accords" of the postwar institutional structure represented reforms that helped stabilize the economy, mute class conflict, and ensure relative social harmony.[22] Success in meeting these goals required that the state increase its share of the overall economic product. Total government spending, at all levels, as a percentage of the gross national product (GNP) rose from the 18.9 percent average between 1934 and 1939 to 34 percent between 1980 and 1982,[23] with federal government spending stabilizing at 20 to 22 percent of the GNP, about double the percentage of the 1920s.[24] But the proportion devoted to military expenditures—much larger than in Japan or West European countries—led critics to label the growing size of the state sector "bastard Keynesianism." As a percentage of GNP, military spending rose from 1.3 percent in 1939 to 10.7 percent in the high Cold War period of 1951–1959.[25]

Justified by Keynesian principles, state responsibility for managing the economy became more acceptable after World War II. The function of the "built-in stabilizers" forged during and after the Great Depression was demand management—the use of fiscal policy to maintain a high level of aggregate demand. Economists thought that inflation and unemployment could be kept at low levels, rendering the boom–bust cycle of earlier capitalist eras anachronistic. The heyday of this approach was probably the Kennedy–Johnson era, with the tax cuts of 1962 and 1964, which gave investment credits to business and lowered income taxes, serving to stimulate demand and reduce unemployment, even at the risk of running budget deficits. But this was a conservative application of Keynesian methods, relying on economic growth itself to meet social needs. Rather than directly targeting government spending on priority areas, money was placed in the hands of businesses and individuals to spend as they wished. In effect, given the bias of tax policy and the skill of tax lawyers, wealth was being redistributed upwards in the hope that it would be used to stimulate growth from which all would benefit: classic "trickle-down" economics. This approach harmonized with and was influenced by leading business groups in the 1960s, especially the Committee for Economic Development and the Business Council.[26]

In the area of class relations, the postwar years saw the forging of an accord between capital and labor whereby the government recognized the right of workers to form unions, wage gains were tied to productivity increases in major industries, and the AFL–CIO was incorporated as a junior partner in the Democratic Party coalition. Providing capitalists with a stable work force and a growing consumption base, this was a system of labor regulation "that was systematically biased against class-based struggles and demands and that encouraged the reduction of organizational activities to the pursuit of short-term economic interests."[27] While organized labor lost much of its political independence, partly through the purge of leftists from union leadership positions in the late 1940s, the working class did make gains in its economic position relative to capital. Real after-tax wages per worker rose at an average rate of 3.4 percent annually between 1965 and 1973, according to one computation, while real after-tax net profits per worker declined at an average rate of 0.6 percent, a dramatic reversal from the previous decade.[28] Coming in the context of recession and international pressures, the profit squeeze led business to open a frontal attack on working-class gains during the 1970s. As we shall see, many of the policy-planners' proposals implicitly or explicitly argue for the redistribution of social wealth from labor to capital in order to restore growth and profitability.

The third element of the domestic institutional structure was the role of the state in income insecurity, business subsidization, and social and economic regulation. Among the major programs were social security, welfare assistance, unemployment compensation, food stamps, medical benefits, housing, and education programs. Business was also protected through a variety of government programs of regulation, purchasing, taxation, guarantees, and subsidies. Thus both private citizens and corporations were shielded from market forces in the phase of "security capitalism."[29]

As a proportion of total government spending, social welfare expenditures increased from 32.7 percent in 1955, to 42.2 percent in 1965, to 57.9 percent in 1975, representing a percentage of GNP in the same three years of 8.6, 11.7, and 19.9.[30] In addition, the early 1970s saw the government take on new regulatory functions through, for example, passage of the Occupational Safety and Health Act (1970), creation of the Environmental Protection Agency (1970), and extension of various civil rights and affirmative-action measures. While these programs were limited in many ways, they did provide the working class with benefits that attenuated the disciplinary effect of the labor market, while imposing new costs on capitalists, and thus they became the objects of intense contestation by business groups as the economic crisis deepened. Citizen rights secured through the liberal democratic state now loomed as barriers to the restoration of the conditions for capitalist accumulation. Neoconservative intellectuals began to bemoan the "excess" of democracy and the "overload" of government, calling for a reassertion of state authority and a reduction in social welfare expenditures and business regulations.

Before these strains became apparent in the 1970s, energy resources and raw materials needed for an expanding economy seemed to be in abundant supply at low prices in the postwar period and were easily accessible even if located in Third World regions. Physical constraints imposed by the ecological balance did not appear to be a limit on industrial production in the 1950s and 1960s, and U.S. military power stood poised as a threat to radical nationalists who might seek to rewrite the terms of trade. In a context of favorable resource and environmental conditions, the three demand-supporting aspects of the domestic institutional structure prevented the relapse into stagnation that many policy-planners feared would occur after World War II in the absence of system-stabilizing reforms. As it was, the most formidable economic leap forward in American history took place.

The relative prosperity generated by a growing economy in the first two postwar decades combined with a Cold War foreign policy to form what Godfrey Hodgson calls the "ideology of the liberal consensus." The global outlook stressed the threat of communism and the promise of American enterprise to the free world. In tandem, the domestic ideology touted the democratic nature of U.S. capitalism, whose continual growth provided the abundance in which social conflicts and class struggles were dissolved, as all parts of society recognized their common interests in making the system work. Remaining problems were more technical than political, to be solved by transfusions of federal money and the skills of social scientists.[31] This "end-of-ideology" ideology was expressed perfectly by President John F. Kennedy in 1962:

> Most of us are conditioned for many years to have a political viewpoint. . . . The fact of the matter is that most of the problems . . . that we now face are technical problems, are administrative problems. They are very sophisticated judgments that do not lend themselves to the great sort of passionate movements which have stirred the country so often in the past.[32]

These technical problems were thought to center on fine-tuning the economy, and the apparent success of economic policy in the 1960s led to a belief that the crisis-prone pattern of unregulated capitalism was a thing of the past. Thus the 1965 Council of Economic Advisers report stated that "both our increased understanding of the effectiveness of fiscal policy and the continued improvement of . . . our economic information strengthens the conviction that recessions can be increasingly avoided and ultimately wiped out."[33]

By the early 1970s, the defining accords of liberal democratic capitalism in the United States were increasingly torn, provoking a search for new policies and ideas to justify them by rapidly mobilizing business elites and their allies. As in other periods of crisis and transition, like the Progressive Era or the New Deal, the intellectual paradigms and institutional arrangements of the past were criticized as outmoded. While there was a widespread sense of a critical turning point after 1973 among those with power, there has been disagreement about the sources of the crisis and about the new policies needed to restore economic growth, reduce the claims on government, and maintain social stability. These disagreements among elites are reflected in the divergent assessments and proposals of policy planning organizations.

Here my approach would interpret the positions of leading policy organizations as class-based elite strategies of crisis-management. Addressing a range of key issues, such strategies aim to reorient policies and restructure institutions—especially as they bear on the relationship between the state and the economy—so that the social relations of capitalism are reproduced on a domestic and international level. But this process must take into account the specific political context of postwar America, the public arena in which policies are articulated, shaped, and implemented.

Impasse: the Political Context

We have traced the foundations of America's postwar economic growth and global power, because their decline in the 1970s and 1980s underlies the recent political movement of policy elites. To return to the question posed at the outset of this chapter, we can see the expansion of the policy-planning network as part of an attempt by elites to fashion an effective reply to systemic disorders where established political structures are at an impasse. While there has been enormous pressure for elites to act politically, there are serious questions about the capacity of the U.S. government to serve as a crisis-management vehicle. We shall look briefly at several features of the American political system that limit the state's ability to act purposefully, then turn to elite efforts to break the political stalemate.

Many commentators have noted that the institutional structure of the U.S. government, by eighteenth-century constitutional design, fragments power and authority, making it difficult for the state to formulate policy clearly and to implement it.[34] Within our "Tudor polity," an array of interest groups struggle to define their particular goals as the public interest, or at least to block legislation perceived as damaging to their constituents. Many organized interests have in effect captured parts of the swelling bureaucracy that ostensibly exist to defend broad public concerns.[35]

A second barrier to the decisive pursuit of policy goals is the weak relationship between political parties and the electorate. If American parties pursued coherent programs and enjoyed the durable support of popular coalitions, then built-in institutional barriers could be overridden.[36] But American parties lack the programmatic orientation of European counterparts and confront several other obstacles to strong linkage with voters. Electoral participation in the United States has historically been lower than in other industrial democracies, with turnout declining noticeably since 1960. Party labels seem less and less important in determining voter preferences, while single-issue politics gain force, and elections become devoid of substantive content, instead being "structured by the mass media, individual candidates, and their staffs of pollsters, media consultants, and image manipulators."[37] Since the late 1960s, the New Deal coalition that secured the Democratic Party's majority status since the early 1930s has been visibly splintering.

In many political systems, labor unions aggregate nonelite interests and help develop policy packages that are the basis for social democratic and other party platforms. In capitalist democracies the labor movement has a political representation role that goes well beyond meeting the immediate economic needs of union members. There is a strong correlation between the strength of a nation's labor movement and such policy results as the tolerated level of unemployment, the proportion of the budget spent on social security and welfare programs, and the degree of inequality in income distribution. Nations with strong labor unions have less joblessness, more social spending, and a narrower range of inequality.[38]

In the United States the political role of the labor movement has been comparatively weak.[39] There is no major party of the left in American politics, and labor has been but one interest—and a declining one at that—among others in the Democratic Party. Since the 1950s, the percentage of the labor force organized in unions has been falling and is now around 20 percent. As we shall see, organized labor has been facing a concerted business offensive in recent years that has thrown it on the defensive as a political and economic force. But American labor leadership has never developed broad political alternatives and, in the instance of foreign policy, has been a faithful supporter of the Cold War since the late 1940s.[40]

With elections remote from substance, parties dominated by business and other interests, and nonelites lacking instruments of independent political action, it might be asked where the challenges to elites come from, at least on the domestic level. Could not the problems of the 1970s have been handily resolved through the consensus-forming approach of the Council on Foreign Relations, the Business Council, and the Ford Foundation? When elites are united, with identical economic interests and ideological orientations, conflicts are more easily resolved. But they are divided on defense spending, foreign trade, tax policy, budget deficits, and any number of other issues. Furthermore, the 1970s and 1980s are a period in which politics as usual have broken down, just because so many accumulating problems have developed. Consensus politics is most orderly when levels of economic growth and international hegemony are sufficient to co-opt or to vanquish threats to stability, and these conditions have not been obtained in recent years.

Finally, it is essential to recognize that, whatever the built-in elite biases of American politics, capitalists perceived themselves as having lost control of the political agenda in the 1970s to forces unsympathetic to their imperatives.[41] Growing out of the 1960s dissatisfaction with all major American institutions, and skeptical of the value of unlimited economic growth, the 1970s witnessed the partial political empowerment of a "loose coalition of middle-class based consumer and environmental, feminist and civil rights organizations, assisted on occasion by organized labor, aided by a sympathetic media and supported by much of the intelligentsia," which was "able to influence both the terms of public debate and the outcomes of government policy in a direction antithetical to the interests of business."[42] Public-interest groups succeeded in winning new regulations over business and greater representation of nonbusiness groups in economic policymaking on air and water pollution, occupational safety and health, consumer protection, affirmative action, and other issues. While there is much dispute about the actual costs imposed on business by these measures, capitalists saw them as especially burdensome in the context of declining profit margins and intensifying international competition.

We have described a set of conditions that, by the early 1970s, had eroded the stability of the postwar political economy. Political institutions appear to be ill-suited to act at the necessary level of purpose and authority, at the same time that new government policies obstruct the resolution of the economic crisis and the restoration of American power from a capitalist standpoint. What developed in the 1970s was a political mobilization of business and allied elites to redefine the terms of political debate and redirect the ends and content of policy. In this campaign, policy-planning organizations played no small part.

Processes of Elite Mobilization

Any number of public opinion polls conducted in the mid-1970s showed a sharp drop in the confidence in major institutions expressed by the American people. Business was no exception to public disenchantment, a fact that was not lost on corporate leaders. Much was at stake as the economic crisis intensified and America's global position became uncertain. From the standpoint of the ruling class, the correct resolution of crises depended on a change in public opinion toward the capitalist system, in the perception of the national interest, and in the general ideological climate surrounding the shaping of public policy. These are the grounds on which elites have mobilized for more than a decade in a contest over policy, though not always with identical interpretations of problems or solutions.

Three examples of the connection between elite networks, policy organizations, and the changing terms of political debate may help us understand the policy-formation process. The first took place in the mid-1970s, when a policy current opposed to U.S.–Soviet détente was endeavoring to publicize an alarmist reading of Soviet behavior in world affairs. Serving as the organizational expression of this tendency was the Committee on the Present Danger (CPD), which was formed in

1974 and would later place many of its members in the Reagan administration.

In 1976, under pressure from the CPD hawks, President Ford directed Central Intelligence Agency (CIA) Director George Bush to establish an outside panel to evaluate the national intelligence estimates that the CIA makes of Soviet capabilities. The seven-member panel, which came to be known as Team B, was comprised of hard-liners only, four of whom were members of the CPD, including Richard Pipes (the chair) and the ubiquitous Paul Nitze.[43] Though their report was not published in full, its contents were deliberately leaked to the press and widely disseminated just before Jimmy Carter took office. Essentially the report argued that the Soviets were engaged in a massive military buildup, were outspending the United States on defense 2 to 1, and were developing a civil defense program on the assumption that they could survive a nuclear war, and that, therefore, the United States must abandon illusions of détente and counter these moves with its own military buildup.

There are notorious difficulties in estimating the Soviet Union's defense spending, and recent CIA studies have shown that Soviet percentage increases in military outlays from 1976 to 1983 were lower than the increases in American military spending.[44] The Team B report itself was criticized in 1980 as extremely misleading by former State Department and CIA official Arthur Macy Cox.[45] While not denying that the Soviet Union has been increasing its military strength, Cox argues that Soviet defense spending rose at a steady 3 percent annual rate in the 1970s. Although Soviet defense expenditures may be a greater proportion of their gross national product than previously believed, this is because the CIA had overestimated the efficiency of Soviet military production. Cox also points to the significant asymmetry between the contributions of U.S. allies in Nato and Soviet allies in the Warsaw Pact: In 1976 the NATO powers and France spent $96 billion on defense while the Warsaw Pact powers outside the Soviet Union spent $17 billion. In addition, a large portion of the Soviet Union's defense effort is turned toward China. If these points are taken into account, "the share of the Soviet defense budget allocated to the forces facing the United States and its allies is less than 75 percent of the combined budgets of the NATO powers." Cox concludes, "The claim of Soviet military superiority is an illusion based, in large part, on a misunderstanding of the facts."[46] But by 1980 the arguments of the CPD and its allies in other hard-line policy groups were increasingly shaping American perceptions of the Soviet Union. However, it was not long before a counterreaction emerged within the foreign-policy establishment.

The second example concerns the relationship between business Democrats and the nuclear freeze movement, which has been documented by Thomas Ferguson and Joel Rogers.[47] In the early 1980s a number of multinationally oriented Democrats were disturbed by Reagan's CPD-style defense policies, which they viewed as disruptive of relations between the United States and Europe, damaging to prospects for business dealings with the Soviet Union, and potentially threatening to American economic interests in the Third World. In response, the business Democrats, together with a number of major foundations on which they were overrepresented, poured support into the growing ranks of arms control policy groups that received much favorable coverage in the major media. Additional support came from real estate interests and professional groups who were adversely affected by spending cuts that were made to make way for Reagan's military buildup. In the view of Ferguson and Rogers, this proliferation of establishment policy groups took the critical edge off what was originally a grass-roots freeze movement, cutting short discussion of the relations between multinational business, the use of force in U.S. foreign policy, and social class.

A third instance of policy institutions at work to shape opinion centers on domestic social policy and the impact of Charles Murray's well-known critique of Great Society programs, *Losing Ground*. In Reagan's Washington, Murray's arguments provided justification for the slashing of federal antipoverty programs. Journalist Chuck Lane of the *New Republic* looked beyond the contents of *Losing Ground* and found a well-orchestrated conservative campaign to publicize Murray's work.[48] Previously the author of a Heritage Foundation pamphlet, Murray was invited to expand his paper into a book by the Manhattan Institute, a conservative New York think tank. To cover his salary and extensive promotion for the book, $125,000 was raised, mainly from the right-wing Scaife and Olin foundations, the latter with the help of leading neoconservative Irving Kristol. Made possible by the funding was a nationwide series of meetings between Murray and editors, journalists, academics, and television interviewers, and other publicity efforts. While this account does not speak to the validity of the ideas in *Losing Ground*, it does suggest that intellectual debate is often linked to the power moves of policy elites.

What these examples depict is a greatly heightened degree of political activism by national security and economic policy elites. In part, this elite mobilization centers on the creation and dissemination of ideology and sanctioned interpretations of problems. Because political ideas that gain currency enter into the restructuring of ideas and institutions, it is crucial for would-be hegemonic actors to position themselves to influence the authoritative understanding of events.

Since the early 1970s, the American business community has engaged in a multifaceted campaign to wrest control of the policy agenda from adversaries and shift the balance of power in procapitalist directions.[49] In response to declining public confidence in business, perceived threats from labor, environmental, and public-interest critics, and the constraints of diminishing profits in the face of serious international competition, all segments of American business stepped up their political activity in ways that went well beyond traditional pork-barrel lobbying for specific benefits. Operating through strengthened industry trade associations and Chamber of Commerce networks, business contested broad political legislation that affected the economy. Perhaps the most significant development was the formation of the Business Roundtable in 1972, an organization that engaged in direct lobbying on such legislative issues as labor law reform, taxation, and banking regulation.[50]

In addition to lobbying, after 1974 corporations and trade associations established political action committees (PACs) and increased campaign contributions at a rate far beyond the efforts of organized labor. Business PACs increased in number from 248 in 1974 to 1,100 in 1978,[51] while the expenditures of corporate and trade associations PACs grew from $8.0 million to $84.9 million between 1972 and 1982, a tenfold increase that was more than double the rate of increase in organized labor's PACs' expenditures.[52] Contributions have gone to incumbents of both parties or, in a competitive election, to the more conservative Republican candidate.

A third area of the business offensive was a drive to weaken organized labor.[53] This involved formation of antiunion groups like the Committee for a Union-Free Environment, the growth of union-busting consulting firms, and the increased willingness of business to violate the National Labor Relations Act in union representation elections. Management has also resorted to decertification elections in growing numbers, in which workers are asked to get rid of their unions entirely. These moves mark a change from the relatively cooperative business–labor relations of the postwar years.

Finally, capitalists moved ahead on the ideological front by increasing expenditures for the type of probusiness advocacy advertising pioneered by Mobil Corporation and by subsidizing sympathetic intellectual and research projects at universities.[54] For our purposes, the most important aspect of the business interest in ideas has been the accelerated funding of policy institutions that espouse pro-free-market positions. In the 1970s the major conservative policy organizations, such as the American Enterprise Institute, the Heritage Foundation, the Hoover Institution, and the Institute for Contemporary Studies, received increased corporate funding. Other more specialized groups whose analysis supported probusiness tax and regulatory policies were also strongly backed, including the National Bureau of Economic Research, under Martin Feldstein, the Center for the Study of American Business at Washington University, led by Murray Weidenbaum, and the American Council for Capital Formation, led by longtime business tax lobbyist Charls E. Walker.[55] By 1978 the business ideological offensive seemed to be paying off as Congress passed tax legislation weighted in favor of business and upper-income groups and defeated an AFL–CIO–backed labor law reform, despite a Democratic President and Democratic majorities in both houses of Congress.

The corporate politicization process shows business acting less as a collection of individual profit seekers and more as a class cognizant of general business interests. In part this was due to the complacency-shaking circumstances of the 1970s, but it was also rooted in the evolution of the corporate structure that has created an "inner circle" of capitalists. These business leaders are defined by their connections to a business system that is increasingly integrated by patterns of intercorporate ownership and interlocking directorates. These broad-based ties have allowed business leaders to achieve greater coherence in defining problems and imperatives, formulating policy recommendations, and charting a political strategy for achieving business goals.[56]

The politics of business does not explain everything we need to know about policy formation in recent years. Many other interests remain organized, business itself is often divided or simply unclear on the issues, intellectual and ideological currents have their own autonomy, and international problems cannot be reduced to economic considerations. However, there are real world dynamics that affect the policy-planning process, by shaping policy institutions whose ideas find elite support and public expression. In the United States during the 1970s and 1980s, elite mobilization has been spurred principally by a declining economic situation, the political obstacles posed by forces that are at odds with business positions, international economic and foreign-policy disarray, and a political system unable to cut through the knot of problems pervading the U.S. political economy.

We now have some sense of the context in which policy-planning organizations have been functioning. Postwar arrangements were breaking down by the early 1970s. Centrists of the corporate liberal stripe struggled to keep ahead of crises, while new and revitalized conservative forces positioned themselves to take charge, even as the capitalist accumulation process and international conflicts ceaselessly threw out new challenges. We now turn to a look at how policy organizations have offered plans to manage events, while often being overtaken by them, starting with the broadest international dimensions in which American politics is played out.

3

International Economics, National Politics

IN THE 1950S AND 1960S, during the height of the Cold War, discussion of international politics within the United States was dominated by America's tense relationship with the Soviet Union. In the early 1970s there was a noticeable shift in discourse about international affairs. Economic matters came to the foreground, while national security concerns of a military or strategic nature receded by comparison. This reversal was spurred, on the one hand, by the Nixon administration's policy of détente with the Soviet Union, embodied in the first SALT treaty in 1972. In the same year, Nixon reversed long-standing U.S. hostility to China by traveling to Peking despite the continued U.S. military presence in Vietnam.

On the other hand, the immediate pressure from monetary disorder, trade imbalance, and the 1973–74 oil embargo and price hikes by OPEC producers impelled a shift in the international policy agenda. Trilateral Commissioner and Senator Walter F. Mondale captured this shift in an essay entitled "Beyond Détente: Toward International Economic Security." Writing in the Council on Foreign Relations' quarterly *Foreign Affairs*, Mondale stated in 1974:

Economic issues are now front and center for the world's political leaders, topping the agenda of both domestic and foreign policy concerns. While the major international security issues of the last quarter century are still with us, . . . these are now being overshadowed by the risk that the operation of the international economy may spin out of control.

In response to this threat, Mondale argued, "The priority we have accorded for years to traditional political and security concerns must now be given to international economic issues."[1]

International Dimensions of the U.S. Economy

It is in the nature of a capitalist economy to expand beyond the boundaries of the nation–state in which it is based. Although foreign activity on the part of American corporations and banks is not a recent development, a qualitative expansion in the U.S. penetration of the world economy occurred in the post–World War II era. This mushrooming presence can be measured in several ways, revealing the material foundations for the concern with economic issues by Mondale and others in the early 1970s.

Between 1950 and 1974 the value of U.S. private investment abroad went from $19 billion to $196.6 billion.[2] After adjusting for inflation, this tenfold increase represents a 7 percent annual growth in U.S. foreign investment. During this period, investment was increasingly directed to Western Europe, though Latin America continued to be an important area for U.S. firms.

After 1945 foreign business activity played a stronger and stronger relative role in the U.S. economy as a whole. Between 1950 and 1972 the value of direct foreign investment doubled, from 5 percent to 10 percent of total corporate investment assets (at home and abroad). This reflects the faster growth rate of foreign investment, compared with domestic investment. From 1960 to 1970, for example, domestic investment by American firms increased by 119 percent, while foreign investment increased by 247 percent.[3] The return flow of profits to the United States from these investments far exceeded new capital outflow. There was also a rise in the share of foreign profits in total after-tax corporate profits, from about 7 percent in 1950 to nearly 25 percent in 1972. Partly this indicates the high profit rates on foreign invested capital: an average rate of between 12 and 17 percent from 1950 to 1972, compared with an overall (including domestic) profit rate ranging from 5 percent to 11 percent in the same period.

The booming foreign involvement of financial institutions has paralleled the expansion of multinational corporations. In 1960, eight U.S. banks had a total of 131 foreign branches with combined assets of $3.5 billion. By 1978 there were 137 banks operating 761 branches with assets of $270 billion. Paul Sweezy and Harry Magdoff commented: "Nothing like this ever happened in the history of banking in the United States or anywhere else."[4]

In addition, foreign economic activity is concentrated in the largest U.S. corporations and banks, and they derive an increasing proportion of their profits from operations abroad. Thomas Weisskopf estimated that by 1970 the income drawn from foreign operations by the top 10 U.S. industrial corporations represented 30 percent of the total foreign earnings of all

U.S. industrial corporations, and that the income derived by the top 50 accounted for roughly half the total.[5] Similarly, the share of foreign earnings in the total earnings of the 13 largest U.S. banks grew from 18.8 percent in 1970 to 49.6 percent in 1976, an increase of 164 percent in 6 years.[6]

The United States is not the only advanced industrial nation whose economy has expanded internationally. As we shall see, the growing "interdependence" of the various sectors of the world economy is a development of great importance for the policy organizations. Here, it may be noted that investment by foreigners in the United States has expanded rapidly, from $8.0 billion in 1962 to $26.7 billion in 1975. The value of foreign bank assets in the United States rose from $5 billion in 1965 to $42 billion in 1974.[7] These upward trends continue in the 1980s.

Other measures of the importance of global economics could be given, such as resource dependency or a breakdown of foreign investment and earnings by industrial sector. It should be clear for now that the role of the U.S. economy in the world capitalist system swelled in absolute and relative importance in the postwar decades, as well as in structural importance. America's global economic thrust rested on the political foundations of the Bretton Woods system and the security networks made possible by U.S. hegemony.

As we saw in the last chapter, enormous strains were plaguing the Bretton Woods system by the early 1970s, continuing through the decade at the same time the United States was increasingly integrated into the international economy. The most ambitious elite attempt to make political adaptations to these changed global realities was the Trilateral Commission project, launched in 1973. Essentially the Trilateralists and their allies at the Brookings Institution and other internationalist forums wanted to fashion a new "world order" to manage the contradictions of world capitalism in the 1970s that would, in its own way, be as politically far-reaching as the Bretton Woods system was in the 1940s. But a reordered world political economy was bound to arouse domestic opposition from groups who feared a loss of power as policy decisions were relocated in new institutions. At least some of these policy differences are expressed by the American Enterprise Institute, the Institute for Contemporary Studies, and the Heritage Foundation, even as they support an open, classically liberal international economic system.

To capture this debate, let us first look at the over-all Trilateralist perspective on the international political economy. Then we shall break this approach down and discuss its application in four specific areas, noting contrasts with conservative, free-market views. It is clear that the Trilateral project was at something of an impasse by 1980, and this opened the way for conservative positions associated with the Reagan administration. Finally, we shall look at the continuities and discords in international economic policy during the first half of the 1980s, as they are embodied in policy-planning organizations.

Origins of Trilateralism

In 1971, with international economic pressures rising, the Nixon administration implemented a number of policies, such as withdrawing the gold backing of the dollar and imposing surcharges on imports, that struck foreign and American critics as rash, nationalistic, and dangerous. In his drive for the presidency, Nixon had received some support from leaders of the Business Council and the Committee for Economic Development, and his national security adviser, Henry Kissinger, had long-standing ties to the Rockefeller family and the Council on Foreign Relations. Still, Nixon's appointment patterns and bases of support were drawn less from the corporate-financial elites of the Eastern Establishment than were those of his Democratic predecessors.[8]

By the early 1970s, parts of the globally oriented sector of the American business community were deeply disturbed by the direction of economic trends and the drift of U.S. policy. In this context David Rockefeller, chairman of the Chase Manhattan Corporation, found fertile ground for initiating a private international organization that would aim at promoting the common interests of the United States, Western Europe, and Japan. In 1972, in various meetings, articles, and exchanges of opinions, Rockefeller and other representatives of corporate internationalism pushed the concept of a trilateral commission. Rockefeller found support for his ideas at the high-level Bilderberg Conference, which met in Belgium in the spring of 1972.[9] There he encountered other corporate and political leaders who were concerned about the deterioration in relations among the great industrial powers and were receptive to a new approach to international problems. This meeting, and others like it, served to establish contacts and to develop the nucleus of the Trilateral Commission's membership.[10]

Similar ideas on the necessity of a "community of developed nations" had been put forward by Columbia University professor Zbigniew Brzezinski in his book *Between Two Ages*, published in 1970, and in several essays in *Foreign Affairs* and *Foreign Policy*. Brzezinski wanted to widen the concept of the Atlantic Alliance to include Japan, a growing world power and the subject of his book *The Fragile Blossom*. Brzezinski was skeptical of the Nixon administration's balance-of-power approach to world affairs in the 1970s. He thought that Nixon had seriously neglected and undermined alliance ties while giving undue priority to relations with the Soviet Union and China. The administration was also criticized for its implicit indifference to the mounting problems of the less-developed nations.[11] In contrast, Brzezinski advocated a trilateral partnership of the United States, Western Europe, and Japan in order to "create a stable core for global politics" that would cooperate in work on common problems and critical issues confronting the world.[12]

In late 1971 and early 1972 Brzezinski helped organize a series of "Tripartite Studies" sponsored by the Brookings Institution and including scholars from Japan and Europe. He was joined in this project by a group of "transnational theorists" associated with Brookings: C. Fred Bergsten, Richard Cooper, Richard Gardner, and Philip Trezise.[13] Arguing for the centrality of "interdependence," they attacked Nixon's policies as a capitulation to economic nationalism that could lead to trade wars and a world depression. Bergsten, writing in *Foreign Affairs*, expressed the burgeoning trilateralist critique of Nixon:

> In the summer of 1971, President Nixon and Secretary Connolly revolutionized U.S. foreign economic policy. In so doing, they promoted a protectionist trend which raises questions about the future of the U.S. economy at least as fundamental as those raised by abrupt adoption of wage-price controls. In so doing, they have also encouraged a disastrous

isolationist trend which raises questions about the future of U.S. foreign policy. . . . Both the U.S. economy and U.S. foreign policy for the relevant future hang in the balance.[14]

The Brookings Institution studies influenced David Rockefeller, who had known Brzezinski previously, and encouraged him to organize the Trilateral Commission. After the Bilderberg meeting, Rockefeller, working with Brzezinski, Robert Bowie, George Franklin, and Henry Owen, developed further support in North America and held a preparatory trilateral meeting in the summer of 1972, at which the decision to go ahead was made. Over the next year leadership, members, and staff were selected, and the Commission was formally launched on July 1, 1973, with Brzezinski as director and Rockefeller as chairman of the executive committee.[15]

From 1973 to 1976 a relatively coherent global analysis of international problems was worked out under the auspices of the Trilateral Commission and the Brookings Institution. It was marked by a high degree of awareness that the post–World War II international political economy was at a turning point and that bold new initiatives were needed to fend off the threats of war, economic depression, and social breakdown.

The Trilateral Commission and the Brookings Institution operate within the same intellectual and political framework, and the concepts and content of their analysis are very similar. This is not surprising, given the membership overlap between the two groups. As we have seen, Brookings scholars helped lay the groundwork for the Trilateral Commission and reappear as co-authors of several "Triangle Papers." These two organizations were in the forefront of the effort to restructure the international economy in the 1970s, pursuing their goal thoroughly and self-consciously.

In contrast, the American Enterprise Institute and the Institute for Contemporary Studies were less innovative and less far-reaching in their analyses of the same problems. Their greater commitment to free-market economics and wariness of state-imposed organizational solutions made it difficult to develop new paradigms for analysis. For its part, the Heritage Foundation devoted its growing resources to domestic affairs and national security concerns, while occasionally attacking liberal arguments for reforming the international economic system. During the 1970s the "world order" framework of the liberal center seemed unable to manage events, and elites in the business community came to believe that the risks outweighed the likely benefits of plans that would involve greater state commitments or substantial changes in the organization of the international economy. This process of disillusionment played into the hands of conservative forces, despite, or because of, the fact that they offered no bold, new policy prescriptions.

Given this asymmetry of inventiveness between the two groupings, let us first outline the key features of the Brookings–Trilateral interdependence perspective, and then examine its specific application to four crucial problem areas in the world economy: monetary relations, trade issues, the North–South struggle, and energy policy. In the discussion of each issue the divergent orientations of the more conservative policy-planning organizations will be described. As the 1970s wore on, an increasingly plain political reality was the impasse and frustrations of the globalist position. In its last two years the Carter administration jettisoned some of its early Trilateralist baggage, moving rightward under pressure from an invigorated new conservatism that reemphasized national security and military preparedness in the international arena. Vacillating between the policy perspectives of managerialism and militarism, Carter gave the appearance of indecision and opportunism that helped to prepare his demise. In 1981 the Reagan team entered Washington armed with its distinctive ideology to confront the intractable world disorders of international capitalism.

Global Interdependence and Trilateral Managerialism

Underlying the analysis of specific issues by the Brookings Institution and the Trilateral Commission is a particular framework for understanding international developments that carries with it definite political implications. In a Brookings-supported study, C. Fred Bergsten, Robert O. Keohane, and Joseph S. Nye Jr. distinguish between two levels of analysis in international political economy. The "process level" deals with "short-term behavior within a constant set of institutions, fundamental assumptions, and expectations," while a "structure level" has to do with "long-term political and economic determinants of the systemic incentives and constraints within which actors operate."[16] Trilateralists and interdependence theorists place great importance on attending to the latter "second face of power," for the early 1970s were marked by a growing questioning of basic postwar structures and rules, resulting in an "increased politicization of international economic affairs."[17] In response to the threat of disorder and chaos, the Trilateral Commission asserts that "new forms of common management" must be devised, since short-term adjustments are inadequate for purposes of holding the system together.[18]

The Brookings–Trilateral position sees the international political economy as an interconnected regime defined by specific rules, institutions, and operative assumptions. Nations are interlocked through economic, technological, political, and military processes in such a way that developments in one area of the international system have important ramifications ("linkages") in other areas. Politics and economics, thoroughly conjoined, cannot be analyzed or treated separately.

The political structure of the international economy has typically been a "hegemonic system," by which Bergsten, Keohane, and Nye mean "one in which one state is able and willing to determine and maintain the essential rules by which relations among states are governed."[19] During the nineteenth century, Great Britain played this role, while after 1945 the United States was the pivotal power, providing leadership that sustained a liberal order supporting free trade and promoting economic growth and political stability. The analysts from the Brookings Institution and the Trilateral Commission view the postwar order as a highly positive achievement. More than conservative free-marketers, they stress the role of political volition and constructive planning as crucial ingredients in the successful reconstruction of the war-torn world. The summary statement of the Trilateral Commission says: "The system shaped after World War II was created through an act of will and human initiative in a relatively restricted period of time."[20] The raison d'être of the Trilateral Commission is to reshape the system through renewed political initiatives in the areas of advanced capitalism. The election of Jimmy Carter in 1976 was seen by some American Trilateralists as a history-making opportunity. Brookings Institution scholar C. Fred Bergsten, co-author of a Trilateral Commission report and assistant secretary of the Treasury for International Affairs under Carter, expressed this hope well: "After every major war in this century Americans sought a new world order. Wilson pushed the League of Nations; Roosevelt and Truman constructed the UN–Bretton Woods system; and now, Jimmy Carter gives us the Trilateral plan."[21]

This sense of urgency was sharpened by the volatile international economy of the 1970s. The economic growth of Japan and Western Europe was eroding American hegemony, as the first Brookings–Tripartite Report made clear: "It is no longer feasible for the United States to assume predominant responsibility for making the system work. This responsibility must now be distributed so as to more nearly reflect the diffusion of economic power that has occurred over the past two decades."[22]

The need for joint, cooperative leadership is a constant refrain in Brookings–Trilateral statements. While this would represent a move to "collective hegemony," analysts of interdependence are clear about limiting managerial power to a select circle. A report entitled "Toward a Renovated International System," summing up the initial three years of the Trilateral Commission's work, provides frank recommendations for the new basis of international leadership. The report denies that a trilateral approach is intended to create a "closed club" of rich nations; rather, "It is essential that the trilateral countries not only remain sensitive and responsive to needs and problems elsewhere in the world, but that they also be flexible in their approach to each particular issue, consulting frequently with others and participating with them as the particular issue permits or requires."[23]

However, the report stops well short of suggesting the kind of general North–South negotiations for a new international order that less-developed countries pushed for in the 1970s. Instead a plea is made for "piecemeal functionalism," in which issues are broken down into parts and dealt with by those most concerned.[24] According to the report, "wide participation may impede action on important issues and produce solutions too complex or compromised to be effective. Greater progress can be made when smaller groups of like-minded or similarly situated countries collaborate together."[25] In practice this amounts to hegemony of the richer nations in the world economy: "Close trilateral cooperation, which must be responsive to the needs and problems of others, will improve the chances of a smooth and peaceful evolution of the global system."[26] The management of international monetary arrangements, for example, "involves relatively few countries, although all countries have an interest in it."[27]

The ideas of Brookings Institution scholars and Trilateral Commission authors are sometimes seen as quite change-oriented on international questions. But in order to make a more discerning political assessment of this policy current, it is important to examine just what changes are recommended and which ones are ignored or excluded. Capitalism as a closely meshed, expanding world economy is viewed as a system whose growth will benefit rich and poor nations alike. There are no proposed changes that would seriously restrict the most globally oriented firms or the international institutions (IMF, World Bank) that work in tandem with developed capitalist interests. As we have seen, the leadership "core" of the global political economy is to rest within the advanced capitalist nations.

Those changes that are called for, in the Brookings–Trilateral perspective, are mainly political or organizational in character, meant to managerially adapt to and adjust the capitalist economic relations already in place: the "management of interdependence." In this view politics tends to lag behind dynamic economic developments that create the facts of interdependence, leading a major Brookings Institution study to state that "timidity is the main danger" for American foreign policy.[28]

The sources of this lack of foresight and gumption on the part of policymakers are traced to narrow nationalist interests pressuring government to protect their relative position in the domestic economy against international competition.[29] The actions of the Nixon administration in 1971 are often pointed to as negative examples of shortsighted and threatening nationalism.[30] Subservience to protectionist forces must be avoided, lest the delicate interplay of international economic mechanism comes unhinged. Policymakers must act in terms of the larger, systemic imperatives that increasingly determine domestic consequences: "The economic officials of at least the largest countries must begin to think in terms of managing a single world economy in addition to managing international economic relations among countries."[31] Such is the scope of transition in the policy agenda proposed by the Trilateral Commission and the Brookings interdependence theorists, given the postwar order's critical condition.

The quotations in this chapter show that the two policy groups present their views as being in the general interest and not as the specific outlook of a particular sector of society or an ideological grouping. Trilateral Commission spokespersons like David Rockefeller take pains to describe their organization as reasonable and moderate—certainly not a "bankers' club"—and unfairly subjected to misleading and paranoic attacks by both the left and the right.[32] Without falling into either economic reductionism or conspiracy theory, it is possible to analyze the Brookings–Trilateral position on international economic issues as consistent with a policy current in American politics that is ideologically and economically grounded. Essays by Robert W. Cox and Jeff Frieden are useful for this purpose.

In a review of the voluminous literature on the New International Economic Order (NIEO), stimulated by the demands of the non-aligned movement, Robert Cox identifies five schools of thought: establishment, social democratic, Third World, neomercantilist, and historical materialist.[33] Each sets out a mode of analysis and a strategy for action with regard to the international political economy. Cox, a self-described conservative with sympathy for the left, undertakes an "ideological analysis . . . against the prevailing orthodoxies which, when stripped of their putative universality, become seen as special pleading for historically transient but presently entrenched interests."[34]

For Cox, schools of thought are materially linked to networks which bring like-minded individuals together to help build a consensus around an analysis and a set of policy prescriptions. At the center of networks are private organizations—"mobilizing and coordinating agencies" that sponsor research and provide funds for studies, conferences, and other forums.[35] The dominant view of the NIEO in the industrialized countries is the establishment position of "monopolistic liberalism." From Cox's view, "the Trilateral Commission is the most important formal organization coordinating this network."[36] He describes the world-view of monopolistic liberalism as follows:

> The fundamental commitment of the establishment perspective is to an open world market with relatively free movement of capital, goods, and technology. Government interventions should be of a kind that support this goal, and such interventions as would impede it are to be condemned. Powerful governments are to enforce this code of conduct upon weaker governments, using for this purpose especially the international organizations they control.[37]

Most of the Brookings–Trilateral writings on international economics are squarely within this framework. There is some variation. Certain contributions shade into what Cox would call a social democratic perspective, sympathetic to Third World claims for more equity and decision-making power, while retaining the liberal ideal of progress through the open market. A good example of this stance is Seyom Brown's 1974 book, *New Forces in World Politics*, published by Brookings. Both the establishment and the social democratic perspectives are far removed from Third World and Marxist positions, which oppose capitalist economics and envision a radical redistribution of political and economic power between and within the First and Third Worlds.

Cox's ideological analysis of Trilateralism can be complemented by Jeff Frieden's emphasis on the class basis of policy ideology. In Frieden's view, the liberalized international economy of the 1950s and 1960s was presided over, in the United States, by a distinct bloc of forces. "The internationalists," he argues, "concentrated their theoretical work in the Brookings Institution and the Council on Foreign Relations, their political work in the White House, and their economic work in the world's money markets."[38] Trilateralism is the organized 1970s representative of this same policy current. It is the political expression of those banks and corporations with growing international commitments that need a forum for discussion and decision-making in a period of instability. A new and concentrated assertion of capitalist imperatives on an international basis must be undertaken, lest economic nationalism increase and cut off the freedom of capital to flow into profit-making opportunities.[39] Frieden is blunt: "The Trilateral Commission is the executive advisory committee to transnational finance capital."[40]

Frieden notes that a domestically oriented section of finance capital opposes the thrust of Trilateralism. Included are such industries as steel, textiles, and footwear, which are not significantly involved in international markets, have been hurt by foreign competition, and are active in seeking protectionist legislation. Clearly this faction is at odds with the move toward continued world economic integration and transnational liberalization. To what extent does it find expression in conservative policy-planning organizations like the American Enterprise Institute and the Institute for Contemporary Studies?

The American Enterprise Institute has organized a number of studies on international economics as symposia, and it often includes Brookings Institution scholars among the participants. The title of a 1979 AEI study, *Challenges to a Liberal International Economic Order*, suggests the standpoint. Liberal economics is seen as the virtuous path to progress, while economic nationalism and protectionism are viewed as vices to be resisted and defeated.[41] Similarly, the Institute for Contemporary Studies published a volume in 1979 on the politics of protectionism, the basic perspective of which was that tariff wars were "a threat to the very basis of the postwar global economy."[42] Thus it can be said that the AEI and the ICS do not constitute a clear opposition to the liberal interdependence school of the Brookings Institution and the Trilateral Commission on the issues of free trade and open markets. But while conflict over the goal of a liberal global economy is not a line of demarcation between these policy organizations, their chosen political means to this end reveal differences.

The AEI and the ICS focus on the unhindered free market as the basis for policy, but the Trilateralists are more apt to be concerned about the socially and politically disruptive side-effects of the economics of interdependence. Their analysis allows for more political steering mechanisms to be brought into place. To some extent this replicates the differences over state intervention in the domestic economy between "conservatives" and "liberals." The Reagan administration, for example, has attempted, with much backsliding, to uphold free trade while being very cautious about any political departures that would require new commitments to, or coordination with, other states or international organizations. From the standpoint of some Trilateral managerialists, the unwillingness of free-market advocates to alter the political structure and operative rules of the international economy is as great an obstacle to forestalling crisis as the growing forces of protectionism.

The policy organizations differ in how they view the Third World in the world economy. The AEI and the ICS are more openly hostile to Third World demands, while some Brookings and Trilateral statements at least verbally counsel limited accommodation. The conservative groups also stress the dangers posed by Soviet power and revolutionary movements in the Third World to U.S. economic security, including the threat to international shipping, access to vital natural resources, trade patterns, and debt repayment. This has consequences for their preferred national security policy (see Chapter 4). Examination of the four institutions' perspectives on monetary and foreign trade issues, North–South relations, and energy policy will help in comparing and contrasting their underlying political outlooks. Crises in these four areas in the 1970s marked both the decline of U.S. hegemony and the changing global economic context in which American policy was exercised.

Monetary and Trade Issues

In the Brookings–Trilateral framework, monetary and trade issues are closely related. The Trilateral Commission task force report on trade, drafted in 1974 principally by Brookings Institution Senior Fellow Philip H. Trezise, states that "liberalized trade will facilitate the orderly functioning of the monetary system, just as it is true that a well-working monetary system will promote trade."[43] Since there is no room for regional or national insulation from world economic processes, the goal must be "to make interdependence, which is inescapable in the modern world, a more manageable and less troubling condition."[44]

In the early 1970s, distress over the international economy often focused on the challenges to established monetary relations. After several years of debate about its overvaluation, the dollar was devalued by more than 8 percent in December 1971, at the Smithsonian Agreements, proclaimed by President Nixon to be "the most significant monetary achievement in the history of the world." Some fourteen months later that agreement was shattered, as the United States devalued its currency by another 10 percent, following a massive speculative outflow of dollars early in 1973. Just ahead was the huge transfer of funds to OPEC states, and the general pattern of floating exchange rates, leading to widespread uncertainty about the future ratios of currencies, upon which trade and investment decisions depend. Over the decade the largely unregulated and volatile Eurocurrency market expanded more than tenfold to over $600 billion, nearly three-quarters of which was in Eurodollars. Finally, the debt burden of many Third World countries reached astronomical proportions by 1980, producing fears of a repayment crisis with reverberations throughout the world economy.

These ominous monetary developments indicated that the international economy as a whole was faced with crisis. Richard Cooper argued, "Ideally, monetary relations should be inconspicuous, part of the background in a well-functioning system. Once they become visible and uncertain, something is wrong."[45] In an increasingly interdependent system, where the growth of national economies is strongly tied to the international movement of capital, unstable monetary relations cast a pall over economic prospects. It is significant that the first report of the Trilateral Commission, published in 1973, dealt with this issue.

The monetary task force argues that, with the downfall of Bretton Woods, "there is an urgent need to restore some systematic, mutually agreed international monetary order." Mutual confidence between the major powers is needed for this task. Though the report represents the viewpoint of the advanced capitalist regions, the Trilateral Commission authors are confident that their recommendations for orderly agreements are in the best interests of the poor countries, the Communist states, and the oil-producing nations, organized in OPEC.[46]

The proposals aim to prevent "monetary anarchy" by curbing wide swings in exchange rates and by smoothing the balance-of-payments adjustment process. These measures would require greater coordination of domestic economic policies and an expansion of the IMF's lending facilities in order to counter speculative movements of funds. Excess dollar holdings would be converted into a new international currency, "bancor," and be used by the IMF to even out foreign exchange imbalances. By "multilateralizing" international monetary arrangements, the IMF would become a true "central bank for central banks."[47] This approach is characteristic of the Trilateral Commission's emphasis on institutional and managerial solutions to problems.

A 1977 report reiterates the theme that a "core" of five to ten countries should establish the basic features of the international financial system. Important tasks include bolstering the reserve role of Special Drawing Rights, preventing erratic movements of exchange rates, monitoring the Eurocurrency market more closely, and coordinating the economic policies of the Trilateral states.[48]

The unstable nature of monetary relations in the 1970s was made plain by the fate of a 1979 Trilateral Commission report entitled "Major Payments Imbalances and International Financial Stability." The 1979 oil price rises temporarily reversed a decline in OPEC surpluses, and the debt burden of the poorer countries grew much worse, contrary to the predictions of the Trilateral draft report. Overtaken and tarnished by the onrush of events, the report was withdrawn from publication.

During the 1970s, because of several important developments, foreign trade became a much debated political issue in the United States. By 1980, exports and imports each represented more than 10 percent of the gross national product, double the proportions from twenty years before. Yet the direction of trade seemed to go against the United States, as trade deficits of more than $25 billion a year—and climbing—became the norm from 1977. The shares of world markets controlled by American exports shrank, while foreign firms increased their cut of the U.S. market. Declining U.S. industries and defensive labor unions lobbied Congress for protectionist legislation.

All the four policy-planning organizations strongly oppose protectionism. The Trilateral Commission trade report calls for GATT negotiations to reduce industrial tariffs as much as possible over the long run. Restrictions on exports, safeguards against disruptive imports, and other nontariff distortions of trade are to be discouraged through tighter rules of international conduct, advance consultation, and other GATT reforms to be codified and regulated by the core powers.[49] The report also endorses special attention to the trade interests of the Third World, though it warns of "a danger that the developing countries could make of the negotiations a grand debating session . . . rather than a conscientious and often tedious effort to find workable answers to hard questions."[50]

The Trilateral Commission's co-thinkers at the Brookings Institution concur that economic policy is bounded by the facts of interdependence, making an insular approach unrealistic. In a 1976 prospective of the next ten years, Edward Fried and Philip Trezise contend that international consultation must go much further than the stabilization of exchange rates by central banks, to include the coordination of domestic demand policies by the advanced industrial nations. For this approach to work, noninflationary American growth is needed, given the size of the U.S. economy and the continuing reserve role of the dollar. Growth, efficiency, and innovation in the world economy will be fostered if trade restrictions are progressively lifted. In particular, tariffs on manufactured products should be reduced, because "they impede the integration of the developing countries into the international industrial system."[51]

In 1980 Ralph Bryant and Lawrence Krause write, along similar lines, "The trend toward increasing economic interdependence should be accepted, but stronger collective efforts should be made to manage that trend, and a corresponding evolution of national and intergovernmental institutions should be actively promoted."[52] Organizations that facilitate this process should be strengthened, but no structural economic changes are needed. In the Brookings–Trilateral view, the social facts established by international capitalist development set the parameters of policy toward monetary and trade relations. The orderly rationalization and integration of transnational capitalism should be overseen by those international institutions (the IMF, the World Bank, GATT) already dominated by the trilateral powers.

While the "interdependence" paradigm is clearly dominant in the Brookings–Trilateral partnership, contrasting views of the policy implications of international economics contend at the American Enterprise Institute. Marina v. N. Whitman, a Trilateral Commission member and former AEI academic adviser, takes interdependence as the inescapable foundation of U.S. policy toward the world economy. Like the Brookings scholars, she argues, "If we are to reap the full benefits of international economic integration, some globalization of the management of macroeconomic policy problems is required."[53] But for the AEI's chief economist, Herbert Stein, "The introduction of international considerations and participants in a major way into the making of macroeconomic policy would overburden what is already a very weak process."[54]

Typical of the AEI mainstream are Gottfried Haberler's economic analyses in the annual "Contemporary Economic Problems" series. For Haberler, probably the leading AEI international economist, "Turbulence in the foreign exchange markets in recent years have their roots not in a basic defect of the system of floating exchange rates but in the failings of national policies in some of the leading countries."[55] In line with this premise, Haberler attributes the declining dollar and worsening trade deficits in 1977–1978 to the Carter administration's expansionary policies, which led to a crippling "inflation differential" between the United States and strong-currency countries like Japan and West Germany. He views as inflationary the "locomotive strategy," promoted by Trilateralists like Richard Cooper, Carter's under secretary of state for economic affairs, which sought to induce strong countries to stimulate their economies, thus drawing in imports from the United States. The lesson Haberler draws is this: "The single most important, nay indispensable, measure to prevent a further weakening of the dollar and of the whole international monetary system is that the United States bring down its rate of inflation."⁵⁶ This is to be accomplished not through wage-price controls or an incomes policy, but through restraining monetary and fiscal policy, curbing the demands of unions and other interest groups, and adopting free-market policies generally.

Adherence to market principles as the basis for international monetary and trade policy is also underlined by John T. Cuddington and Ronald I. McKinnon in key essays developing policy positions for the Institute for Contemporary Studies.⁵⁷ They strongly support liberalized trade, as do other ICS economists, employing the arguments of classical liberal political economy on the benefits of unrestricted markets, while accepting minimal adjustment assistance to displaced workers. More than Trilateralists or Brookings Institution analysts, the ICS economists see consistent free-market policies as the tonic for both international and domestic troubles. Cuddington and McKinnon believe that the Federal Reserve should focus less on domestic interest rates and more on the value of the dollar in foreign exchange markets, while calling for greater monetary coordination among the central banks of the United States, Japan, and West Germany.

To restate an earlier point, the AEI and the ICS do not, in general, take the changing nature of the international economy, and the U.S. role within it, as the touchstone of economic policy. While systemic liberalization is a goal and some policy coordination is desirable, their agenda focuses on restoring growth and profitability to the domestic economy through conservative, probusiness measures, whose benefits will then spill over into the global arena. By contrast, the Trilateralists and many Brookings scholars begin with the processes of the world economy, under which are subsumed the prospects for national political economies. Simply put, the "internationalism" of the two camps has somewhat opposed intellectual and political foundations. The specific proposals of all four organizations should be understood against the background of contending strategies for adapting U.S. policy to a changing world capitalism.

North–South Relations

Relations among the advanced capitalist nations are at the center of monetary and trade issues, but the economic ties between the First World and the less-developed countries of the Third World have also entered into the debate over international policy. Clear differences of strategy for dealing with the Third World are evident among policy elites. The contrast between reformist and revanchist approaches is reflected in Trilateral Commission reports and certain essays by AEI and ICS analysts.

In a seminal 1973 essay in *Foreign Policy*, C. Fred Bergsten urgently stated the case for instituting a new economic relationship with the Third World. Against the view that regarded poorer countries "solely as pawns on the chessboard of global power politics," Bergsten maintained that a stance recognizing the growing economic interdependence of North and South was needed.[58] A posture of indifference by the richer states would only encourage a radical economic nationalism that could seriously disrupt trade, finance, and resource supplies. Bergsten's main conclusion was that, in conjunction with its European and Japanese allies, "the United States must, in its own national self-interest, adopt much more cooperative and responsive policies toward the Third World."[59]

Bergsten's essay was written before OPEC's price hikes and before the U.N. special sessions in 1974 and 1975 that endorsed the Third World call for a New International Economic Order (NIEO). Rather than decrying these events, the Trilateral Commission took the enlightened self-interest position of Bergsten, endorsing the concept of a new economic order, while defining it in a nonthreatening, system-securing way. The poorer countries "need the aid, technology, know-how and markets of the Trilateral world" while "Trilateral countries increasingly need the developing countries as sources of raw materials, as export markets, and, most important of all, as constructive partners in the creation of a workable world order."[60] The idea is to persuade Third World leaders that they have a positive stake in reforming, rather than transforming, existing relationships. This will be in their interest because "extreme measures could have a self-defeating effect by threatening to throttle the goose which can lay the golden eggs of growth" and "expansion of the global economic pie rather than redistribution of a pie of unchanged size is the most hopeful means of improving the relative economic position of the poorer nations."[61]

On the issue of basic commodity resources, for example, the Trilateral Commission proposes measures to stabilize international transactions while making provisions for new actors on the commodity market scene. As the relevant task force report states, "It would be shortsighted for any nations to expect to be able to isolate themselves from world commodity developments and at the same time to see the broader world economy evolve in an orderly, constructive direction."[62] Nonindustrialized, commodity-exporting nations are to be integrated into the world economy in a way that is beneficial to their economic development, while industrialized commodity-importing nations gain secure supplies at predictable prices.

The global political economy foreseen by the Trilateral Commission is a tiered order, with the trilateral countries and the multinational corporations and banks at the core. It is their economic imperatives that are to shape the contours of a global framework. Accommodations made to the developing countries will be on terms that ensure conditions favorable to the needs of multinationals for stability and profits. Confrontation politics vis-à-vis the Third World must give way to subtler inducements to establish a favorable global business climate.

During the 1970s an intellectual and political current ranging itself against the trilateralist outlook gathered force. Daniel Patrick Moynihan's diatribes against Third World posturing at the United Nations echoed mounting sentiments hostile to demands from the southern hemisphere and eager for a reassertion of unapologetic American power and leadership.

Opposition to calls for a New International Economic Order are strongly expressed by contributors to an ICS volume, *The Third World: Premises of U.S. Policy*. Published in 1978, it anticipates the Reagan administration's approach to the Third World. The editor, W. Scott Thompson, who was a Defense Department official in 1975–1976, has worked on building support for Reagan's foreign policy through a high position at the U.S. Information Agency.

In addition to opposing NIEO plans, the ICS writers take aim at "important elements in the American foreign policy establishment" who accept "the West's responsibility for Third

World poverty and a complementary responsibility to solve that poverty by massive wealth transfers."[63] It may be presumed that the somewhat caricatured targets were Carter administration liberals, Robert McNamara's World Bank, and the Trilateralist–interdependence school. They are charged with sowing illusions about the Third World that have contributed to Western weakness.

The conservative position is well stated in an essay by Peter Bauer and Basil Yamey in the ICS volume.[64] Bauer has been an important figure in polemicizing against the Trilateralist type of thinking from the right, with several important essays appearing, appropriately, in *Commentary* magazine from 1975 on. Bauer and Yamey argue that the main obstacles to Third World economic development are internal and that commercial contact with the West, far from being exploitative, has been enormously positive. Further economic progress requires abandonment of state planning efforts and adherence to capitalist market principles. The developed countries should lower barriers to Third World exports and not subsidize economic inefficiency through foreign aid. If aid is granted, Bauer states elsewhere, it should not be through multinational programs. He prefers "bilateral straight cash grants to governments that perform the essential tasks of government without controlling the economy too closely and without trying to politicize life in their countries."[65] Advanced capitalist countries should purge themselves of guilt for the plight of the poor and cease making conciliatory gestures toward upstart Third World elites.

In less harsh terms, this view is held by the leading AEI international economists, who see the NIEO package as a threat to a liberal world order. A prolific AEI scholar, Thomas Willett, perceives the demands of the less-developed countries as an expression of resentment, rather than as a reasonable economic program. Like Bauer and Yamey, he suggests that "much of the LDC [less-developed countries] rhetoric on the NIEO proposals may have become an expensive luxury for the gratification of political and social objectives of elites in the developing countries at the expense of improvement of the economic well-being of their general population."[66] By undercutting the humanitarian high ground of Third World demands, conservatives can repudiate concessions as both economically unwise and morally unprincipled. Although there are powerful criticisms of the NIEO program on the left,[67] the very different right-wing critique has increasingly shaped policy in the United States, dovetailing with a resurgent militarism in national security affairs.

Energy Policy

Gradations of accommodationist and hard-line policy tendencies can also be observed on the energy issue. The embargoes, cutbacks, and price rises emanating from OPEC in 1973–74 only intensified an energy problem that had been developing for years. Availability of abundant supplies of oil at relatively low prices helped fuel postwar growth in the United States. With this relationship altered, policy elites put energy on the political agenda. In the 1970s the Trilateral Commission published four reports on the energy problem.[68]

From the Trilateralist standpoint, the energy crisis threatens worldwide economic and political turmoil unless effective policies are cooperatively implemented by the industrial countries. The era of cheap and plentiful oil is over, and the three trilateral regions need a common, long-range energy strategy. Part of the response is to begin conservation programs, emergency sharing plans, and joint research and development of new energy sources, including nuclear energy. Equally important is the relationship with the OPEC producers, whose desire to own and control their resources is seen as "legitimate."[69]

Ensuring steady supplies of imported oil in the 1970s could be done only through a common strategy that avoided confrontation with OPEC. Even though Western Europe and Japan depended on imports much more than the United States did, no separate deal was to be cut with the producers, since a unified Trilateral front was necessary if OPEC's new-found power was to be responsibly harnessed to the world economy. Both economic warfare and military action against OPEC were ruled out, for they "court political disaster without bringing the desired results."[70] Rejected were the proposals for military intervention in the Persian Gulf to seize control of the oil fields, made by some Western strategists after the war of October 1973.

The initial Trilateral Commission approach also differed markedly from Secretary Kissinger's hopes of forcing down oil prices and disrupting the cartel through a confrontationist U.S. position, despite Arab and Iranian calls for dialogue. Kissinger's approach was sharply criticized by Trilateralist George Ball at a Commission meeting in December 1974, and six months later the secretary of state was sounding a softer note toward OPEC.[71]

The Trilateral policy toward the energy crisis involves an attempt "to create a many-sided structure of cooperation with the producers."[72] Economic ties between OPEC and the developed consuming nations should be tightened through cooperation in the national development programs of the producing states, encouragement of OPEC investment in the industrialized countries, and provision of greater power for the OPEC states in international organizations. The producers should also be prodded to contribute to a special fund for recycling revenues to debt-strapped less-developed countries.

Security ties should also be improved, using arms sales as an opening wedge and reducing balance-of-trade deficits in the process. Stationing of Western forces might also be acceptable to OPEC elites—or so it was hoped at the time, since "their newly-acquired wealth may serve as an invitation to subversion, revolution, or intervention from outside."[73] A settlement of the Arab–Israeli conflict is seen as a component of a new energy and economic relationship. A solution to this vexing dispute should be "based essentially on the principle of non-acquisition of territory by force and the right of all nations to secure existence."[74] Presumably this would involve a withdrawal of Israel from land occupied in the 1967 war, in return for Arab recognition of the Jewish state, along the lines of U.N. Security Council Resolution 242. A similar view, worked out in more detail, is contained in an important 1975 Brookings Institution Middle East Study Group report funded by the Rockefeller Foundation;[75] the study group included Zbigniew Brzezinski. The report supported Palestinian self-determination, possibly in the form of an independent state.

These conclusions are quite similar to those reached by Richard Erb, an energy analyst for the American Enterprise Institute.[76] Believing Saudi Arabia to be the key to OPEC policies, Erb calls for a better climate toward Saudi foreign investment, more U.S. corporate involvement in the desert state's economic program, and stronger ties between the Saudi central bank and the U.S. Federal Reserve Board and Treasury Department. Saudi membership in multilateral financial organizations, including the OECD, is suggested. Like the Trilateralists, Erb looks to the integration of new oil wealth into the world economy and is critical of moves by Congress to restrict this process. He also sees a resolution of the Arab–Israeli conflict as a precondition for secure, long-term energy supplies from the Middle East. The AEI on this question tends to be more sympathetic to Arab concerns than are those of the neoconservative intellectuals, with whom the AEI otherwise has much in common. Perhaps this is in part because of the Lebanese background of the Baroody family.[77]

Strongly believing in the problem-solving power of the market, the AEI and the ICS see the decontrol of oil and gas prices, along with removal of other disincentives to domestic production, as the keys to reducing dependence on exports. In contrast, the Trilateral Commission wants market forces to provide much of the "motive power" on energy, but it states that the "overall strategy must take the form of public policy based on the conscious choice and dedicated efforts of governments and peoples."[78]

Richard Sweeney of the ICS discounts the negative impact of OPEC on the dollar and, like Erb, focuses on orderly investment and financial arrangements with the Saudis.[79] But absent from ICS discussion of energy is any urgency about coordinating policy with other countries or about making room for the producing states in new international relationships. Instead, diversifying supplies and building up strategic petroleum reserves in preparation for a crisis are emphasized. Managerial approaches to energy problems give way to militarism at the ICs, as an alleged "Soviet threat" to Persian Gulf oil supplies in the 1980s is invoked, to be met by an expansion of U.S. military forces.[80]

Since 1981 the Reagan administration has pushed deregulatory energy policies domestically, while attempting to undercut Middle East conflicts by molding a strategic consensus" around the purported Soviet menace to all states in the region. The 1982 war in Lebanon revealed the inadequacy of this approach, and the United States remains without a coherent approach to the oil-producing region. For its part, the coordinated energy plans promoted by the Trilateral Commission were disrupted by political instability abroad and the 1979 price increases. When the Shah of Iran, the regional ally of the United States, was overthrown in 1979, discourse about international dimensions of the energy crisis was remilitarized, even though worldwide demand for oil was down by the early 1980s, new supplies were appearing, and OPEC was internally divided. While the Carter administration played into this trend, and the Trilateral Commission fortified the military and strategic aspects of its thinking on the energy issue, this shift favored political currents represented by the ICs, the AEI, the Heritage Foundation, and other conservative policy organizations.

The World of the 1980s

By 1981 the conditions for realizing the Trilateralist system-managing strategy were dissipating, as the inertia of national political interests held back those establishment forces seeking to rationalize the international political economy. Leaders of the seven top capitalist powers have met at annual economic summits since 1975, but the actual extent of policy coordination appears to be small. In the early 1980s, governments routinely accused one another of undermining their respective economic programs, as high U.S. interest rates drained capital from Western Europe, putting a damper on economic growth there and keeping the value of the dollar up, leading to massive U.S. balance-of-trade deficits of over $100 billion.

Since the early 1970s, America has become more intertwined with the international economy. In addition to cheapening imports, the overvalued dollar has attracted foreign investment in government bonds and bank deposits, which help finance the federal budget deficit, and the United States is now a net debtor nation, owing more to foreigners than foreigners owe to it. Total foreign investment of all kinds in the United States is moving toward $1 trillion.[81] Developing countries of the Third World are increasingly vital to U.S. business, accounting for more than 40 percent of U.S. exports in 1982.[82] In the early 1980s, rising U.S. interest rates added to already crushing debt burdens, while the recession in the trilateral regions deprived developing countries of export markets, foreign exchange, and capital for internal development. Third World countries now owe creditors nearly $1 trillion, with many of the most-indebted states in Latin America, where private U.S. banks have made huge loans whose repayment prospects are doubtful.

During the Reagan years, the Trilateralist current has had some presence within the administration, but mainly it attempts to influence policy from the outside. An effective allied voice on issues of exchange rates and debt has been the Institute for International Economics (IIE), established in 1981 with a $4 million, five-year commitment from the German Marshall Fund of the United States. With a board of directors sprinkled with Trilateralists, the IIE is headed by former Carter administration official C. Fred Bergsten, whose past affiliations include the Brookings Institution, the Carnegie Endowment for International Peace, the Council on Foreign Relations, and the Trilateral Commission. Also intersecting with liberal Trilateral thinking to promote a sympathetic view of Third World assistance needs is the Overseas Development Council (ODC), founded in 1969 to raise awareness of the growing interdependence of the United States and the developing world.[83] Funded by many internationally oriented corporations and corporate foundations, the chair of the ODC board is Robert McNamara, himself the co-author of a 1983 Trilateral Commission report on Third World development.

Recent Trilateral deliberations continue to stress the interconnection of economic and security issues and the need for policy coordination by the states of the trilateral regions.[84] Trilateralists see the international monetary system as distorted by the overvalued dollar, which is itself a product of high interest rates caused by the budget deficits that are one legacy of Reaganomics. To reduce the deficit military spending reductions will be necessary in the United States, and so the burden should be more evenly shared by the trilateral countries. In the debt-strapped Third World, some austerity measures must be installed, but not so harshly that they cause political explosions. Private Western banks must accept some write-off of loans, while multilateral institutions increase their aid resources. Above all, political leaders in the advanced sector must understand the global pattern of the relationships in which they are enmeshed, so that their policy decisions are made in light of their broadest international political and economic ramifications. Ritual devotion to free-market verities are no substitute for a political sensibility attuned to managing the process of the global capitalist political economy. These ideas have some support in elite policy circles, and possibly in corners of the Reagan administration and the American Enterprise Institute, where a few Trilateralists reside. But other policy-planners and conservative supporters of Reagan have different priorities and ideological commitments that clash with any movement toward world order management.

Consider the Heritage Foundation, which in November 1980 delivered its encyclopedic recommendations to President-Elect Reagan and his transition team, including a set of proposals on international economic policy whose spirit animated much of the Reagan approach for five years. Like the AEI and ICS, the Heritage Foundation sees the route to international economic adjustment as based on domestic revitalization, to be achieved by consistent free-market policies. Barriers to foreign trade and investment are to be removed, export subsidies abolished, and import curbs resisted. Intervention in foreign exchange markets to alter the value of the dollar should also be discontinued. The Heritage Foundation has also been a persistent critic of foreign aid programs, and of any measures that would increase the resources of the IMF or the World Bank. Third World countries should adopt free-market measures, reduce their state sector, and open their economies to the free flow of private foreign capital.[85] The Heritage approach requires no messy new levels of political coordination or institution-building, and for that reason it fits in nicely with the nationalist unilateralism that marks segments of the American right.

In the 1980s Reagan administration officials have advocated

a return to free-enterprise policies in international policy arenas as an antidote to the ailments of Third World economies. But the sheer enormity of the debt crisis has led the United States to make modest proposals for expanding the role of the World Bank, as with Treasury Secretary James Baker's October 1985 proposals, which caused consternation at the Heritage Foundation. In 1986 Baker also secured agreement at the Tokyo economic summit for stabilizing exchange rates through a "managed float." But these measures are small in proportion to the full, interconnected dimensions of world economic problems, and the conservative forecast for recovery remains grounded in business satisfying domestic policies.

In the 1980s the policy agenda for global affairs was the reverse of that adumbrated by Mondale in 1974. Under the shadow of a world recession in the early 1980s, and with negotiations on comprehensive North–South economic agreements virtually dead, a new "world disorder" of economic crisis, interstate wars, and revolutionary movements had emerged in the Third World, against the earlier hopes of the Brookings–Trilateral policy current. In the midst of political, economic, and cultural frustrations in the United States, contradictions and crises of the international political economy were seen more and more as national security dilemmas caused by heightened Soviet assertiveness and flagging American will and military preparedness. This view of international politics was guiding U.S. policy in the 1980s.

4

Foreign Policy: From Détente to Cold War

IN 1973 the Trilateralist vanguard of the U.S. foreign-policy establishment was urging a redirection of attention from national security to "global" issues, especially those having to do with the international economy. In 1976 Richard Ullman could write, "In the U.S., among elites, at any rate, trilateralism has become almost the consensus position on foreign policy."[1] But by 1981 the Trilateralist–interdependence policy current was on the defensive, and the foreign policy agenda was quickly being reshaped along Cold War lines. In 1980 Ronald Reagan had stated in pointed terms the perspective behind the hard-line national security policies he would adopt: "Let's not delude ourselves. The Soviet Union underlies all the unrest that is going on. If they weren't engaged in this game of dominoes, there wouldn't be any hot spots in the world."[2]

Statements and policies of the Carter administration over its four-year term reflect the waning of early Trilateralism and a shift to Cold War militarism. Jimmy Carter, who was educated in foreign policy through his participation in the Trilateral Commission, came into office in 1977 as an advocate of military spending cutbacks, human rights, a conciliatory approach to the Soviet Union, and international policy coordination among the major nations. Many of Carter's initial liberal themes were sounded in a famous speech delivered at Notre Dame University on 22 May 1977. He rejected the Cold War mentality, "with Vietnam the best example of its intellectual and moral poverty." President Carter proclaimed: "We are now free of that inordinate fear of communism which once led us to embrace any dictator who joined us in our fear." With the threat of conflict with the Soviet Union subsiding, a newly confident United States could shape a foreign policy that would "encourage all countries to rise above narrow national interests and work together to solve such formidable global problems as the threat of nuclear war, racial hatred, the arms race, environmental damage, hunger, and disease." Carter's purpose was undoubtedly to regain the moral highground for the "great democracies," especially the United States, over and against the "totalitarian countries."[3] But if this was a consistent aim throughout his term in office, by 1980 the strategy for achieving it had changed considerably.

A changed stance was apparent in the President's State of the Union Address on 23 January 1980. Carter spoke gravely of the "threats to peace" represented by the hostage crisis in Iran and the Soviet invasion of Afghanistan, asserting, "Tonight, as throughout our generation, freedom and peace in the world depend on the state of the American union." He referred to three basic challenges to America's position as the "strongest of all nations": turmoil in the developing world, typified by the revolution in Iran; continued dependence of the industrial democracies on imported Middle Eastern oil; and, at the top of the list, the "steady growth and increased projection of Soviet military power beyond its borders." These challenges seemed to converge on a particular area of the world, leading Carter to say: "An attempt by any outside force to gain control of the Persian Gulf region will be regarded as an assault on the vital interests of the United States. It will be repelled by use of any means necessary, including military force."[4]

The new Carter Doctrine was part of a post-Afghanistan package that included reinstatement of draft registration for young men, an embargo on grain exports to the Soviet Union, withdrawal of U.S. participation in the Moscow Summer Olympics, sales of military-related equipment to China, and new levels of support for U.S. client regimes in the Third World. Taken together, these policies indicated a hardening militarist retrenchment in U.S. foreign policy. However, the policy shift predates the crises over Iran and Afghanistan, to which it is often seen as a response. In March 1978, Carter had called for a real increase in military spending. Over the next year and a half his administration made Cold War issues of alleged Cuban involvement in the Shaba rebellion in Zaire (1978) and the presence of a Soviet brigade in Cuba (1979), supported development of the MX missile system, and hastened to build the interventionist Rapid Deployment Force, all prior to the hostage seizure in Teheran or the Soviet move on Kabul. Inside the United States an elite-level conflict over the direction of foreign policy was pushing Carter to the right.

Intra-Elite Conflict and the Breakdown of Consensus

An increasingly fierce debate within the foreign-policy establishment gathered force from 1973 to 1980. At stake was the whole orientation of the United States to the rapidly changing world of the 1970s. Given the importance of American international hegemony after 1945 for domestic policies, alternative foreign policies were bound to affect the character of the United States as a liberal democratic capitalist society. As we shall see, political considerations of this sort were never far removed from arguments about national security policy.

This elite-level debate, with a right-wing position gaining more visibility and credibility as it progressed, was a major force pressuring Carter to adopt the above-mentioned policies in the second half of his term. In 1980 Ronald Reagan capitalized on the mood of resurgent militarism already in place, claiming that Carter's born-again hawkishness was too little, too late. But the conservative impact on national security policy needs to be set in the context of two enabling trends. One is a set of unfavorable developments including continued economic crisis in the later 1970s, a series of revolutionary Third World upheavals, and the erosion of U.S. military superiority by the Soviet Union, which were perceived as threatening U.S. security. The other trend is the ambiguity of the Trilateral program, particularly on the issue of U.S.–Soviet relations that divided the Carter administration internally. Over time the hard-line proponents were able to interpret events to the Congress, the media, and the public in a way that strengthened their world-view and weakened the Trilateral center.

The struggle to define security issues took place in a range of settings, including private policy organizations, opinion-shaping journals, and the wider media. The five policy-planning organizations examined in this book played important roles in the foreign-policy debate. While the Trilateral

Commission, the Brookings Institution, the American Enterprise Institute, the Heritage Foundation, and the Institute for Contemporary Studies were not uniquely influential or necessarily the key agenda-setters, they were representative of the two main camps in the foreign-policy debate, published studies that had high-level impact, and overlapped in personnel with the other important actors.

The notion that the main directions of public policy in post-1945 America were shaped by an elite establishment welding together an amalgam of private and public groups and class interests is now familiar. In his famous Trilateral Commission paper, Samuel P. Huntington wrote:

> To the extent that the United States was governed by anyone during the decades after World War II, it was governed by the president acting with the support and cooperation of key individuals and groups in the Executive Office, the federal bureaucracy, Congress, and the more important businesses, banks, law firms, foundations, and media, which constitute the private establishment.[5]

Foreign policy has been even more of a province for the pinnacle of the ruling coalition than economic, social welfare, or civil rights policy. The goal here was to advance, in Jerry Sanders' words, "the commingled objectives of stabilizing an international economic climate favorable to capitalist expansion, and maintaining political hegemony in areas defined as vital to U.S. geopolitical interests."[6] Around this agenda a national security elite attempted to marry the political and economic goals of the Pax Americana, a task for which their extensive experience in the realms of diplomacy and business had prepared them well. Through discussions in such key locales as Council on Foreign Relations (CFR) study groups and the CFR's journal *Foreign Affairs*, a workable consensus was achieved on the grand design of the American Century. But by the mid-1970s the subterranean rumblings of Vietnam-era intra-elite discord had emerged into sharp debate between increasingly distinct camps.[7]

Following Jerry Sanders, I shall term the two main competing foreign-policy ideologies within elite-planning settings as "managerialism" and "militarism."[8] This usage is almost identical to the Trader–Prussian distinction made by Michael Klare, which was outlined in Chapter 1. The managerial approach emphasizes international economic problems as a root of political instability and deemphasizes the U.S.–Soviet conflict. Promoting trade and rationalized financial institutions, the managerialists are strongly associated with the Brookings–Trilateral partnership and allies in the CFR 1980s Project and the Carnegie Endowment's journal *Foreign Policy*. The early outlook of the Carter administration, expressed in the Notre Dame speech, typifies the approach of this policy current.

In opposition stand the militarists, who think the rhetoric of "global interdependence" obscures the continuing need for the United States to improve its military defenses against international conflict instigated or encouraged by the Soviet Union. The most important organization of the Cold War network is the Committee on the Present Danger, flanked by old-line "strong defense" groups like the American Security Council and the National Strategy Information Center, as well as several New Right organizations that attempt to organize public pressure on Congress to uphold tough anticommunism defense and foreign policy positions. Intellectual backing comes out of Georgetown University's Center for Strategic and International Studies, *Commentary* magazine, and the *National Interest*, as well as Old Right publications like the *National Review* and the once-liberal *New Republic*. Some Cold Warriors are members of the Committee for the Free World, led by neoconservative Midge Decter, and a number are active at the American Enterprise Institute, the Heritage Foundation, the Hoover Institution, and the Institute for Contemporary Studies. Many prominent strategists and analysts of this network have been members of or advisers to the Reagan administration. It is well known that Jeane Kirkpatrick was at the AEI when she wrote the essays that caught the eye of Ronald Reagan, leading to her post at the United Nations. Even within the militarist camp, however, there are differences over definitions of U.S. interests, the prudence of intervention, and appropriate strategy toward the Soviet Union, which will be explored later in this chapter.

Much more than on the issue of international political economy, we shall see a direct confrontation of the center and the right on national security policy, with disarray and contestation more evident than consensus in foreign-policy planning for the changed world of the 1970s and 1980s. But the debate during the years under consideration (1973–1985) has a clear direction, revealing a militarization of strategic thinking and a decline of an initially ambitious and confident centrist position. By 1980 the foreign policy of the United States was being defined in national security terms that stressed anticommunism and military readiness, with deep skepticism about arms control and other negotiations with the Soviet Union. Many of the political themes from the early Cold War period were being replayed, intensified by the deadly and seemingly inexorable logic of the nuclear arms race.⁹

Less than a decade earlier, in 1973, the agenda for U.S. foreign policy looked very different, as the détente policy of a Republican administration was in place, American forces were largely withdrawn from Vietnam, and economic and energy crises evoked new concern. Thus a historic shift in U.S. foreign policy must be accounted for. The leading policy-planning organizations both reflected changing perceptions about national security and helped to bring these changes about. Their published writings and statements are both a point of entry into an understanding of recent politics and a material force helping to shape actual policy.

The impact of the groups' conflicting analyses reflects on the state of the intra-elite debate within the foreign-policy establishment at various times. We shall now proceed through these exchanges chronologically to see how the views offered were responses to ongoing real-world developments. I will use the inauguration of Jimmy Carter in January 1977 as a rough division line in the stages of the debate, unraveling particular issues such as nuclear weapons, alliance relations, posture toward China and the Soviet Union, and Third World intervention as they develop over time. The first period sees the Brookings Institution and the Trilateral Commission articulating the postdétente, post-Vietnam position begun by Nixon and Kissinger while a conservative opposition to those same policies begins to organize itself. The second stage is marked by the dilemmas of Trilateralism in a disorderly world and a strengthening national-security camp sounding alarms about an alleged loss of American superiority.

Détente, Interdependence, and American Foreign Policy

We have already noted that analysts affiliated with the Brookings Institution and the Trilateral Commission saw the early 1970s as a turning point in postwar global relations, one that demanded a reorientation of American foreign policy. President Nixon's trips to Moscow and Peking in 1972 seemed to confirm the need for a new foreign-policy agenda, given the decline of a world order structured by the Cold War. This perspective was stated by Brookings President Kermit Gordon, who concluded that Nixon's actions "strengthened the belief that the issues dividing the great communist powers and the United States, however serious, are unlikely to lead to war. For the rest of this decade, it seems likely that the leading U.S. foreign-policy issues will arise increasingly from relations with the noncommunist world."[10] Gordon's remarks came in his foreword to a collection of essays entitled *The Next Phase in Foreign Policy*, published by the Brookings Institution in 1973. With essays by such future Carter administration officials as Zbigniew Brzezinski, Leslie Gelb, and Henry Owen, editor of the volume, it can be read as a useful articulation of Kermit Gordon's argument from the standpoint of the liberal–centrist policy current that Trilateralism draws on. We shall look at several of the essays in conjunction with Seyom Brown's 1974 Brookings study entitled *New Forces in World Politics*, an early version of which appeared in the Owen volume. Widely used in world politics and international relations college courses in the mid-1970s, Brown's book laid out the prodétente, interdependence paradigm for a post–Cold War generation of students.

In his lead essay, Henry Owen argued that the early 1970s were "a time of major transition" marked by "the partial breakup of a world order in which the nature of power and authority had seemed reasonably clear."[11] One response at the time was growing public questioning about America's global role and a "diminishing confidence in our ability to influence the course of events in all parts of the globe."[12] For Owen and the Brookings scholars, this is an understandable but regrettable reaction that must be opposed. They are liberal internationalists who want to maintain U.S. influence on a global scale while changing its modus operandi in the face of new conditions. As the Vietnam War dragged on and other crises struck, they worried about the erosion of legitimacy surrounding the conduct of foreign policy. Carter's human rights policy, influenced by some of these people, was in part an attempt to win public support for maintaining global commitments on a remoralized basis in a wary post-Vietnam era. In 1973 the liberal consensus on what to do was centered on three strategic aims: the main focus of U.S. foreign policy in the decade ahead should be the creation of close trilateral relations with Western Europe and Japan on economic problems and policies; security policies toward the Third World should be downscaled, with more effort going into multilateral defense approaches; the United States should continue "patiently seeking common interests with the U.S.S.R. and China, without expecting rapid or dramatic breakthroughs."[13]

These recommendations rested on an analysis of the changes in world politics underway in the 1970s that overlaps with the perspective on international political economy discussed in Chapter 3. Indeed, underlining the close connection between economics and foreign policy is itself a defining feature of the

Brookings–Trilateral school. The erosion of Cold War coalitions and nation–state sovereignty by the economic and political changes wrought by global "modernization" sets the parameters of Seyom Brown's study. Since this process is unfolding haphazardly, threatening international stability and weakening legitimacy, Brown's approach to "the tasks of global management" was based on the perceived need to "anticipate developments . . . in order to channel them in accordance with the imperatives of social order and justice."[14] Moderate reforms satisfying the claims of justice are seen as functional to the maintenance of the "order" and "stability" so essential if an interdependent world-capitalist economy is not to be thrown off balance by political conflict. Thus Henry Owen advocates the "transfer of substantial resources from rich to poor nations," because this is "one of the few ways in which useful actions can be taken to reduce the risks of growing violence and chaos in the developing world."[15]

This brief summary highlights several important aspects of the managerial way of thinking. First, with the decline of U.S. hegemony and the growth of international interdependence, leadership of the world political economy must be based on common management by the advanced capitalist states, though the United States is actually to be first among equals. Second, policies and institutional changes should take place on a planned rather than an ad hoc basis, wherein political strategy rests on forecasts of the near-future requirements of system maintenance and rationalization. Third, the needed long-range solutions are seen as opposed by various narrowly based but powerfully entrenched interests. Such obstacles are to be overcome not by political democratization or a redistribution of power, but through institutional streamlining, rearrangement of priorities, better use of research, and more pragmatic wielding of power. In short, the Brookings–Trilateral outlook contains many elements of a liberal technocratic ideology, characteristically laced with a fear of the "politicization" of global issues and a desire to accommodate conflicts within more flexible versions of existing arrangements.

In *The Next Phase in Foreign Policy* this framework is applied to a number of regional and functional problems. For example, it is recommended that the United States lower its military profile in Asia and Latin America and develop ties with former pariah states like China and Cuba. Normalized relations with radical regimes can blunt their revolutionary impulses and open up profitable economic opportunities. It is significant that, given its importance for foreign policy in the mid-1970s, Africa receives no separate discussion. In general, the Third World is seen as an economic problem rather than a security concern. Multilateral approaches and acceptance of "creative pluralism" are seen as most likely to create the conditions for trade and investment in the Third World.[16]

The managerial approach of the Brookings Institution to foreign policy is well exemplified in an important 1975 study group report entitled *Toward Peace in the Middle East*.[17] In the wake of the 1973 Arab–Israeli war, the OPEC price hikes, and Kissinger's shuttle diplomacy, the elite sixteen-member study group went beyond the immediate negotiating agenda to consider U.S. interests in the whole region and the global implications of a particular approach to the conflict. The economic stakes for the United States include assuring oil imports to itself and to its European and Japanese allies and maintaining the growing volume of trade and investment in the area. Given the vital importance of the Middle East to international capitalism, the United States should secure ties with Israel and the Arab states and press for a durable settlement that will meet the needs of all concerned. A resolution of the Middle East conflict is viewed as key to realizing the grand design for a liberal capitalist world: "Efforts by the United States to establish greater global stability and to help manage the growing economic interdependence among nations more effectively are likely to be frustrated as long as conflict and confrontation seem probable in this area where so many national interests converge."[18]

This framework shapes the specific recommendations. What is needed is a comprehensive settlement that exchanges land acquired by Israel in the 1967 war for security guarantees from the Arab states. It is recognized that Palestinian self-determination must be a central component of the agreement, possibly taking the form of a new Palestinian state, though the role of the Palestine Liberation Organization is left unclear. Finally, the negotiation and ratification forum should be as broad as possible and include roles for the United Nations and the Soviet Union.

These proposals went well beyond both prior U.S. positions and the Camp David accords that Carter would strike with Begin and Sadat in 1978. It is partly because of the politically induced limitations on the traditional U.S. relationship with Israel that the proposals seem ambitious. On this issue and others, the managerial emphasis on resolving destabilizing political conflicts through enlightened self-interest was not fully realized, even when an administration shaped by this outlook came to power in 1977.

Constructing a new foreign-policy consensus responsive to the changing world political economy required abandoning the bipolar world-view of the Cold War, so that the anatagonism between the United States and the Soviet Union would no longer dominate international politics. With ideological hostility abating and military alliances loosening, the United States could then deal with countries on a case-by-case basis, rather than through the prism of Cold War manicheanism. In its more reformist versions, a managerial strategy would be better suited to a decentered, polyarchical world of multiple coalitions, marked by a new set of problems that went beyond national security: resources, economics, the North–South struggle, and the problems of uneven capitalist interdependence generally.[19]

While affirming the need for closer trilateral ties and for devoting more attention to new global issues, Zbigniew Brzezinski was more cautious about the future of U.S.–Soviet relations in his 1973 essay for the Brookings Institution study. He stressed that conflict would continue, warned against overoptimism about détente, and argued that "deterring occasional clashes with the Soviet Union is likely to require a continuing and substantial defense effort."[20] Brzezinski's views are important because they reveal boundaries within the Brookings framework against moving too far away from traditional security policies. In his capacity as Trilateral Commission Director and National Security Adviser to Carter, Brzezinski was in a position to have a strong influence on the specific blend of managerial policies the United States adopted.

The managerial–Trader approach to foreign policy taken by the Trilateral Commission and the early Carter administration was worked out by Brookings Institution analysts in the era of high détente. From the new Cold War period a decade later, it is striking how the liberal scenario of declining militarization and eased superpower relations has been shattered. But even in 1974 Seyom Brown noted the presence of skeptics about détente for whom "the essential cold war persists and nothing crucial has really changed (except the emergence of a neo-isolationist mood in the United States)."[21] This hard-line current congealed into a combative opposition to the managerialists and helped reshape the debate over foreign policy into the mold of Dean Acheson and John Foster Dulles. Even before Carter's election in 1976, the American Enterprise Institute, the Institute for Contemporary Studies, and other conservative policy organizations were updating traditional views of power and diplomacy in order to defend the threatened American empire.

The Conservative Attack on Détente

As foreign-policy currents in the 1970s, managerialism and militarism were shaped in response to the decline of U.S. hegemony and in reaction to the Nixon administration's strategy for dealing with this decline. As a complex approach to the maintenance of U.S. leadership the Nixon–Kissinger policy of détente sought to tame the Soviet Union and China, limiting their power to regional rather than global spheres. Meanwhile, the costs of U.S. involvement in the Third World would be reduced, assuaging domestic opposition while reducing pressures on the dollar stemming from overseas military expenditures.[22]

The aim of the Nixon Doctrine, enunciated in 1969, was to replace direct U.S. military intervention abroad with a heightened emphasis on training and funding allied forces in the Third World. The immediate case was "Vietnamization," where U.S. combat troops were withdrawn in phases, leaving the ground-fighting to U.S.-equipped South Vietnamese units, backed up by intensified bombing of North Vietnamese–National Liberation Front forces. Elsewhere, American interests would be attended to through the use of regional allies, the most important of which was the Shah's Iran. Thus, returning home from signing the SALT I treaty in Moscow in May 1972. Nixon and Kissinger visited the Shah in Teheran, pledging to back his destabilization of neighboring Iraq, then a Soviet ally.[23] In 1974–75 the Shah sent several thousand Iranian troops to Oman to help suppress a left-wing struggle in Dhofar Province. Other potential regional gendarmes included Brazil, Zaire, Indonesia, and Saudi Arabia. Backed up by CIA covert operations, such as those against Allende's Chile, this low-profile method would keep insurgency under wraps and secure what were deemed to be the geopolitical interests of the United States.

As for relations between the superpowers, the Cold War was to be replaced by a more traditional balance of power. Recognizing the Soviet buildup of arms since the Cuban missile crisis, the United States negotiated a nuclear arms treaty with Moscow based on the principle of strategic parity. However, the SALT I treaty still permitted the United States to undertake the qualitative modernization of its nuclear forces, allowing deployment of multiple-warhead missiles to continue, for example. At the same time, relations with the People's Republic of China began to normalize, partly in order to play China off against the Soviets and to prevent either from blocking a U.S. settlement of the Vietnam War. The Soviet Union could also purchase needed technology and obtain credits from U.S. corporations and banks, contingent on curtailed support for Third

World allies. This was the famed policy of linkage, a behavioristic strategy extending political and economic incentives that would positively reinforce Soviet good behavior.

By the 1976 election both managerialists and Cold Warriors had grown critical of the Nixon–Kissinger strategy for a new world order, as foreign policy crisis and international instability continued. Democratic candidate Jimmy Carter embodied the Trilateralist agenda. For the managerialists of the Trilateral Commission, the policy of détente was welcome, as was the restraint on the use of military force. Kissinger himself became a member of the executive committee of the Trilateral Commission shortly after leaving office. But Trilateralists like Brzezinski argued that Nixon and Kissinger had attached too much importance to superpower relations.[24] Rather than the balance of power, the international economic system should be the touchstone for foreign policy. Relations with European and Japanese allies had soured, despite Kissinger's 1973 "Year of Europe" speech, while the economic position of the Third World went largely unaddressed. Kissinger's indifference to economic issues was well known. A foreign policy recognizing the centrality of interdependence was needed, along with an ideological and moral facelift, which could be provided by the untainted former governor of Georgia.

Ronald Reagan, who challenged Nixon's successor, Gerald Ford, for the Republican nomination in 1976, represented a hawkish tendency, with different objections to Nixonian foreign policy. Gaining surprising support in the primaries, Reagan drew on the bellicose anticommunism of the Republican right wing, which had been in eclipse since the Goldwater debacle of 1964 but beginning a revival process in the mid-1970s. However, his attack on détente ran parallel to the views of new groups espousing a tough anti-Soviet line and drawing support from many Democrats and nominal liberals.[25]

In 1972 the Coalition for a Democratic Majority (CDM) was founded by Cold War liberals, some with close ties to George Meany's AFL–CIO, who were upset by George McGovern's nomination over Hubert Humphrey and by the growing influence within the Democratic Party of a "new class" sympathetic to antiwar, feminist, ecological, and countercultural movements. The Coalition's Foreign Policy Task Force, headed by former under secretary of state Eugene V. Rostow, issued a sharp critique of détente in 1974. Two years later the Committee on the Present Danger was formed by Rostow, along with such other CDM luminaries as Richard Pipes, Midge Decter, Norman Podhoretz, Leon Keyserling, Jeane Kirkpatrick, Max Kampelman, and John P. Roche.

Many members of the new strong defense party continued to think of themselves as true liberals. some attacking American corporations for ignoring the public interest in their eagerness to do business with the communists. The Jackson–Vanik Amendment of 1974, tying increased U.S. trade with the Soviet Union to the eased emigration of Soviet Jews, brought together Cold War liberals, supporters of Israel, and others resentful of OPEC impetuousness. The rise of Arab militance, the "fall" of Southeast Asia in 1975, Soviet–Cuban activity in Angola, and the growth of Eurocommunism were collocated and interpreted to mean that détente had become a one-way street. Pressure from the containment militarists caused Ford and Kissinger to cease using the by now unpopular term détente during the 1976 campaign.

It is against this background of the challenge to détente from the right we can consider the role played by the AEI and the ICS up to 1977. Again, their part in questioning the centrist managers from the right was not unique; other "Prussian" agents have been identified. But as research and discussion organizations dealing with a broad range of policy issues, they helped meld a renewed "strong defense" position with a broad array of other conservative concerns, forming a many layered right-wing program based on what seemed to be thorough analysis. In publishing anthologies, the AEI and the ICS helped collate critiques of specific defense policies into a distinct foreign-policy world-view.

In 1976 the AEI published a book of readings entitled *Détente and Defense*, edited by Robert J. Pranger, followed in early 1977 by the ICS's first venture into international affairs, a thirteen-essay collection entitled *Defending America: Toward a New Role in the Post Détente World*.[26] The AEI volume contains a number of documents by participants in détente policy, along with both supportive and critical evaluations. Although a clear line is not imposed editorially, the impact of the book as a whole, with its generous representation of conservative criticism, is to engender wariness about détente, suggesting that its contribution to international order has been overplayed and that power based on military force or its threat must continue as a vital part of American foreign policy to check unrestrained Soviet ambition.

Even more powerful as a collective statement against foreign policy trends is the ICS study, which forcefully states the militarist view that had been developing from 1972 to 1976. All contributors were well known as anticommunist defense and foreign policy analysts, familiar to readers of *Commentary*, *Encounter*, and *Survey*. Several, such as Paul Nitze and Eugene

Rostow, were leaders of the recently formed Committee on the Present Danger, and a number of them would become advisers to Ronald Reagan in a few years time. Lending his imprimatur to this "powerful antidote to the complacency which marks so much recent thinking about America's foreign and defense policies" was Senator Henry M. Jackson, probably the most important source of opposition in the Senate to the relaxed posture of Nixon and Kissinger toward the Soviet Union. An introduction was contributed by James Schlesinger, who had formed a de facto alliance against détente with Nitze, Rostow, and others while he was still secretary of defense under Nixon and Ford.[27]

Disagreements between managerialists and militarists are rooted in sharply contrasted images of the mainsprings of contemporary international politics. In essays reprinted in the AEI reader, Zbigniew Brzezinski and Stanley Hoffmann, who disagree in other respects, concur that the relationship between the United States and the Soviet Union is no longer the fulcrum of international politics, having been surpassed by a range of global issues that involve many new actors.[28] Just such a framework is reflected by the hard-line critics. For Charles Burton Marshall, a CPD executive committee member with essays in both the AEI and ICS volumes, "The relationship between the United States and the Soviet Union—and this is a point of cardinal import—will continue to set the great strategic frame."[29] A paradigm that obscures this fact is dangerous because it leads the United States to lower its defenses at a time when the Soviets are on the offensive. For the right, the Cold War has never ended.

Détente is judged by the conservative critics to have been oversold. Theodore Draper, Gregory Grossman, and a group of anticommunist scholars connected with *Survey* argued that few economic gains would accrue to the West from détente, but Soviet militarism would be subsidized through extension of credit and the sale of advanced technology.[30] Unlike the Traders, the hawks do not see economic interdependence creating the conditions for stable, reformist Soviet policy. "Kissinger's détente amounts to giving the assets away without requiring any strategic benefits in return," argued G. Warren Nutter of the AEI. He proposes "business-like bargaining based on the principle of unimpaired security" as part of a "revitalized diplomacy," including "selective strategic targeting" that will "help raise Western morale and confidence and lay the way for repairing our crumbling ramparts and alliance."[31]

For the right, remilitarization is necessary because the Soviet Union remains the "focus of evil" in the world, as President Reagan put it. Détente and peaceful coexistence mask the goal of global domination which Marxism–Leninism sets out as the task for Kremlin occupants. Articulating a common conservative belief, Eugene Rostow concluded:

> There has been no change in the nature of Soviet policy, and no improvement in Soviet-American relations. On the contrary, Soviet policy is more ominous than at any earlier period; it is sustained by a far larger and more threatening armory, and by a political will more ruthless and more reckless than that of Stalin.[32]

It follows that little can be expected from negotiations between the United States and the Soviet Union, because the Soviets, unlike the United States, do not and will not accept limitations on their geopolitical pursuits unless they are confronted with political unity and military force.

Failure to maintain Western strength and to fortify global

containment is of major concern to the ICS writers. Their explanation of Western laxity sounds many neoconservative themes about cultural and moral disarray. Military capabilities are in danger of becoming inferior because of the crisis of the political spirit. Thus W. Scott Thompson writes that the most important factor in the worsening international balance has been "the collapse of Western will."[33] CPD member Paul Seabury, in his concluding essay in the ICS study, traces flagging will to domestic discontent over Vietnam, which led many citizens and members of the elite to biases against intervention and in favor of keeping a low global profile. Our Vietnam defeat, Seabury contends, was "self-inflicted," with the result that "America's credibility as an ally has accordingly been impaired."[34] This self-flagellating "Vietnam syndrome" will lead to "appeasement" and "Finlandization" in the West, according to Rostow, who in typical neoconservative fashion draws an analogy between the fate of Western democracies in the 1930s and the 1970s.[35] Nazi Germany, of course, becomes the Soviet Union. If the United States is to toughen up, sacrifices that go against the liberal grain will have to be made. Government has come to be a "service enterprise," says Charles Burton Marshall, where "the concept of rights becomes a notion of entitlement to the satisfaction of any ambition or appetite whatever." This leads to the circumstance in which "the general welfare, in a hugely expanded version, has become a claimant against the common defense."[36] The spirit of the 1960s must be reversed and domestic priorities rearranged, so that America can rearm to meet the present danger.

Unlike the 1930s, today's international contest has nuclear arsenals as a component. According to the doctrine of mutually assured destruction (MAD), these weapons are not to be used in actual military combat in order to gain political advantage. Their purpose is to prevent an enemy attack by holding out the prospect of devastating retaliation that would inflict "unacceptable damages" on the aggressor, thus keeping the peace by denying any potential gain from a first strike. When both sides have this capability, nuclear war is deterred.

Looked at in this way, nuclear weapons are qualitatively different from conventional forces. "What in the name of God is strategic superiority?" Henry Kissinger once asked. But for Paul Nitze and others, in *Defending America*, nuclear superiority is a meaningful concept, directly linked to the ability of the United States to wield its influence on a global basis:

> For many years U.S. strategic nuclear preponderance has made it possible to offset Soviet military superiority at the periphery and to deter its offensive employment. It has also made it possible for the U.S. confidently to use the seas for projection of its supportive power despite the Soviet Union's always very real sea-denial capabilities.[37]

In effect, attainment of Soviet nuclear parity is seen as a threat to America's hegemonic role, including its ability to project military power worldwide. This reversal must be righted by reattaining a decisive U.S. edge.

In a critical discussion in *Foreign Policy*, Alan Tonelson wrote, "Nitze clearly regards nuclear weapons as similar to conventional weapons, in the sense that both are tools of foreign policy whose use can, must, and will be contemplated.[38] This position is premised on the belief that "military force is the prime level of influence in international affairs,"[39] a view that saturated the now legendary NSC-68 document of 1950, a founding statement of Cold War containment militarism that Nitze shaped as head of the Policy Planning Staff in the State Department.

Nitze builds his case by attributing to the Soviet Union a stance that his critics say he actually desires for the United States: a strategy of nuclear war-fighting. Through the use of mathematical models of a Soviet nuclear attack, Nitze claimed that most of the U.S. intercontinental ballistic missiles (ICBMs) would be taken out in a Soviet first strike, leaving few counterforce weapons with which to fire back at Soviet military targets with the necessary pinpoint accuracy. If American leaders struck back at Soviet population centers, a destructive reciprocal attack on U.S. cities could be unleashed by reserve Soviet nuclear forces. Thus our strategic "vulnerability" creates a situation where Soviet nuclear blackmail could force a surrender by the United States, a devastating political defeat for the free world. Furthermore, Nitze contends, the Soviets have an elaborate and workable civil defense program, proving that they take the possibility of a winnable nuclear war seriously.[40]

These arguments were and are vigorously disputed in defense policy circles, where the charges about missile vulnerability and Soviet civil defense are rejected by many. But they fed into an emerging militarist current in the mid-1970s that was deeply suspicious of arms control agreements and strongly supportive of building new weapons systems to modernize the American nuclear triad. Nitze himself resigned from the U.S. SALT delegation in 1974 and went on a campaign against any weakening of American defenses. His 1976 *Foreign Affairs* and *Foreign Policy* essays, reprinted in the AEI and ICS volumes, were widely discussed, added fuel to the hawks' fire, and portended Nitze's emergence as the leading opponent of SALT II.

In *Defending America* Nitze was joined in this project by Albert Wohlstetter, one of the original "wizards of armageddon" at the RAND Corporation who coined the phrase the "balance of terror."[41] Wohlstetter's lengthy essay is an attack on the view that the strategic arms race is dangerously out of control. In Wohlstetter's perspective, this "Luddite" way of thinking, all too prevalent in discussion of defense issues, obstructs the needed technological innovations that "will permit new forms of mobility for strategic forces, making it easier for deterrent forces to survive." Like Nutter's call for "selective strategic targeting." Wohlstetter's hope that improvements in accuracy and control will "increase the range of choice"[42] in strategic conflict looks to critics like an endorsement of a nuclear war-fighting capability and a first-strike potential. It contrasts with the spirit of the explicit rejection of weapons systems that threaten a first strike, by Jerome Kahan of the Brookings Institution, who adheres more strictly to deterrence theory.[43]

For the hard-liners the ICS has gathered, conventional forces must also be strengthened in order to counter the Soviet menace. Because, according to Eugene Rostow, the Soviet goal of controlling Europe rests on a strategy of gaining control of the Middle East and Mediterrancan area, the U.S. presence in the Middle East must grow. In Europe itself the American commitment to NATO must be reaffirmed and the tendency to look with sympathy on Eurocommunism rejected. On an ideological level, the United States should make the most of Soviet abuses of human rights, so as to win the struggle for moral hegemony.[44]

These goals rested on a view of the Soviet world role based partly on analysis but also on an ideology that used the diverse challenges to American hegemony in a national security threat. Several ICS authors refer to the 1975–76 events in Angola as proof that the Soviets violated the rules of détente. Yet the Soviet and Cuban backing for the Popular Movement for the Liberation of Angola resumed only after the CIA, aided by Zaire and South Africa, stepped up support for pro-Western factions. In any event, the Angolan revolution had a long internal history rooted in the struggle for independence from Portugal. It was not a simple East–West affair, but it was perceived by the critics of détente as a sign of a dangerous blow at the international balance. Coming on the heels of defeat in Indochina, the refusal of Congress to approve funds to fight Soviet and Cuban allies in a Third World conflict was seen by the right as a disastrous evasion of U.S. global responsibilities. A pattern had been established. The current represented by the AEI and ICS would have many opportunities in the second half of the 1970s to paint internally generated Third World upheavals into a picture of global Soviet expansion.[45] The "disrespect" shown by Third World political movements for the "rules of détente" fed into calls for the remilitarization of American foreign policy. Additional grist for the militarist mill was generated by the contradictions of Jimmy Carter's Trilateral plan.

Trilateral Managerialism in Crisis: The Carter Years

When addressing foreign policy, Jimmy Carter employed the language of liberal interdependence and Trilateralism during his early months as President. But we have noted that, by 1980, his rhetoric had moved much closer to the militarist current, and his actions followed suit. In part this shift reflects the continued growth of the right, whose 1977–1980 offensive will be discussed in the next section. But we need to explain why the CPD, AEI, ICS, and their allies gained such political credence, pulling the national security debate sharply right. To this end, we shall first describe the contradictory foreign-policy ideology bequeathed to Carter by the Brookings Institution and the Trilateral Commission and explain how its torsions were reflected inside the Carter administration. Second, we shall analyze how domestic and international political and economic developments undermined the realization of a liberal, Trader version of the Trilateral program and drew out the anticommunist elements. Finally, we shall see how key spokespersons of the Trilateral Commission and the Brookings Institution accommodated the remilitarization of American foreign policy and reverted to classic containment doctrine.

A 1977 summary of the Trilateral Commission's "broad strategy for the management of interdependence" included "keeping the peace, managing the world economy, contributing to economic development and the satisfaction of basic human needs, and promoting human rights."[46] This was a program of self-interested reform, the success of which depended on Trilateral cooperation, domestic public support, and steady economic growth in order to present the Soviet Union and the Third World with a politically united front and material incentives for accepting the developed capitalist nations' agenda.

In 1976 the Brookings Institution focused on the policy tasks of the next ten years in its annual *Setting National Priorities* survey, which was widely viewed as a blueprint for a new Democratic administration. The volume's editors, Henry Owen and Charles Schultze, were appointed to high-level positions by President Carter. In his chapter on "Peace and War," Owen, a Trilateral Commission member, surveyed potential military conflicts with assumptions that were very similar to those in *The Next Phase in Foreign Policy* three years earlier: U.S. military intervention should be renounced, except in extreme circumstances, and more attention paid to economic relations. Exceptions are Northeast Asia, the Middle East, and Europe, where vital U.S. interests are at stake and the commitment of the United States to their defense needs to be made clear, even though no actual confrontation is likely. Ties with China should improve, but not in a way that antagonizes Japan or the Soviet Union.

At the same time, Owen and Schultze refer to the "overblown hopes that accompanied détente," arguing that the main threat to the United States remains a military conflict with the Soviet Union, a fact that has not been superseded by new economic and social issues.[47] The Soviet Union is described as a heavily armed, totalitarian state with which the United States will have both competitive and cooperative relations if it remains strong, adopts a sober, businesslike attitude, and does not expect too much in the way of improved ties. According to Barry Blechman, this posture requires a "new consensus in defense policy" on the need to increase defense spending once again.[48]

Both Owen and Blechman note that their goals may appear to be contradictory and, with no breakthroughs impending, marshaling public support could prove difficult. From a vantage point in the 1980s they appear vulnerable to the kind of alternative analysis that the right leveled at Carter. The continuing economic slump undermined the ability of the "community of developed nations" to impose world leadership, and whole areas of the Third World skimmed over by the Brookings survey did not yield to managerial solutions and became crisis spots. In 1976 Barry Blechman thought it "difficult to imagine that . . . events will occur in Latin America or the Caribbean to threaten this nation's security to a degree or in a way that would require a significant military response."[49] In accounting for world disorder and America's frustration, many would find the explanations of the right easy to accept.

Within the Trilateral Commission there were similar ambiguities about where the main challenges to U.S. foreign policy would come from and about what blend of cooperation and confrontation would be possible with the Soviet Union. After concerning itself mainly with problems of the advanced capitalist countries, OPEC, and the developing regions in its first three years of existence. the Trilateral Commission issued two reports on relations with the communist powers in 1977 and 1978. Taken together, they suggested uncertainty and division within the foreign policy establishment about U.S.–Soviet ties. As we shall see, these disagreements were present within Carter's foreign-policy team.

Collaboration with Communist Countries in Managing Global Problems, drafted principally by Henry Owen, along with Andrew Shonfield of Britain and Chihiro Hosoya of Japan, was hopeful about prospects for cooperation with the Soviets and the Chinese.[50] Promising areas for collaboration included food, nuclear proliferation, oceans, and trade policy, along with earthquake warning and energy-warranting exploration. Development aid, space, and weather offered less potential. Achievement of progress in these areas would ease the Trilateral task of global management and brighten the long-term prospects for East–West cooperation. Negotiations on any of the problems should rest on mutual interests and be devoid of threats or attempts to reshape communist societies internally.

In contrast to such relative optimism was the outlook of *An Overview of East–West Relations*, heatedly discussed within the Trilateral Commission and published in early 1978. Two of the authors, Jeremy Azreal, a former RAND Corporation strategist of the University of Chicago, and Richard Lowenthal of Berlin, were known as hard-liners.[51] Along with Tohru Nakagawa of Japan, they argued that, despite the rise of major new international problems in the 1970s, the East–West contest remained "the main axis dividing the contemporary world."[52]

The authors upheld a limited conception of détente, defining it simply as "necessary and useful efforts to limit the forms and range, the risks and burdens of a continued conflict by negotiation and partial cooperation."[53] Détente has encouraged an illusion of stability in the West that "tends to confine its holders to defensive objectives and to a reactive political attitude." The report argues for a more aggressive posture in shaping the world order and containing the Soviet Union. The West "should seek to influence the natural processes of change worldwide in a direction that is favorable to its fundamental values."[54] Political developments that restrict Western purposes and maneuverability are threats. Thus Eurocommunism is dangerous not to democratic politics but to "the political cohesion of Western Europe and the Atlantic alliance."[55] Even the appearance of strategic nuclear superiority by the Soviets is threatening, for it may remove their fear of U.S. retaliation, opening up paths of intervention by conventional force in Third World spots where they enjoy local superiority.[56] Among other means to be taken, a closer alliance with China can help box in the Soviets, buttressing Trilateral unity and international hegemony: "The present degree of Sino-Soviet hostility . . . tends to benefit the West; and the West should help ensure that the present situation continues to be worthwhile for China."[57]

Within the Carter administration there were different foreign policy tendencies that disagreed about whether a revitalized containment policy toward the Soviets was necessary in order to achieve the larger Trilateral goals.[58] One group, associated with scholars and former officials centered around *Foreign Policy*, was accommodationist toward the Soviet Union, which they saw as a cautious, problem-ridden nation that, at most, sought parity and security assurances from the United States. Strongly committed to the Trader vision of an adaptable world capitalist political economy guided by a discerning, remoralized American foreign policy, their number included Cyrus Vance, Richard Holbrooke, Leslie Gelb, Paul Warnke, Marshall Shulman, Anthony Lake, and Richard Moose at the State Department, along with Andrew Young at the United Nations and C. Fred Bergsten at the Treasury Department.

Representing elements of both the Trilateral and the militarist outlooks was another current headed by Zbigniew Brzezinski and the National Security Council. While Brzezinski favored stronger Trilateral ties and an improved North–South dialogue, he also took a more aggressive stance toward Moscow and strongly supported playing the "China card" as a U.S. counterweight against the Soviets. Drawing Brzezinski and eventually Carter to the right was the antidétente current in the Committee on the Present Danger, largely outside the administration but represented within it by Energy Secretary James Schlesinger.

Initially Carter seemed to favor the "soft-line" Trader view, or at least to be evenhanded with the two groups. Presidential

Review Memorandum 10 (PRM-10), from the summer of 1977, characterized U.S.–Soviet relations as combining traditional competition with growing cooperation. PRM-10 advocated holding to an "essential equivalence" in the nuclear weapons balance while calling for U.S. military superiority in Europe and the Middle East, two regions deemed vitally important by the Trilateral Commission. The memorandum thus appealed both to the prodétente forces and to the hard-liners in the Carter administration.[59] Over time, however, the balance of power within the Carter camp shifted in favor of the hard-line position, as evidenced in the exits of Paul Warnke, Andrew Young, and Cyrus Vance. Some manifestations of this policy direction were mentioned at the beginning of this chapter. Other actions included the NATO decision to station 572 new medium-range nuclear missiles in Europe, increased arms sales and military aid to Saudi Arabia, Israel, Egypt, Morocco, and Pakistan, overlooking human rights violations in Iran, the Philippines, and other authoritarian regimes, and calls for freeing the CIA from the little public accountability it had. By 1980 the particulars of Carter's foreign policy were being shaped by the general condition of renewed East–West rivalry.

Assuming Carter was sincere in his Trilateralism, we need to explain why he moved from a foreign policy based on "interdependence" to neo–Cold War containment militarism. One widely accepted explanation is that the shift was a necessary and rational response to Soviet adventurism in the Third World and to the related Soviet buildup of conventional and nuclear forces. Leaving aside the assumptions this position usually makes about the benevolence of American power, I would argue that while the Soviets had indeed improved their military position, their foreign policy in the late 1970s was but one element among several contributing to the new Cold War. Moreover, the U.S. interpretation of their actions was deeply colored by the exigencies of domestic American politics, which interacted with economic problems and Third World crises to create a political context ripe for resurgent militarism.[60] As we saw in Chapter 2, the Team B report on Soviet strength reflected the contestable views of the hard-line camp, yet deeply affected elite discussion of the superpower balance of forces in the late 1970s.

The Team B report constituted an opening shot by the "Prussian" faction against Carter's "global interdependence" approach, in what would become an increasingly fierce intraelite conflict. The CPD and their allies in the AEI, ICS and elsewhere were determined to keep up the pressure against managerial and Trilateral ideology, which they regarded as a rationalization for the "loss of will" among the leadership class.[61] The CPD had submitted fifty-three names to President Carter for possible appointments and failed to receive a single one. "My views are unprintable," said Rostow in reference to the new Carter team, while Nitze added, "Every softliner I can think of is in government."[62] These Cold Warriors were determined to reverse Richard Ullman's judgment that trilateralism had become the new consensus world-view of foreign-policy elites, and they would resort to political mobilization to do so.

Throughout Carter's term, an opposition coalition of traditional conservatives, neoconservatives, and the New Right banded together to attack what they saw as sellout policies. From the fight over Paul Warnke's nomination to head the Arms Control and Disarmament Agency, through the Panama Canal treaty battle, to the conflict over SALT II, Carter gave ground, finding it more and more politically difficult to adhere to a liberal Trilateral program. In a period of growing international crisis, the complex approach to "world order" offered by the Brookings Institution and the Trilateral Commission had less appeal than a visceral conjuring of the Soviet threat. Unlike post-1945 American hegemony, the Trilateral policy did not coincide with an expanding domestic economy or the implementation of new programs to benefit the working class. It was not difficult to develop a right-wing populist critique of Trilateralism, accusing the big corporations and banks of following a self-interested foreign policy that forsook the national security needs of the United States. President Carter's statements and Trilateral ideology were replete with appeals to the age of limits, the need for sacrifices, and diminished expectations of government. Offering little to a confused public, these were hardly effective rallying points. But, after Vietnam, public support for foreign policy could not be ignored, something the Cold War current capitalized on more than the managerialists.

According to Thomas Ferguson and Joel Rogers, moving toward Cold War militarism would have been more difficult if the economic dividends of détente and Trilateralism had been greater.[63] In the early 1970s, détente was seen as an opportunity for profitable investment in the Soviet Union by U.S. banks and multinational corporations. The prodétente American Committee for East–West Accord included officials from Pepsico, Coca Cola, El Paso Natural Gas, Control Data Corporation, and Wall Street's Brown Brothers Harriman and Company, among other corporate interests involved.[64] But it soon became apparent that the Soviet Union offered no economic bonanza to U.S. business, whereas southern Europe and the Third World held brighter investment, trade, and loan prospects. This shift in foreign economic focus had two results that fed into resurgent militarism: the costs of disrupting U.S.–Soviet relations were lowered, and the enhancement of military intervention capabilities seemed necessary to protect economic interests, given the politically explosive effects of uneven capitalist development in the Third World periphery. The heightened rivalry of advanced capitalist powers in the late 1970s, contrary to Trilateral Commission prescriptions, also encouraged the belief that military strength might spell political leverage. Empowered as a result of these mounting pressures were interests inside the United States that had never accepted détente and that had a stake in increased arms spending, protection from international economic competition, and maintenance of U.S. support to client states, especially Israel, which was promoted as a defender of Western civilization amid the barbarous Third World.

A more general explanation of policy can be drawn from this interpretation of détente's rise and fall. Changing international economic conditions help to restructure the terrain of domestic political debate, in this case on defense policy. Especially in unstable periods like the 1970s, policy currents coalesce around divergent agendas and assessments of the root causes of economic crisis and global turmoil. These currents represent a bloc of actors that include, but are not reducible to, key economic interests and encompass a range of other social, political, and cultural forces. Policy-planning organizations help to articulate the long-term goals of these shifting configurations of power. The direction of political debate sets limits on the range of possibilities considered in the mainstream institutions, protestations of objectivity and analytic disinterest notwithstanding.

The pressure of both domestic politics and international developments affected the discussion on national security within centrist policy planning, agenda-shaping organizations. Winston Lord, president of the Council on Foreign Relations, noted in his 1978 report that discussions on U.S.–Soviet relations within the Council "seemed to reflect the toughening of attitude in the nation as a whole."[65] Within the Trilateral Commission differences existed, but the general direction was clearly toward rearming and emphasizing a Soviet threat. Typical of the tenor was a 1980 overview of foreign policy in *Trialogue* by Robert Bowie, a founding member of the Commission. Bowie argues that "the overselling of détente in the 1970s fostered Western illusions about Soviet policy."[66] Because mutual interests of the United States and the Soviets are few, and because Moscow is bent on extending its power, the superpower relationship must be "antagonistic and competitive," contends Bowie, and backed up in the West by a refortified containment policy involving new foreign base facilities and improved means of intervention.

In a similar vein Brzezinski told *Trialogue* just before leaving office that Soviet ambitions were at the root of the new Cold War: "It is because of that lack of restraint that détente today is in a poor shape."[67] While denying that he wanted confrontation and an arms race, Brzezinski rejected "the McGovernite fear of the use of American power and the inclination to acquiesce to Soviet expansionism." He endorsed Carter's Presidential Directive 59 from the summer of 1980, which formally approved counterforce nuclear targeting, stating that PD-59 was "designed to give us greater flexibility to manage a war, to fight it on alternative levels, and thereby to deter more effectively the Soviets from initiating a war in the first place."

Many of the security fears in Trilateral deliberation came to focus on the Persian Gulf and the Middle East. By 1978 this area was the source of 34 percent of U.S. petroleum imports, 61 percent of West European imports, and 72 percent of Japanese imports and the site of over half the world's proven oil reserves.[68] A volatile area in transition, wracked by political instability, the Gulf is located at the intersection of Europe, Asia, and Africa, and is close to the underside of the Soviet Union.

In line with both the Nixon Doctrine and the Trilateral Commission strategy of acting through regional surrogates, Iran played a key role on behalf of U.S. security interests in the Gulf during the 1970s, using the $20 billion worth of weapons purchased from the United States to act as an area policeman. The Shah's regime was also seen as a model of semiperipheral capitalist modernization, pro-Western and open to foreign investment. Despite a record of human rights violations described by Amnesty International as one of the world's worst, the Shah was toasted in Teheran by President Carter on 31 December 1977: "Iran under the great leadership of the Shah is an island of stability in one of the more troubled areas of the world. This is a great tribute to you, your majesty, and to your leadership and to the respect, admiration and love your people give to you."[69]

The collapse of the Shah in early 1979 was an absolutely shattering blow to U.S. foreign policy, leading to a rapid speedup both in political pressure and in military intervention preparations, to ensure the continued flow of oil and to persuade Arab states that their best hopes lie with moderation and an alliance with the United States rather than with radicalism and ties with the Soviet Union.[70] In February 1979, Secretary of Defense Harold Brown visited Saudi Arabia, Jordan, Israel, and Egypt to discuss military cooperation. In March the administration rushed arms to North Yemen, a Saudi client then involved in a clash with pro-Soviet South Yemen. American naval forces in the Indian Ocean were beefed up, and pressure was exerted on Israel and Egypt to sign a peace treaty, which they did in March.

Even before the Islamic revolution, contingency plans were being developed for direct U.S. intervention in the form of a rapid deployment force (RDF).[71] In 1977 both Carter and Brzezinski approved the idea of a quick strike force specifically for the Persian Gulf, but the Pentagon feared the plan would divert resources from Western Europe, while the State Department believed that the RDF would be too politically provocative.[72] Thus, little was done in 1978 to push the force forward until the debacle in Iran converted the skeptics into believers. The development of the RDF signaled the decline of the Trader–managerial strategy, with its low-profile, economic-inducement mode of controlling key regions. It indicated that the United States was overcoming its "Vietnam syndrome" of reluctance to intervene directly to protect its interests.

At the official level, most interpretations of this turn emphasize the dangers of Soviet expansionism, with alleged Soviet designs on the oil-rich Gulf region being an especially strong rallying image. But occasionally Trilateralist statements set forth a more candid structural analysis of political conflict in the Third World, revealing the material basis for the shift from managerial to militarist modes of control. Thus, in the Defense Department's Fiscal Year 1981 Annual Report, Secretary Harold Brown, a former Trilateral Commission member, warned of the spread of uncontrolled turbulence in the Third World and noted that these disorders "have many and varied causes" beyond Soviet adventurism.[73] The underlying sources include failure of the United States "to provide for the basic needs of people and narrow the explosive disparity between wealth and hunger" as well as "differences about the proper world distribution of income and natural resources." Brown noted that "the particular manner in which our economy has expanded means that we have come to depend to no small degree on imports, exports, and the earnings from overseas investments for our material well-being." Middle East oil supplies are the foremost source of dependency. Given this intertwined system, "international economic disorder could almost equal in severity the military threat from the Soviet Union." Of the measures the United States must take to ensure stability, Brown put the formation of the RDF at the top of the list.

In a speech before the Council on Foreign Relations in March 1980, Brown elaborated on the new Carter Doctrine, indicating the situations in which the United States would use military force in the Persian Gulf:

> What is important is the ability rapidly to move forces into the region with the numbers, mobility, and firepower to preclude initial adversary forces from reaching vital points. It is not necessary for our initial units to be able to defeat the whole force an adversary might eventually have in place. It is also not necessary for us to await the firing of the first shot or the prior arrival of hostile forces; many of our forces can be moved upon strategic warning, and some upon receipt of even very early and ambiguous indications.[74]

Under this doctrine the United States would have extremely wide latitude in the kinds of political conflicts it would respond to. Various pretexts could be given to justify preemptive U.S. intervention. Indigenous revolutionary movements in the Gulf states or elsewhere that contested for power could be pointed to as evidence of a serious threat to vital U.S. interests.

For example, Reagan administration policy in Central America can be seen in this light as an application of national security principles laid down by Carter officials.

My point is not that the Carter and Brown doctrines are an overt expression of a strategy previously worked out in the inner recesses of the Trilateral Commission. Rather, the toughening of official policy in 1979 and 1980 is consistent with the evolving views of important Trilateralists and, more important, is a logical outcome of the failed managerial strategy of empire management, threatened by Third World "turbulence" and domestic political pressure. Under these conditions, elites saw remilitarization and anti-Sovietism as central to political consensus-shaping and to defending U.S. hegemony in a way that is consistent with past practices. Conceding ground to the right was a more natural reflex to national security managers than rethinking the policy of containment itself.

The drift of establishment thinking about foreign policy is visible in the 1980 issue of *Setting National Priorities*, completed by the Brookings Institution at about the same time Harold Brown was addressing the CFR. Like the 1976 predecessor, it looked at policy prospects for the next decade, rather than merely for the coming fiscal year, and it was subtitled "Agenda for the 1980s." The chapters on defense and foreign policy validated the trend toward looking at national security increasingly in terms of military preparedness. It was in the Persian Gulf region that the superpower contest and the threat to U.S. security were most intense, where "turbulent political events, intense Western economic interest, and the close proximity of the Soviet Union combine to produce potential security problems for which U.S. forces are poorly positioned."[75] To meet this purported challenge, the Brookings study recommended a "significant" real increase in defense spending for several years and a "greater capability for moving forces by air and by sea to distant parts of the world."[76] Although diplomatic and economic approaches to problems were also advocated, the remilitarization of foreign policy, and the political interpretation on which it rests, were endorsed by the foremost liberal policy-planning organization, at the beginning of the new decade.

"From Weakness to Strength": AEI, ICS, and Heritage

During the Carter years the American Enterprise Institute experienced rapid growth, bringing many influential scholars into its fold and attracting new sources of corporate funding.[77] By 1980 it was the policy-planning organization perhaps most representative of U.S. business. While the AEI had long been known for its studies of economic and regulatory issues, foreign and defense policy studies expanded greatly in the second half of the 1970s. The Public Policy Project on National Defense was established in 1976. Its advisory council, chaired by former Secretary of Defense Melvin Laird, included political figures such as Clark Clifford, William Colby, Barry Goldwater, Jack Kemp, and Paul Nitze, corporate leaders R. E. Kirby, chair of Westinghouse Electric, and Thomas Murphy, chair of General Motors, and military men like Admiral Thomas Moorer, former chairman of the Joint Chiefs of Staff, and Lieutenant General George Seignious, who (symptomatically) replaced Paul Warnke as director of the Arms Control and Disarmament Agency in 1979. In 1978 a project on the Future Conduct of American Foreign Policy began at AEI, with George Bush chairing an advisory council whose twenty-four members ranged from conservative to moderately liberal. The *AEI Defense Review* began publishing six times a year in 1977 and soon took its place as a leading elite journal of debate on national security issues. In 1979 it upgraded its title to *AEI Foreign Policy and Defense Review*.

The ideological center of gravity at the AEI could be described as moderately conservative Republicanism, as indicated by the affiliation of George Bush, Gerald Ford, and Melvin Laird. But in the 1970s the AEI's political and intellectual expanse was broadened when a number of disenchanted liberals from the Coalition for a Democratic Majority were brought into AEI projects: Peter Berger, Nathan Glazer, Jeane Kirkpatrick, Irving Kristol, Seymour Martin Lipset, Michael Novak, Ben Wattenberg, and others.[78] As AEI resident scholars, Kirkpatrick and Novak helped develop the neoconservative critique of Carter's foreign policy, especially on the human rights issue, and were later appointed by Reagan to the U.S. mission to the United Nations, armed to combat leftist positions.

Unlike the Institute for Contemporary Studies, which published a single, massive volume on national security in 1980, the AEI's foreign-policy studies number in the dozens and often include opposing viewpoints. But it is possible to discriminate, drawing upon certain authors and publications to compose a profile of where the AEI's foreign-policy analysis was headed from 1977 to 1980. We shall consider AEI thinking in the areas of defense posture and military spending, global security strategy, and the approach of the United States to the Third World.

In his annual analysis of the projected defense program for

the next five years, Lawrence J. Korb provided a running commentary on President Carter's defense policy. Before being appointed to the Defense Department by President Reagan, Korb was resident director of defense policy studies at AEI and co-editor of the *AEI Foreign Policy and Defense Review*. In his 1978 survey Korb stated that NATO central forces were being overemphasized, to the detriment of "other capabilities," such as those needed to confront "many unstable situations to our south." To meet these challenges there was no way to avoid increased military spending.[79] This emphasis on stepped-up defense outlays and rebuilt intervention potential was backed by a warning that "we have consistently underestimated the capabilities of the Soviet Union."[80] By 1980 there was an urgent tone to Korb's analysis: "This nation is at a crossroads.... The choices we make about this current defense program will, in large measure, determine the future of the international system."[81] While approving of Carter's and Brown's spending hikes, Korb thought it was still not enough to offset growing Soviet advantages, so if spending for social programs had to give way, that would only be a tough-minded recognition of priorities.

In the crucial election year of 1980, Korb's position was supported by Herbert Stein, AEI Senior Fellow and former chair of the Council of Economic Advisers under Nixon and Ford. In the January 1980 issue of the *AEI Economist*, which Stein edits and largely writes, he argued that higher military spending would not necessarily be a burden on the economy, since defense expenditures as a percentage of GNP had declined from 11.4 percent between 1954 and 1960 to 4.6 percent between 1977 and 1979. According to Stein, increasing the ratio of defense to GNP to 10 percent is necessary because of growing Soviet power and the threat of new actors, such as OPEC. While the latter challenge should ultimately be met through greater U.S. energy independence, "In the short run our security against the use of the oil weapon depends not on our energy position but on our general military–economic–political strength."[82] Access to foreign resources by the "great powers" must be secured by military force if necessary, including, Stein implies, outright seizure of OPEC oil fields. In this view, such a policy will win support when Americans cease doubting their society's virtue and renew their confidence and pride in the system.

Neither Korb nor Stein is considered an ideological right-winger. As leading spokespersons for the AEI on defense and economic issues, their calls in 1980 to cut income support programs to accommodate a massive military rearmament effort reflected a new consensus on national security policy in most sections of the political spectrum.

This consensus was nurtured, among other places, in the AEI defense project, where a better-defined and stronger military role in the overall design of U.S. foreign policy was advocated. In *Civil-Military Relations* (1977), General Andrew J. Goodpaster, former NATO Supreme Allied Commander and a CPD member, and Samuel P. Huntingon, soon to be an AEI adjunct scholar after coordinating security-planning at Brzezinski's National Security Council, stated the case for overcoming Vietnam-era suspicions of the military and achieving a more respectful relationship between the armed forces and civil society.[83] In *Grand Strategy for the 1980s* (1978), four generals and an admiral advocated a more cohesive national security strategy in the face of resource dependency and growing Soviet power. General Maxwell Taylor foresaw North–South conflicts becoming as important as the East–West confrontation, given the importance of trade and foreign resources to the U.S. economy. Taylor, a CPD member, proposed a large defense-spending increase tied to improvements in conventional rather than nuclear forces, to protect sea lanes and market regions in the Middle East, sub-Saharan Africa, Southwest Asia, and the western hemisphere.[84] Taylor's proposals reflected the views of other contributors who also saw superpower conflict being displaced onto the Third World, where U.S. economic interests were expanding and where revitalized conventional forces might spell the difference in who exerts power and influence.

Since the proposals for mushrooming defense expenditures and greater military intervention capacity went against the "Vietnam syndrome," an ideological justification for taking a hard line was important in the bid for public support. At the AEI Jeane Kirkpatrick, Michael Novak, and other neoconservatives laid the basis for a reassertion of U.S. "will." It was while Kirkpatrick was an AEI resident scholar that she wrote "Dictatorships and Double Standards" for *Commentary*, the essay that so impressed Ronald Reagan, as well as "U.S. Security and Latin America" and other essays, which have been collected and published by the AEI.[85] Kirkpatrick was bitterly critical of Carter's human rights policy, and that aspect of Trilateralism that encouraged an opening to the "forces of change" in Third World countries. In Kirkpatrick's eyes, such moderate positions rested on a fatalistic view of history and only served to undermine the confidence of pro-U.S. "authoritarian" allies like the Shah of Iran and Somoza of Nicaragua. This policy opened the door to far worse "totalitarian" regimes of the left. While acceptance of this approach reflected "an attitude of defeatism, self-doubt, self-denigration, and self-delusion" within the Establishment, "President Reagan's election was a watershed that marked the end to a period of retreat."[86] Just as Carter had attempted to put a moral gloss on his post Vietnam managerial policies, so too did the intellectual exponents of Reaganism and remilitarization argue that their world-view rested on stringent ethical responsibilities: "We have now entered a period when the moral and political will of our nation will be tested as never before."[87] For the battle against totalitarianism to succeed, widespread attitudes in American public life would have to change and the purveyors of détente and liberal interdependence would either have to accept the new Cold War realities or be politically and intellectually routed.

For the AEI neoconservatives, a positive view of American democratic capitalism must be rekindled to win support for a decisive foreign policy. A celebratory public philosophy of the American system will discredit domestic critics and encourage its extension abroad. This effort reaches its apogee in the writings of Michael Novak, whose analysis of the large corporation as a spiritual community will be discussed in Chapters 5 and 6. Novak draws on the supposedly positive relationship between capitalism, democracy, and spiritual culture in the United States to polemicize against the "liberation theology" developed by sections of the Roman Catholic Church in Latin America who are active in organizing peasants and are sympathetic to socialism. Roger Fontaine, a former associate of Novak's at the AEI who became the Latin America specialist at the National Security Council in 1981, argues against church radicals in Kirkpatrick-like terms: "In the name of liberation, some reinvent tyranny."[88] From this perspective, confronting the secular and religious left in the Third World, either directly or through assistance to friendly regimes, offers opportunities for scoring moral and political triumphs for the American way of life. The drive for a tougher foreign policy forms part of the larger task, for AEI thinkers, of reordering American political culture, a struggle that will take place on many fronts. Thus Novak has been a key organizer of the Institute on Religion and Democracy, set up partly to battle political activists within the Protestant churches and the Roman Catholic Church.

We find then, by 1980, a number of separate AEI studies converging on a program of increased defense spending and a more interventionist policy in the Third World. While some at the AEI, such as Robert Pranger, worried that defense policy was becoming "highly politicized and increasingly ideological,"[89] the AEI consensus favored a foreign policy based on liberal free trade coupled with a remilitarized opposition to the Soviet Union and radical Third World nationalism.

While the AEI's ruminations on foreign policy are scattered in a number of policy statements and analyses, the Institute for Contemporary Studies weighed into the national security debate with a 524-page study released on 20 May 1980. *National Security in the 1980s: From Weakness to Strength* carried on the analysis of *Defending America* (1977), but with the intent to "set forth a positive agenda for policy."[90] With its publication coinciding with the presidential election campaign, the volume can be read as a set of proposals designed to shape policy in a forthcoming conservative administration, as can the Heritage Foundation's *Mandate for Leadership* or the Hoover Institution's *The United States in the 1980s*. Most of the seventeen contributors were to serve Ronald Reagan as foreign-policy advisers during his campaign and/or as officials in his administration.

The ICS, which began organizing the book in the fall of 1979, clearly intended it to have a political impact in 1980 by systematically articulating a critique of defense policy under Carter, offering an alternative strong defense agenda that a Republican candidate (preferably Reagan, who had ties to the ICS) could adopt as program. When the book was released, the ICS sponsored a media blitz in Washington and elsewhere, briefing leading newspaper and television journalists, as well as leaders from business, labor, the academic community, Congress, and the executive branch. The book's editor, W. Scott Thompson, and prominent contributors like Richard Burt of the *New York Times*, defense consultant Edward Luttwak, and retired Admiral Elmo Zumwalt led panel discussions based on the book's conclusions, fielding questions that "reflected a nearly unanimous concern about U.S. military posture," according to the ICS. Later the Institute noted with satisfaction that more than fifty newspapers around the nation had used excerpts from the book for editorial opinions, fulfilling the ICS goal of "enlightening opinion leaders throughout the country about the status of national security."[91]

Much of the discussion in *National Security in the 1980s* is an updated version of *Defending America*; Edward Luttwak, Charles Burton Marshall, Paul Nitze, W. Scott Thompson, and Albert Wohlstetter reappear as authors. This group of men represents a hard line position within a broad trend toward militarism. Among those who became Reagan advisers or officials are Kenneth Adelman, Richard Burt, Fred Ikle, Geoffrey Kemp, Nitze, Thompson, and William Van Cleave. If, as Thompson argues, strategy involves the use of means ranging from the "diplomat" to the "soldier," these analysts are overwhelmingly concerned with advancing the role of the soldier in defending U.S. interests.[92] Since their collective foreign-policy ideology has already been described, we shall turn to some of the more important points these contributors were making in the winter of 1980.

National Security in the 1980s is, among other things, a political attack on what we have called the managerialist policy current. Thompson accuses those who viewed economic interdependence as central in world politics, and military force as increasingly irrelevant, of following a "politics of weaknesses" once they became ensconced in the Carter administration.[93] For the ICS group this outlook is not only descriptively incorrect but also politically dangerous, for it shaped policy at a time when the Soviets were reaching for military superiority. In accounting for the decline of U.S. hegemony ("weakness"), little attention is given to structural changes in the world economy or the international state-system: Soviet expansion and American retreat from responsibility explain the current global tensions.

Another key claim, advanced by CPD executive committee member Zumwalt, is that in the 1970s "the Soviets achieved an exploitable nuclear superiority."[94] While the assertion about Soviet superiority has been repeatedly refuted, a political interpretation of the operative term "exploitable" may provide some insight into the real concerns of the militarists. In my view, what the right wants to recapture is the political advantages in dealing with the Third World that the United States enjoyed in the 1950s and early 1960s as a result of its effective nuclear superiority. In the 1970s, as dependence on OPEC hit home, intercapitalist competition intensified, and a number of radical regimes came to power in the Third World (Ethiopia, Vietnam, Angola, Afghanistan, Iran, Grenada, Nicaragua, Zimbabwe, and others), the Soviet Union's attainment of near parity in the strategic balance was experienced as a reduction in U.S. options for retaining hegemonic control. That nuclear superiority has a psychological and political importance to the militarist current because of the leverage it affords in international conflicts is clear from the remarks of Richard Perle, assistant secretary of defense for international security policy and a colleague of many ICS analysts:

> I'm always worried less about what would happen in an actual nuclear exchange than the effect that the nuclear balance has on our willingness to take risks in local situations. It is not that I am worried about the Soviets attacking the United States with nuclear weapons confident they will win that nuclear war. It is that I worry about an American President feeling he cannot afford to take action in a crisis because Soviet nuclear forces are such that, if escalation took place, they are better poised than we are to move up the escalation ladder.[95]

Many of the specific proposals for rearming the United States in the ICS volume can be seen, in this light, as part of a bid to roll back the new challenges to American superiority, so that the United States can wield its influence and expect to prevail in crises. To this end, military production capability must be improved, the intelligence services given new powers, and both conventional and nuclear forces modernized. Military alliances must be struck anew and power projection potential strengthened, through arms sales and new basing rights, especially around the Persian Gulf region, which is seen as the likely center of superpower confrontation.

Although Scott Thompson denies that the ICS strategists are making "a macho call to arms,"[96] the proposals would clearly cost a great deal of money to implement and might appear to be provocative. But if the public can be convinced that the Soviet Union's "ultimate goal is the subjugation of the free world" (Zumwalt) and that the Soviet Union is "the one truly imperial nation left on earth" (Luttwak), perhaps the effort will be seen as essential.[97] A positive, energizing image for rallying the populace is evoked by Geoffrey Kemp, who calls for "large battle stations in outer space" and other futuristic strategic innovations:

> A concerted U.S. space effort would fire the imagination of a new generation of Americans who were too young to have been influenced by Vietnam but who have been raised in the "Star Wars" environment and who have the energy and scientific talents that need to be tapped. It would give the country a national goal at a time when the absence of such goals, beyond reducing the level of inflation, is very apparent and when there is great confusion about America's future place and role in the world. In short, the United States needs to regain its sense of destiny. If this sounds jingoistic and imperial so be it, for we live, whether we like it or not, in a highly competitive international environment in which the benefits of cooperation are obvious but in which cooperation alone is not enough to insure that the national security of the United States is maintained.[98]

Ronald Reagan's proposals for a space-based missile defense system, contained in his March 1983 "Star Wars" speech, are clearly affiliated with the bold notions of Kemp, who served the President on the National Security Council. It is not important that such developments might violate existing arms agreements, since this group of hard-liners takes a dim view of arms control negotiations anyway.

Space-age warfare aside, the ICS analysts think that conflict is most probable where vital strategic and economic interests are at stake. The ensuing discussion of the relationship of the

United States to the Third World revolves around the struggle against Soviet power, with little exploration of the internal dynamics of developing societies that give rise to revolutionary movements independent of Soviet action. Nor is there any recognition of the limits on or setbacks to Soviet influence in the Third World. Because of this unidimensional focus on strategy and security, human rights quickly drops out as a U.S. concern. Leonard Sullivan states, "We have to substantially broaden our view of what we think is acceptable politically in the world,"[99] meaning that pro–United States authoritarian regimes should fear no criticism from an administration committed to remilitarizing U.S. foreign policy. Rather than decrying an interventionist U.S. policy as imperial, Third World states will welcome our deterrence against the Soviet threat if they are convinced of our "staying power."[100]

Nearly all the hard-line positions developed at the AEI and ICS during the Carter administration were translated into concise policy proposals for the incoming Reagan team in the Heritage Foundation's *Mandate for Leadership*.[101] In the late 1970s, Heritage had ceaselessly attacked Carter's foreign policy in papers, newsletters, and the journal *Policy Review*, reaching a widening circle of would-be policymakers. Expanding from its New Right origins, the Heritage Foundation brought together neoconservatives and old-line hawks into the growing conservative policy network.

In its foreign policy recommendations, *Mandate for Leadership* put the struggle against communism above all other objectives and viewed the Third World as the Cold War arena most in need of decisive U.S. preparedness. Meeting the Soviet challenge in the developing world meant breaking with several themes of the Carter years. Pro-Soviet "totalitarian" forces should be singled out as the worst violators of human rights, while "authoritarian" allies are to be met with nonthreatening "quiet diplomacy."[102] Nongovernmental movements ("terrorists") that threaten friendly regimes should be resolutely opposed. In 1981 the Reagan administration moved quickly to implement these policies in Latin America, South Africa, and elsewhere. Also in line with Heritage thinking was the nomination of *Policy Review* board member Ernest Lefever to be assistant secretary of state for human rights and humanitarian affairs. Lefever's disdain for any recognizable human rights policy, expressed while he was president of the Ethics and Public Policy Center, led to Senate objections, but he was replaced by a man of impeccable neoconservative credentials, Elliot Abrams, a former adviser to Senator Henry Jackson and a frequent contributor to *Policy Review* and *Commentary*.

As an aspect of a new "human rights" policy, Heritage urged the promotion of "economic liberty" throughout the world, understood to mean adoption of free-market economic policies. Alternative Third World programs for economic development are rejected by Heritage analysts, who draw on the work of Peter Bauer and other critics of "statism." Hostility to bothersome Third World views lies beneath a long-running series of attacks that the Heritage Foundation has made on the United Nations, which have met with agreement on the part of some Reagan officials and reportedly influenced the U.S. decision to withdraw from UNESCO in 1985.[103]

A large part of *Mandate for Leadership's* foreign-policy discussion is devoted to Latin America. The Heritage analysis is premised on the view that "The most serious threat facing South America in the near future is Cuba."[104] Central America in particular is seen as a major East–West flashpoint of the early 1980s. Assistance to El Salvador's junta must be stepped up, the misguided anti–free-market land reform halted, and anticommunist states forged into a pro–United States Central America bloc. Even before Reagan took office the Heritage Foundation was calling for support to anti-Sandinista forces in Nicaragua, and it has remained a staunch advocate of greater Contra funding. Heritage positions on Nicaragua reflect adherence to the Reagan Doctrine of attempting to "roll back" radical regimes in the Third World.[105] Thus, in 1984, the Heritage Foundation spoke for "sustained attention to Grenada in order to assure the long-term success of the 1983 rescue mission"[106] and favored the development of "low intensity conflict" forms of unconventional warfare against enemy Third World states, in conjunction with internal (or CIA-sponsored) anti-Marxist insurgencies.[107] Repeal of the Clark Amendment barring support to Jonas Savimbi's UNITA forces fighting the leftist Angola government is another long-time Heritage objective, one that was accomplished in 1985 by congressional action.

Other conservative policy-planners were also charting a more aggressive U.S. policy toward the Soviet Union in the early 1980s. Several authors in an ICS book, *Beyond Containment*, argued for measures to weaken the Soviet Union internally. Editor Aaron Wildavsky proposed a stance of "maximal containment" aimed at "pluralizing" the Soviet system through political means "before it grows so threatening that all that is left to us is capitulation or nuclear war."[108] Extending containment entails opposing "Soviet proxies" around the world. One of the ICS authors, noting the lack of public support for intervention, argued that it must be overcome through "an emotional, almost physical counterforce. In other words, the campaign to protect a policy of containment must resemble, to a considerable degree, an advertising campaign."[109] In 1984 the ICS followed up on this point by publishing a selection of documents seized by U.S. forces in the invasion of Grenada, designed to show the American people that the New Jewel Movement of Maurice Bishop had been "bent upon imposing comprehensive totalitarian controls upon the people of Grenada by methods meticulously copied from its mentors in long-established Communist states."[110]

As I have argued, the nuclear buildup advocated by conservative policy-planners is aimed at securing American political hegemony in face of a diverse set of challenges. In the 1980s a new barrier to remilitarization emerged in the form of substantial citizen opposition to the arms race. Military-oriented policy analysts responded by stating "the moral case for the arms buildup," to use the title of an essay by ICS official Patrick Glynn.[111] For its part, the Heritage Foundation was one of the most active promoters of space-based missile defenses prior to President Reagan's acceptance of the idea in 1983. A common argument of "Star Wars" supporters is that the new system would be a humane alternative to the mutually assured destruction deterrence strategy, with its deliberate population-targeting.

The 1980s have witnessed the deepening of the new Cold War that set in during the late 1970s. A conservative foreign-policy network had helped reshape the terms of debate. A Soviet scholar captured this in a 1981 essay: "Few in the politically relevant spectrum these days would challenge the assertion that the Soviet Union is a menace. Yet there is still disagreement about the nature of the beast and how to tame it."[112] To be sure, defense analysts at the Brookings Institution worried about skyrocketing defense budgets and Reagan's nuclear program, while many Trilateralists supported arms control, a gradual renewal of détente, and a negotiated settlement of Central American conflicts through the Contadora process.[113] But it seemed to matter little that representatives of centrist policy-planning organizations like the Council on Foreign Relations and the Trilateral Commission found positions in the Reagan administration. There are not a few militarists in those groups, coexisting with the managerialist majority, and the center had itself moved to the right.

This process was rooted in the increasing pressure to which the postwar position of the United States was subjected in the 1970s. To the extent that they were embodied in policy, managerialism and Trilateralism were unable to stabilize the international political economy and to sustain a post-Vietnam consensus on foreign policy. The militarist current, well funded and well organized, was able to rally forces around an image of an America beseiged, but ready to recoup its rightful place under strong leadership. This political shift was noticeable in the increased budgets and prominence of conservative policy-planning organizations like the American Enterprise Institute, the Institute for Contemporary Studies, the Heritage Foundation, and other institutionalized co-thinkers. No longer were the Brookings Institution and the Council on Foreign Relations without serious competition in the elite policy-planning process. But there is no reason to believe that the militarist current will be more successful in forging a world order, though the climate it has helped to create is fraught with danger. Very real problems in and pressures on the United States, which have been displaced onto a misrepresented Soviet threat, persist and will not be resolved by summoning up a steely "will." To understand the real sources of the crisis in U.S. hegemony, it is necessary to examine the decline of the domestic economy and the failure of various policy-planners to restore stable growth.

5

Economic Stagnation and Domestic Policy Conflict

THE FOUNDATIONS OF LIBERAL democratic capitalism in the United States—as we have termed the post-1945 political economy—were constructed of both domestic and international components. Chapters 3 and 4 analyzed the challenges to the hegemonic role played by the United States in international affairs. Proceeding from the facts of the mounting crisis in the 1970s, we have examined the efforts of five policy-planning organizations to devise political strategies, based on their own analysis of problems, to manage the disorder in international economics and foreign policy in ways that would secure the interests and values these organizations and their members represent.

At the end of Chapter 4, I suggested a close interconnection between the threat to global American leadership and the declining strength of the U.S. economy. A temporal parallel between the two processes is evident: from 1973 to 1980 a growing international crisis coincided with a downturn in all the leading indicators of the health of the U.S. economy. The political fallout from the crisis in both spheres was also quite similar: the consensus of the center that had guided economic policy from 1945 to 1973 broke down, as contenders to the orthodoxy emerged on the right and left. As with foreign policy, the debate on the economy featured a rapidly growing conservative position that, promoted by corporate backing and right-wing policy groups, fed into Ronald Reagan's 1980 victory. Ideology also connected foreign and domestic decline, as economic weakness was frequently attributed to foreign causes, such as OPEC or Japanese impertinence, while exhortations to rearm functioned both as a talismanic restorer of America's international potency and as a psychological compensation for the frustrating inability of the government to stabilize the economy.

Just as America's leaders were in a state of panic about global events in 1980, so too were they deeply troubled about the collapsing economy in that year. As the election neared, the GNP growth rate fell to zero, productivity continued its apparent decline, and inflation and unemployment rates rose sharply. Discussion in the media of economic crisis and the need to "reindustrialize" was inescapable.

This mood was reflected in Reagan's first national address on the economy as President. On 5 February 1981, he declared, "I regret to say that we are in the worst economic mess since the Great Depression."[1] While Reagan's explanation of why the crisis had developed was as contested as his prescriptions for overcoming it, his sense of the gravity of the situation was widely shared among economists, policymakers, business people, and citizens alike. Their anxiety about the future stood in sharp contrast to the sunny horizons of continuous growth forecast by most economic policy experts in the 1960s. In the intervening decade of the 1970s, confidence in the fine-tuning policies of postwar economic management sagged badly. By 1981, just ten years after Richard Nixon declared that he too was a Keynesian, a program that had been derided as "voodoo economics" or "Hooverism" not long before was being implemented as the economic policy of the Reagan administration. Analyzing this new economic conjuncture and responding to it were major concerns of the American Enterprise Institute, the Brookings Institution, the Heritage Foundation, the Institute for Contemporary Studies, and the Trilateral Commission, along with many other business-oriented policy groups that grew up in the 1970s. All these organizations saw resolving the economic crisis as a key to achieving their other policy goals. Failure to do so was viewed as portending still deeper social and political crisis. As I define these organizations' developing and contrasting views of the economy, I shall attempt to draw out the social and political changes entailed in their positions, especially as they bear on the larger shape of liberal democratic capitalism in the United States.

Turning Point: The 1970s

The advanced capitalist world enjoyed two decades of rapid economic growth after World War II. In the United States this was made possible by a set of social and political arrangements that intertwined with and buttressed the capitalist accumulation process. Central to the postwar regime was the increased role of the state in fine-tuning the economy and structuring the relationship of business, labor, and citizens. After a somewhat laggard period in the late 1950s, the expansion of the early 1960s convinced many economists and policymakers that the mechanisms to promote a process of steady economic growth had been found.

The style of economic management associated with the Kennedy and Johnson administrations came to be identified with the liberalism of the Brookings Institution. Kermit Gordon, president of Brookings from 1967 to 1976, was a member of Kennedy's Council of Economic Advisers (CEA) and chaired the Bureau of the Budget under President Johnson, as did Charles Schultze, who found a home at Brookings during the Nixon–Ford years and later chaired Jimmy Carter's CEA. The late Arthur Okun, a prominent Brookings senior fellow, chaired the CEA during the Johnson administration. These men considered themselves to be liberals, and the experience of the 1960s helped reinforce perceived linkages between liberal ideas, objective social science, and pragmatic, effective policy.

In contrast, until the 1970s, the American Enterprise Institute was a small and not particularly significant outpost of free-market economics. During the glory years of American Keynesianism, its views seemed anachronistic—even to many corporate leaders. But as mainstream liberalism encountered crisis in the 1970s, the AEI reconstituted itself and began to have an impact in setting the terms of economic policy discourse. The AEI served as a research and recruitment base for the Nixon and Ford administrations. After the Democratic election victory in 1976, which resulted in an inflow of Brookings rivals into the government, former Republican officials like Herbert Stein, Paul McCracken, William Simon, and Gerald Ford attached themselves to the refurbished Institute, helping to raise its profile among business leaders, policymakers, and the opinion-shaping media. The AEI's growth was symptomatic of a broader process of change in which the ideology shaping public debate about the role of the state in the economy moved to the right. The conditions for the existence of a vibrant New Frontier liberalism no longer held in the 1970s. Under the impact of declining economic conditions, discord over policy, and the stepped-up mobilization of elites in the face of what they called a "crisis of democracy," the policy-planning network was reshaped. While establishment thinking on economics and other issues shifted to the right from 1973 to 1980, the groups in this network were often divided, as the institutional arrangements and conceptual paradigms that would determine policy in the future remained unsettled.

The analysis here centers on what I take to be the core statements on economic policy most representative of the approach to domestic political economy by each of the five policy-planning organizations. Their work will be interpreted in the context of real-world political and economic conditions and the ideological drift of the 1970s as it concerned the relationship of the state to the economy. In this period a massive capitalist political offensive, signified by the growth of the Business Roundtable and allied formations, was matched by the expanded influence of the AEI, the ICS, and the Heritage Foundation.

I shall emphasize distinct approaches to macroeconomic management, but I shall also discuss the related areas of energy policy, labor–capital relations, and government regulation, where appropriate. These were important components of the postwar institutional structure of liberal democratic capitalism, which were repoliticized as arenas of conflict in the 1970s, when it was claimed that they had an important bearing on the overall performance of the economy. The proposals of the five groups on this nexus of problems can then be seen as alternative elite approaches to a crisis in which systemic questions are posed.

The response of the Brookings Institution to the crisis of capitalism and democracy in the mid-1970s will be our starting point, followed by a consideration of the Trilateral Commission's broad agenda for restructuring the economy. A critique of economic planning by the AEI and the ICS is next, along with the economic proposals based on traditional free-market conservatism and supply-side economics, which they, along with the Heritage Foundation, published before and during the Reagan years. Both the quandaries of mainstream liberalism and the resurgence of conservative positions will be encompassed. Within a framework that draws out the broader political and social ramifications of economic policy, I shall also lay the foundation for discussing the crisis of the state and democratic politics in Chapter 6.

Keynesian Liberalism in Retreat: The Brookings Institution

Because economic policies associated with the Brookings Institution became the consensus position of establishment liberalism in the 1960s, the response of Brookings scholars to the economic crisis after 1973 is particularly interesting. Established liberalism was confronted with unprecedented problems toward which once-effective policies now seemed inadequate solutions. As the foremost liberal think tank, the Brookings Institution might be expected to articulate the policies that a Democratic administration would pursue after the Nixon–Ford years. In addition, the work of Okun, Schultze, and others reveals a rethinking of liberal views that, intentionally or not, helped bend discussion of economic and social policy to the right.

The dilemmas of Keynesian liberalism are evident in *Setting National Priorities: The Next Ten Years*, a collective work written in 1976 and widely read for indications of the policies Carter would propose, especially because a number of the authors entered his administration in 1977. The tone of the work as a whole anticipates the themes of diminished expectations and the age of limits that Carter would repeatedly invoke. On economic policy, a retreat from Keynesianism is evident, but no coherent framework to guide policy is offered in replacement.

"Ten years ago government was widely viewed as an instrument to solve problems; today government itself is widely viewed as the problem," the Brookings editors say.[2] This "loss of confidence" and "growth of distrust . . . have become far greater than justified by the original causes."[3] Such skepticism should be countered by distinguishing more clearly between the tasks the government can and cannot accomplish and by increasing its efficiency in dealing with legitimate concerns. This is similar to the approach taken to foreign policy, where a stance of selective intervention based on ranked priorities is advocated as a middle ground between imperial overextension and isolationism.

On domestic policy, the Brookings Institution saw itself promoting a pragmatic center position between those who wished to extend and deepen the Great Society and those who saw almost any federal intervention as likely to make things worse. Intertwined with the Institution's concrete analysis in this volume was a concern with restoring public confidence and the legitimacy of the American political system—"with all its faults . . . a marvelously effective tool for providing both freedom and governance."[4] This requires downplaying the ideological bases of politics: "Designing successful policies increasingly requires skills beyond the traditional political ones of negotiation and compromise among conflicting values and interests. In part, the need is for more analytical skills and technical competence."[5] These general themes of the need for trade-offs and fewer demands on government, anxiety over eroded legitimacy, and a technocratic approach to policy formulation were part of the drift of American liberalism in the troubled 1970s.

Arthur Okun, one of the more liberal economists at the Brookings Institution, had already set out the terms of the refocused policy discussion. Okun's widely noted 1975 study, *Equality and Efficiency: The Big Tradeoff*, established in its very title an outer limit against income redistribution programs, which, if taken too far, reduce the material incentives needed to set a capitalist economy in motion. While expressing a preference for greater equality, Okun stressed that "a commitment to equality that ignores what you're dividing up is worth nothing for the rich or the poor. Many plans that are too radical for my taste would shrink the pie so that everybody would get smaller slices even if it's carved up equally."[6] More conservative voices were to use Okun's framework to press for business subsidies and against social welfare outlays, arguing that these were essential steps to take, in difficult times, if the pie from which all partake were to grow.

Confirming the view that Brookings-style liberalism was facing new binds were the specific analyses on macroeconomic policy in the 1976 *Setting National Priorities* survey. In his chapter on stabilization policy, George Perry acknowledged that Keynesian-based policy is in trouble and that the Phillips curve no longer reflects economic reality: "However well demand management worked for much of the post-war period, it is painfully obvious that the conflict between high unemployment and price stability has steadily worsened in recent years."[7] Perry pinpoints inflation as the main barrier to getting the economy out of its morass of stagnation, but he rules out the adoption of wage–price controls, chiefly because they are politically unpopular. He is left to recommend voluntary wage–price guidelines, which the Carter administration was to issue in 1978. In that year a Brookings study proposed a tax-based incomes policy, levied on large employers who grant "excessive" wage increases, as the best way to break inflation.[8] Carter's Council on Wage and Price Stability, headed for a time by Brookings economist Barry Bosworth, had some success in restraining wage gains, though prices proved more difficult to control. George Perry's other remedies, including selective tax reductions, maintaining buffer stocks of inflation-prone raw materials, and reevaluating regulatory policies, were more technical fixes than the structural changes that his own analysis suggested a need for.

Similar conclusions about the limitations of liberal public policy were drawn by Charles Schultze in his chapter on the federal budget. Schultze demonstrated that federal spending as a percentage of GNP had grown only slightly in the previous ten years, while the share of the national budget absorbed by defense had declined relative to expenditures for income security and social programs. Since the Brookings proposals included a reversal of the diminishing defense allotment, and since it was implied that increasing the ratio of federal spending to GNP would be inflationary, there is little room for new programs to create jobs or meet other popular demands.[9] Clearly the Great Society years have passed. It is not surprising that Charles Schultze played a major role in weakening the Humphrey–Hawkins bill of 1978, which originally called for substantial federal efforts to guarantee employment.[10]

Skepticism about government's ability to solve social problems and renewed appreciation of market incentives were recurrent themes in the 1976 *Setting National Priorities* volume, themes that were reiterated by Charles Schultze in his Godkin Lectures at Harvard University, delivered just prior to his entry into the Carter administration. Schultze's *The Public Use of Private Interest*, as the published version was called, is based on the belief "that there is a growing need for collective influence over individual and business behavior that was once the domain of purely private decisions."[11] But past forms of government intervention, labeled "command and control" by Schultze, have been clumsy and inefficient, not based on sound market economic principles. Shifting the focus away from bureaucratic regulation and oversight, Schultze argued for the use of market incentives like taxes and subsidies to bring private decisions in line with the public's interest in improving economic efficiency. A positive effect of this policy mode, from the Brookings standpoint, would be to depoliticize government actions. With the government becoming more of a general administrator, explicit government decisions about allocation would become less necessary, and the ideological charm of the market would be reasserted. In this way, it was hoped, simultaneous progress toward economic growth and political legitimation would take place.

In a 1975 Brookings Institution study, *Pollution, Prices, and*

Public Policy, Schultze and Allen Kneese had already worked out a market-incentives critique of "central regulatory controls" over environmental policy.[12] Under the Carter administration, economic and social deregulation was promoted. Drawing on the advice of Schultze, Carter appointed economists schooled in cost–benefit analysis to regulatory boards, where the claims of business interests that health, safety, and environmental rules were dampening investment, productivity, and growth were treated sympathetically. Alfred E. Kahn, chair of the Civil Aeronautics Board and the Wage-Price Council under Carter, expressed the view shaping policy in the late 1970s: "I have more faith in greed than in regulation."[13]

Responding to the bedeviling political and economic conditions of the mid-1970s, the thrust of the Brookings Institution's economic diagnosis was to make welfare state policies involving increased spending or redistribution contingent on renewed economic growth. In turn, the path to expanded economic output was located in anti-inflation policies, along with various capitalist incentives, whose effect was to impose burdens on working-class citizens. But if the economy fell into a downward spiral, the logic of the Brookings position was to make government policy even more attentive to creating a "favorable business climate" through austerity programs. By late 1978 the Carter administration was faced with an impasse of just this sort.

After initially pursuing expansionary policies, Carter, confronted with galloping inflation, a sinking dollar, and widespread fear of a financial collapse, adopted policies that raised interest rates and pushed the economy into a recession in 1979. "In pursuing a centrist strategy," Alan Wolfe writes, "Carter learned that in an age of austerity, the center shifts to the right."[14] Many centrist economists affiliated with the Brookings Institution endorsed Carter's tight-money, budget-cutting, and wage-restraint measures as temporarily unavoidable actions if inflation was to be wrung out of the economy. But in 1979 and 1980, as unemployment and interest rates rose, energy costs soared, inflation remained high, and budget deficits widened, Democratic constituencies eroded and Carter was widely derided for his economic mismanagement, even as he was tagged the most conservative Democratic president of the century.

Early in 1980, with domestic and international crises deepening, the Brookings Institution produced a lengthy "Agenda for the 1980s" that codified the conservative drift in economic policy debate within the political center. Recognizing that "the nation's problems are interrelated and cannot be resolved piecemeal," the Brookings Institution proposed an anti-inflation policy based on wage–price controls, slow growth in demand, a restrictive money supply, a step-up of economic deregulation, and a significant expansion of tax incentives for capital formation.[15] Believing that the uncertainties of demand-management and regulatory policies in the past have had a "serious destabilizing influence" on the economy, Barry Bosworth argued that "government must pay more attention to the supply-side implications of its actions."[16]

Acknowledging that these "are not easy measures to sell even on a temporary basis," the Brookings Institution was aware that "the problems are as political as they are economic."[17] But because Brookings analysts are technicians working within the assumptions imposed by existing political and economic arrangements, democratic politics enters into their framework only to the extent that "attaining any set of national goals ... depends on public confidence in the competence of the government to make policy and execute it."[18] Viewing 1980 as a turning point involving "painful economic readjustments," the Brookings policy-planners wondered if "it may be that government today can address its problems only within ... a crisis framework."[19]

By 1980 Brookings Institution economic policy analysts increasingly accepted the argument that consumption needed to be reduced and investment raised to fuel a supply-side–led recovery. Rather than managing the crisis through social-democratic domestic reforms, the curtailment of redistributive and demand-stimulating policies was now seen as a precondition for restoring growth. Concerned about the political feasiblity of austerity policies, and the scuttling of liberal programs they required, the Brookings Institution hoped that the crisis of stagflation could be muddled through until economic recovery arrived.

Toward State Capitalism? The Trilateral Commission

The implicit rejection by the Brookings Institution of a neo-Keynesian, social-democratic solution to the economic crisis suggested the direction that liberal policy would take under Carter. While arguments about the need for greater business incentives and reduced social spending won acceptance at Brookings, the changes in political and economic arrangements that would support renewed capitalist accumulation were only implied rather than clearly defined. In contrast, the

Trilateral Commission has been quite explicit about the need to restructure the domestic order. What emerges from Trilateralist considerations on the economic crisis are elements of a corporatist, state capitalist program for rationalizing the political economy in line with the priorities of internationally oriented elites. Beginning with the core intellectual premises and political concerns of this approach, I shall examine the Trilateral plan as it applies to energy, labor relations, and industrial policy.

We have already seen that Trilateralism attempts to approach policy from a systemic perspective that sees both the domestic and the international structures of the postwar period at a turning point, in need of managerial reordering. At such a conjuncture, neither Keynesian fine-tuning nor the invisible hand of the free market can sustain growth and profitability in the U.S. economy. What is needed are structural changes in the institutional bases of accumulation, coordinated with the Trilateral partners, that will stabilize the ongoing integration of international capitalism. Effective policies that will remove the obstacles to this project of capitalist modernization must be implemented.

In its practical recommendations for action and in their analysis of the nature of the crisis, the Trilateral Commission underlines the close connection between politics and economics. Though it is not primarily concerned with economic analysis, the task force report on the governability of democracies (1975) embodies many of the assumptions about the relationship between capitalism and democracy that inform concrete economic policy proposals made by the Trilaterial Commission.

In his survey of the American condition, Samuel P. Huntington argued that the disruption of elite modes of governance by the democratic surges of the 1960s played a causal role in the economic downturn of the 1970s. Claims on government made by a variety of newly politicized constituencies altered the composition of the national budget toward benefit programs and away from national defense. Ultimately these swelling demands caused expenditures to outrun revenues, giving rise to inflation and the fiscal crisis of the state. At the same time, the government's authority to act with resolution has been undercut by the same delegitimating forces that contributed to the onset of the problems. "What the Marxists mistakenly attribute to capitalist economics, however, is, in fact, a product of democratic politics," argues Huntington, inverting James O'Connor's explanation of capitalist crisis.[20]

Since Huntington sees the sources of atrophy lying largely outside an otherwise sound economic system, he is led to call for decreased political participation and increased state authority to resolve the crisis. While some of Huntington's views, which will be discussed more fully in Chapter 6, aroused debate within the Trilateral Commission, most were consistent with the growing mid-1970s ideology that sought to lower demands on government. Linking the prospects for responsible democracy with economic growth, the authors of the governability report endorsed a proposal for a new economic planning agency connected to the White House.[21] As Huntington wrote in 1976, "No 'invisible hand' is going to insure the viability of democratic politics anymore than it ensures the prosperity of market economies."[22]

These calls to rationalize the economy and discipline the polity were central to the Trilateral Commission's forecast of a "reallocation of capital, labor, technology, and available supplies of energy through the economics of scarcity." These changes will occur in the context of "a slower overall growth of the economy, a restructuring of production, a high rate of investment, and a retreat from some of the more extravagant features of our consumer society." Unsure whether the "necessary sacrifices" would be accepted, the Trilateralists understood that their agenda entailed "a considerable degree of voluntary cooperation and of acceptance, voluntary and involuntary, of governmental regulation of an increased sector of personal life."[23]

It was the energy crisis of 1973–74 that concentrated the attention of the elite on the long-term trajectory of the political economy and elicited the terse remarks just quoted. As *Energy: Managing the Transition*, a 1978 Trilateral report, suggested, "The debate over energy policy itself has become a forum for debating the shape of 'post-industrial' American society."[24] In the Trilateralist perspective, managing the energy crisis is a test case for policy, opening into broader efforts to recast the relationship between the state and the economy, while imposing limitations on popular demands.

Energy was already the subject of two Trilateral Commission papers from 1974.[25] In urgent tones the reports spelled out the end of an era of economic growth fueled by cheap, plentiful energy supplies. It was now essential to cut import dependency, reduce domestic consumption, and increase national energy production, lest political turmoil and social disorder follow future energy shocks. Higher oil and gas prices, inducements to conserve energy, and incentives for domestic producers would be needed, but by itself the private market would not suffice to accomplish these tasks. While "market forces will provide much of the motive power, . . . governments will have to set priorities for the use of energy, limit the consumption of certain goods, engage in planning, pass legislation, and vote funds in such fields as mass transit."[26] Anticipating the terms in which President Carter would cast his energy policy, the Trilateral Commission compared the tasks posed by the energy crisis to a "wartime situation" in which the real challenge "is not a struggle with outside adversaries, as in most great crises of the past, but within and among our respective societies."[27]

Persuading the public to view the energy problem as the "moral equivalent of war" was a major preoccupation of Jimmy Carter, whose energy program closely resembled Trilateralist recommendations, as the commission noted.[28] Successful in creating a separate Energy Department, Carter eventually embraced the decontrol of domestic oil and gas prices in order to encourage use-reduction and new production. A tax on the "windfall profits" resulting from decontrol was designed to fund various kinds of energy research and development, provide assistance to low-income energy users, and establish the Synthetic Fuels Corporation. These policies allowed market forces to impose most of the cost of managing the energy crisis on ordinary citizens in the form of higher prices. At the same time, the state was positioned to play an overall channeling role in directing future energy development in partnership with the corporate and financial interests that dominate the energy industry. Carter's four national speeches on the energy crisis framed the issue, with increasingly elaborate symbolic orchestration, in terms of a national emergency in which the moral character of the republic stood in question. As the Brookings Institution would construe it, Carter attempted to manage his energy program by resorting to a crisis framework.

Another crucial policy area bearing on the economy that the

Trilateralists mark for restructuring is industrial relations. Shaping the Trilateral Commission proposals are the objectives of restoring managerial legitimacy, preventing the emergence of class-based politics among the working classes of advanced capitalist countries, and ensuring that trade unions do not become obstacles to technological innovation and international competitiveness. In Trilateral thinking, recovery from the economic crisis of the mid 1970s required a redirection of income from workers to capitalists. As Andrew Shonfield indicated in his address to a Trilateral Commission meeting in December 1974,

> "The class of wage-earners has been managing very nicely—some people think too nicely—to overcome the effects of inflationary rises in the cost of living. The result has been in a number of countries a shift from profit incomes towards wage incomes—the share of profits has diminished—and this is now complicating the conduct of national economic policies."[29]

The 1979 task force report on industrial relations pinpointed the adversarial, contractual system of collective bargaining as a source of inflationary pressures in the economy and a vehicle of antagonism in the social relations of production.[30] What needs to be fostered is "cooperation based upon an ideology that makes it possible to develop constructive industrial relations."[31] Permitting limited participation by employees in aspects of production decisions is a way of reducing anomie and integrating workers into the goal structure of the firm. Forms of worker participation are well established in Western Europe and Japan, but in the United States the confrontational mode of collective bargaining is clung to by most employers and labor officials alike. However, the Trilateral report sees hope in the spread of quality-of-work circles, workers' consultative committees, and employee stock ownership plans, which may dampen potential conflict without unduly restricting managerial prerogatives.[32] Even modest moves from conflictual to consensual labor relations could weaken expression of class conflict in the event of further economic crises, a highly desirable outcome in the view of the Trilateralist system managers.

Like the Trilateral Commission's international policy, which aims to integrate potentially disruptive Third World forces into a structure of reward defined by advanced capitalist interests, the Trilateralist labor policy seeks to adapt industrial relations to capitalist imperatives in a transformed world economy. Unlike the corporate advocates of union-busting and the open shop, the Trilateralist project involves working with existing unions to create an industrial relations environment that is compatible with the need for stability and predictability in the economy.

The economic context necessitating new forms of labor relations is explored in another 1979 Trilateral report on industrial policy. The report makes clear that the Trilateralists see neither free-market economics nor demand-management policy as adequate to meet the myriad problems that developed in the 1970s. What is called for is supply-side restructuring in the shape of an "industrial policy that aims directly to affect the structure of industry rather than influencing it indirectly."[33] While the authors of the report hold no brief for the "invisible hand" of the market, they do stress "that the enterprise sector is the prime mover in the economy."[34] Public policy should help older industries to modernize, while facilitating the development of dynamic, high-technology industries. Industrial policy should not be based on protectionism or "defensive stabilization," which only closes off the ongoing international integration of capitalism and heightens conflicts within and between nations.

While the report leaves specific policies and institutional arrangements open to national variation, it broadly states that "industrial policy should be based on an effective working relationship of government, business, and labor and implemented whenever possible by voluntary concertation."[35] In my view, the Trilateralist response to domestic economic stagnation points toward a political economy girded by corporatist arrangements. As defined by Leo Panitch, corporatism is "a political structure within advanced capitalism which integrates organized socio-economic producer groups through a system of representation and cooperative mutual interaction at the leadership level and social control at the mass level."[36] In the context of calls for lower expectations and austerity, on the one hand, and recapitalization and greater state authority, on the other, corporatist policies can be seen as ingredients of a class-based hegemonic strategy that aims to realign the institutional structures of liberal democratic capitalism.

In the Trilateral Commission reports concerned with national economic policies, the ideological strength of individualism and the free market in the United States are noted by way of contrast with Western Europe and Japan. If the Trilateralist agenda outlined here were to shape policy in the 1980s, it would have had to overcome deep-rooted aversions to an enhanced role for the state. But elite-level conflicts over the long-term orientation of economic policy became evident long before a state-capitalist strategy could be consolidated.

The Free-Market Critique of Planning

During the 1970s, well-placed elites put forth arguments for some form of national economic planning. In 1974 the Initiative Committee for National Economic Planning was founded, co-chaired by United Auto Workers President Leonard Woodcock and Harvard economist Wassily Leontief and supported by a number of prominent academics, political figures, and business leaders. Calling for an Office of National Economic Planning to collect data, map major economic trends, develop alternative plans to meet long-range objectives, and determine future resource, labor, and capital needs, the Initiative Committee was careful to stress its commitment to partnership with private enterprise: "Democratic planning is not a substitute for a decentralized economy nor does it replace the millions of private decisions that are made in the market every day. Rather, to reach democratically chosen objectives, it influences those decisions with a coherent set of economic techniques."[37] These recommendations were drafted into the Balanced Growth and Economic Planning Act, sponsored by Senators Jacob Javits and Hubert Humphrey, and introduced into Congress in the spring of 1975. Around the same time, such businessmen as Henry Ford II and Felix Rohatyn endorsed planning, while the original Humphrey–Hawkins Full Employment Bill included planning as a means to reaching its goal. The Trilateralist agenda apparently intersected with this state-capitalist thrust, and *The Crisis of Democracy* was often read as an outline for an American Bonapartist regime, adapted to the political economy and social structure of late capitalism.

On the left, planning proposals were seen as harbingers of corporatist policies, soon to be put in place by farsighted corporate liberals and their political allies. The planners' self-interested statism, going beyond Keynesianism to "rationalize" crisis-ridden capitalism, was interpreted as an updating of the National Civic Federation's system-stabilizing efforts during the Progressive Era. The notion that ruling-class elements would seek to resolve the crisis of capitalism through an extension of the state's functions was accepted by Paul Sweezy and Harry Magdoff, the foremost Marxist economists in the United States, who wrote in 1975:

> Putting aside for the moment the question of the effectiveness of possible planning arrangements, we can say one thing with reasonable certainty: the present economic crisis and the renewed period of stagnation to which it is the prelude are bound to produce a great leap forward into state capitalism in the United States."[38]

But if a program for restructuring the economy through state planning were to be implemented, opposition from rival capitalist interests and others with the resources to shape public debate would have to be surmounted.

Rather than a consensus developing around the need for corporatist arrangements, an ideological counterattack against statist solutions grew rapidly in the mid-1970s. Both the American Enterprise Institute and the Institute for Contemporary Studies were out front in developing a "free-market" response to liberal crisis management proposals. During the Carter administration, as the economy reverted to stagflation, these policy-planning institutions helped organize a wide-ranging conservative alternative that created a climate in which what came to be known as Reaganomics could be taken seriously. Thus the debate over domestic economic policy within leading policy organizations, and in the nation as a whole, paralleled the foreign policy discussion. Initially bold managerial notions gave way to a right-wing offensive, catalyzed by the hapless efforts of a nominally liberal administration to stabilize conditions over which it had little control.

After the Javits–Humphrey Planning Bill was introduced, the AEI and the ICS prepared extensive rebuttals. A critique by Herbert Stein laid out the line of attack, finding the proposed legislation vague about objectives, unworkable if implemented, and likely to lead to economic and political coercion as key decisions were taken out of private hands.[39] In other words, planning is a form of "creeping socialism." For Stein, the only legitimate kind of planning, if it must be called that, would involve better coordination of current government functions and improved use of statistical data in making policy decisions.

Stein attributed the budding interest in planning as national goal-setting to an overly pessimistic analysis of the economy, seen as intractable to the traditional remedies by certain intellectuals, who in any case have a need to embrace antiestablishment positions. "The proposed planning system is an invitation for the planners to invent goals that the American people do not have," argued Stein.[40] Though planning advocates may proclaim limited objectives, the inevitable failure of the economy to meet their mandated goals of employment, growth, and public services would lead the government to shift from a system of incentives to a system of command. This distrust of state intervention in the economy was stated even more bluntly by Stein's AEI colleague G. Warren Nutter, in another sharp critique of economic planning:

> The serious economic pains now being experienced are symptoms of political ills, not of flaws in the economic system. The basic problem is too

much government, not too little.... The question is whether we wish to be guided in our lives by the invisible hand of freedom or by the visible hand of coercion.[41]

Allying itself with the AEI's perspective against planning was the ICS, weighing into the debate in 1976 with *The Politics of Planning*, a volume of essays by conservative policy analysts. A year earlier the ICS had taken on the liberal planners in *No Time to Confuse*, a critique of *A Time to Choose*, the Ford Foundation's three-year, $4 million study of the energy problem. Since the energy crisis was the issue provoking renewed interest in economic planning, conservative policy institutes like the ICS believed that it was crucial to set out a free-market alternative to those energy policy proposals that broadened the role of the state.

The first two sentences of *No Time to Confuse* established the premises of the conservative case: "Nature's whim causes many of our society's predicaments. Unfortunately, our efforts to alleviate them by applying analysis and advice frequently compound our difficulties and even create additional ones."[42] The second sentence was aimed at what the ICS critics saw as the liberal ideology pervading the Ford Foundation's advocacy of reduced energy consumption through vigorous federal action: the belief that complex policy problems could be managed in the public interest by federal government planning.[43] Moreover, they maintained, this view was held by people who had little understanding of market forces and who aimed to create new bureaucracies for themselves to run, while promoting their antigrowth views as the appropriate ends of society.[44] In attacking liberal energy planners, the ICS was inveighing against an ideology, growing out of the Great Society and counterculture of the 1960s, that threatened to deflect economic and energy policy from supporting the virtues of unfettered capitalism.

Positive proposals for energy policy by the ICS analysts centered on calls for the deregulation of oil and gas prices, thereby inducing both new investment and production and restricted consumption. This was also the conclusion of the first report of the AEI's National Energy Project, issued in 1974.[45] Reiterating this free-market perspective was the AEI energy project's chair, Melvin Laird, who wrote in 1977:

> If we can find the wisdom to treat energy supplies as the important commodities they in fact are, and demand of government only that it establish the framework to permit market forces to work, we will both have redressed the energy imbalance and have relearned the crucial lesson of a free society.[46]

By 1980 it was common to find the AEI described as one of the policy-research organizations most representative of the actual political views of American business leaders. If true, this belies the notion that the capitalist class will seek to resolve the economic crisis through an expansion of the state's role, for the AEI's policy ideology equates public economic planning with a threat to the motive forces of capitalism. But there is much evidence that, despite serious economic problems, only a minority of business leaders favor industrial policy, incomes policy, government guidance of investment, or other extensions of state economic authority.

In 1974 and 1975, the period when economic planning proposals were surfacing, Leonard Silk and David Vogel were allowed to sit in on broad ranging discussions by top U.S. business executives. They found that the business leaders, like

Samuel Huntington believed that democratic principles were in conflict with economic stability. Using the franchise, the public acts through its representatives to secure increased outlays, which siphon off funds from the private sector, reducing the rate of investment and stymieing production. Growing public spending also creates inflation, threatening the very fabric of the capitalist system.[47]

In principle, the fear of democracy that business has is not incompatible with greater state intervention in the economy, if it is tailored to the imperatives of capitalism, as corporate elites perceive them. But Silk and Vogel found an entrenched belief that any move toward national economic planning would threaten managerial discretion and inexorably lead to greater government control of business. Government tends to respond to immediate preferences of the majority, in the executives' view, and is not guided in its actions by the sound precepts of market economics. Summarizing the dominant position on government held by American capitalists, David Vogel states:

> The business community has been remarkably consistent in its opposition to the enactment of any government policies that would centralize economic decision making or strengthen the authority of government over the direction of the business system as a whole. It is only with respect to policies that have their impact on a particular firm or industry that its much heralded pragmatism comes into play. The criterion by which business evaluates government policy has remained quite firm: does the proposed intervention strengthen or weaken the autonomy of management?[48]

In response to the turbulent politics of the 1960s and the unraveling economic situation in the 1970s, capitalists became more politically involved, promoting an agenda centered on business-oriented tax cuts, opposition to economic and social regulation, reduced social welfare spending, hostility to trade union power, and the virtues of free-market economics generally. Policy-planning organizations supportive of these aims expanded in the late 1970s. In the struggle for the ideological hegemony of procapitalist policies, the Heritage Foundation, the Institute for Contemporary Studies, and especially the American Enterprise Institute were increasingly powerful voices.

"Free the Fortune 500!": The American Enterprise Institute

In the years leading up to the 1980 election, no policy organization played a larger role in shaping discussion of economic policy than the American Enterprise Institute. The AEI's impact on domestic economic issues can be compared to the imprint of the Committee on the Present Danger on foreign policy. In both cases a well organized conservative campaign helped push the terms of debate to the right, legitimating free-market and militarist policies respectively.

The success of the AEI in redirecting American politics in the late 1970s is attributable as much to the scope of its activities as to the content of its policy analysis. Chapter 1 described the massive inflow of corporate funds into AEI coffers during the 1970s, which enabled the launching of new study projects and publications, and a huge outreach program involving the media, universities, public conferences, and congressional testimony and staff contact. Much of this agenda-building and opinion-molding effort was directed at domestic economic policy. The breadth and perspective of AEI work is evident in the areas of democratic capitalist ideology, regulatory studies, macroeconomic analysis and recommendations, as well as in the prominent figures active at the AEI.

During the Carter years many top-level economic advisers and officials from past and future Republican administrations became involved in AEI affairs: Herbert Stein, Paul McCracken, William Simon, Arthur Burns, Murray Weidenbaum, Rudolph Penner, James C. Miller III, William Niskanen, and Norman Ture were among those included. Gerald Ford was made an AEI Distinguished Fellow. Joining this free-enterprise chorus were neoconservatives like Irving Kristol, Michael Novak, and Ben Wattenberg—social theorists and polemicists rather than economists. They were able publicists for the conservative economic ideas developed at the AEI, exploiting their ties to the media, from the *Reader's Digest* to *Commentary*, and to the intellectual community, while urging business to fight back against its liberal and radical detractors. As an example of this growing network in action, Kristol helped secure funding from the AEI for Jude Wanniski, a *Wall Street Journal* writer and author of *The Way the World Works*, which is regarded as a seminal statement of supply-side economics. Wanniski had already presented a sympathetic exposition of the famous Laffer Curve in *The Public Interest*, a journal co-edited by Kristol, who is also a regular contributor to the *Wall Street Journal* editorial page and a member of several corporate boards.[49] In turn, the paperback edition of Wanniski's book displayed Kristol's endorsement: "The best economic primer since Adam Smith."

Much of what the AEI is about is rehabilitating the view of capitalism as the bedrock of freedom and democracy while suggesting that socialism must lead to coercion. In its early years, the particlar form of capitalist economics promulgated by the AEI was too extreme even for many business leaders. But in the 1970s the moderating of the AEI's outlook coincided with the heightened politicization of the capitalist class, whose members discovered that "ideas count," as the economic crisis deepened and new social regulations were installed. As a result, the corporate sector found in the AEI a ready source of arguments with which to enter the political arena. These growing bonds between economic interest and policy research were underlined by an official of the Business Roundtable, the leading political group of the corporate elite, who revealed, "It used to be that practically every policy committee meeting would talk about making contributions to support AEI."[50]

The AEI's motto, "Competition of ideas is fundamental to a free society," translates into the promotion of capitalist needs as in the public interest and an attack on policies critical of business that reflect the unrepresentative sentiments of an elitist New Class, based in liberal professions and the state sector. While I shall explore this claim more fully in the next chapter, its force may be briefly noted here by referring to Michael Novak's *American Vision* (1978), which was widely circulated in the business community.[51] Novak argues, "It is in the cultural sphere, in the world of ideas, that democratic capitalism is suffering its greatest losses."[52] He calls for business to wage a "war of ideas" against its "statist," New Class enemies. Novak's strategy for the corporations involves increased funding of public policy research centers, monitoring of public issues by in-house study groups, cultivation of networks of probusiness academics, the clergy, and professionals, and keeping tighter rein over sponsorship of television programs and university grants to ensure that adversarial views are not subsidized by corporate money.[53] Recognizing that capitalism is more than an economic system, Novak and his AEI colleagues understand that the cultural sphere is crucial to the reproduction of bourgeois civilization.

An important part of the AEI's economic analysis is the argument that government regulation has been throttling business by imposing needless costs on production. In 1976 the AEI accelerated its efforts to shape regulatory policy by establishing the Center for the Study of Government Regulation, with an advisory council chaired by Irving Kristol. In 1977 a carefully produced and circulated new AEI journal, *Regulation*, began publication. The first issue contained an article by Kristol attacking the "Naderites" of the "New Class," who have "an ideological animus against the private economic sector" and have acquired a dangerous amount of official power at the Environmental Protection Agency, the Occupational Safety and Health Administration, and the newer regulatory agencies.[54] In a 1975 AEI study, Murray Weidenbaum, later the co-editor of *Regulation*, argued that excessive regulations were a third source of government-induced inflation, along with budget deficits and easy-money policies.[55] Weidenbaum's case against direct environmental control and in favor of indirect price incentives was similar to the position of Charles Schultze, whose *Public Use of Private Interest* was excerpted in *Regulation*. Studies supporting the use of cost–benefit analysis in social regulatory programs were organized by James C. Miller III, co-director of the AEI's Government Regulation Center before heading the Federal Trade Commission under President Reagan.[56] As a result of these combined thrusts, the AEI helped create a political climate responsive to corporate definitions of policy problems and receptive to Murray Weidenbaum's reaction to Big Business Day in 1980: "Free the Fortune 500!"[57] By the time of the Reagan transition the AEI had compiled specific studies and recommendations that were based on liberation of market forces for each of the government agencies charged with social and economic regulation.[58]

Alongside the projects on democratic capitalism and government regulation, macroeconomic policy formed a third area where the AEI mounted a campaign to redirect the economy. In early 1976 the AEI began a Project on Major Economic Problems, whose offspring was a series of annual volumes containing the analyses of leading conservative economists. It has become comparable, and perhaps a rival, to the Brookings Institution's annual *Setting National Priorities*, though the AEI studies have a much wider focus than the budget. In 1977 Herbert Stein, formerly a Brookings analyst before chairing the Council of Economic Advisers in the Nixon administration, began editing and writing the monthly *AEI Economist*. In a format suited to wide distribution, it provided a critical running commentary on economic policy during the Carter years, supplementing Stein's frequent articles in the *Wall Street Journal*. As debates about the effects of taxation on the economy intensified, the AEI set up a program of Tax Policy Studies in 1978, guided by an advisory council chaired by former Treasury Secretary William E. Simon, one of the leading exponents of business ideology in the 1970s and a board member of several major corporations and conservative foundations. Directing the AEI tax program was Rudolph Penner, who became head of the Congressional Budget Office under President Reagan, replacing Brookings policy analyst Alice Rivlin. Finally, in 1980, the AEI organized a prestigious, bipartisan Committee to Fight Inflation, chaired by Arthur Burns, former head of the Federal Reserve System, which contended that inflation was the most dangerous economic problem facing the nation.

While the AEI saw reduced inflation as beneficial to all, the chosen means of budget cuts, deregulation, and unemployment would hit hard at the working class. At the AEI, a rise in the acceptable level of joblessness won support, based on the view that "we have historically high unemployment rates because it has become more tolerable, accepted, and even attractive to be unemployed."[59] Herbert Stein elaborated, explaining:

> [The unemployed] are victims of a society that, because of minimum wage legislation, union scales, and discrimination, has excluded them from jobs they might fill, and a society that has shown them it is possible to live almost as well without working as by working. It has taught them that unemployment is the government's problem, not their's.[60]

The AEI has also brought out a number of studies on the minimum wage that maintain that current legislation is inflationary and reduces both investment and employment opportunities.

Leading AEI economists have distanced themselves from more radical expressions of supply-side economics, especially the claim that large tax cuts would stimulate production to such an extent that the government would reap a revenue windfall and not have to undertake massive budget cuts. Herbert Stein, in particular, has been a frequent and caustic critic of the supply-side "wild men," concerned about massive budget deficits. But the divisions among free-marketers sharpened only after the terms of economic discourse had shifted to the right in the 1970s. The combination of a large outreach effort, made possible by corporate support, and the prestige lent by prominent academics, former government officials, and business leaders made it certain that the AEI's response to the economic crisis would be a potent one, affecting the main lines of public policy.

Toward Reaganomics: ICS and Heritage Foundation

Like the American Enterprise Institute, the Institute for Contemporary Studies quickened its efforts in the late 1970s to produce and disseminate studies supporting conservative economic policies. Whether the growth of the San Francisco–based ICS reflects the emergence of Sunbelt capital, entrepreneurial and antilabor in character, is an open question, but that the ICS has specialized in a strident form of free-market policy-planning and has made every effort to have its proposals translated into government policy is not. The openly ideological ICS, unlike the AEI, makes little attempt to include opposing views in its published volumes and has embraced the term "supply-side economics" to describe its policy perspective.

During the Carter administration, the ICS continued to press for deregulation and business-oriented tax reform. In 1977 the ICS organized a program on regulation at Northwestern University, taking care to invite business representatives to state their case on the malign effect of overregulation on efficiency. The ICS believed that the debate over social regulation had been captured by a policy current that "grew out of the animus against material progress and economic growth which began with the New Left in the later 1960s and became explicit in the environment and no-growth movements of the 1970s."[61] For its part, *Federal Tax Reform*, issued by the ICS in 1978, moved in the wake of California's Proposition 13 property-tax revolt and the slew of tax-reform programs at the national level. Aiming to bolster developing views linking high marginal tax rates and weak capital formation, the ICS authors explored the relations between savings, investment, and taxation.[62]

In the summer of 1980 the strands of ICS economic policy-planning came together in *The Economy in the 1980s: A Program for Growth and Stability*.[63] Like the national security volume described in Chapter 4, this book was strategically timed to enter into the presidential campaign discussion and to shape policy after the November election, when the ICS would claim that "the ideas and policies that are the basis of the Reagan economic program for the future are contained in this institute study."[64] Described by the ICS as "the first presentation of the full program of the 'supply-side' school of economics," *The Economy in the 1980s* was presented by Institute officers, foundation executives, and major media figures, including Irving Kristol, Norman Podhoretz, and leaders of the Council on Foreign Relations and the Trilateral Commission.[65] After Reagan's election victory, ICS authors, who had advised him during the campaign, briefed congressional economic advisers on their recommendations, easing the way for the passage of President Reagan's economic program in 1981. Following the AEI, the ICS had integrated outreach and public relations into policy-planning for a conservative era.

The editor of *The Economy in the 1980s* was Michael J.

Boskin of Stanford University, who had edited two previous ICS volumes. Boskin has been a leading advocate of the notion that savings levels are closely tied to changes in the marginal tax rate, which in turn determines the overall ratio of investment in the economy. In this view, high taxation of personal savings leads to economic stagnation when joined with disincentive-creating regulatory, monetary, and spending policies. These policies must be reversed if stable noninflationary growth is to be restored. In order to remove disincentives that obstruct working, saving, investing, and innovating, tax burdens must be eased, especially for those with a high propensity to save, while monetary policy must be tightened, nondefense government spending slowed, economic and social regulations eased, market mechanisms restored, and trade liberalized.[66]

The ICS authors repeatedly noted the hardships that poor economic performance had imposed on ordinary Americans. They did not strike the pose of big-business advocates. While warning that economic and social disaster loom if past practices are not abandoned, they were confident that their policies will help "to restore that spirit of vitality, creativity, productivity, and resourcefulness with which we so often described our nation and its economy, its possibilities and its accomplishments, in the past."[67] Contrasting this passage with the gloomy outlook of the Brookings Institution's *Agenda for the 1980s* provides some measure of how conservative policy-planning organizations have been able to identify themselves with liberal capitalist visions of progress.

While conservative policy-planners foresaw an unlimited horizon of growth if their measures were implemented, in the short run harsh cuts in government programs were in store. This is clear in the Heritage Foundation's *Mandate for Leader-*

ship, which provided the Reagan administration with a detailed list of government programs to be trimmed, such as food stamps and welfare assistance. At the same time, the Heritage analysts called for tax reductions for business, lifting of price controls on natural gas and oil, and sharp increases in the defense budget. These policies involved a shift in the composition of the federal budget from welfare to warfare and implied a significant upward redistribution of income. The selling point of this package, of course, was the potential of the free-market system to deliver a bountiful supply of goods once the shackles of big government were lifted.

Conflict in the 1980s

A central claim of the business-oriented policy organizations that paved the way for Reaganomics was that the tax system created a disincentive to invest. In line with this premise, the 1981 Reagan tax legislation offered business a number of tax reductions, including accelerated write-offs of new investments in plant and equipment. However, a study by the Washington-based Citizens for Tax Justice found that many of the corporations that had received the largest tax breaks actually decreased investment from 1981 to 1983, contrary to the supply-side expectation. Instead, much of the increased cash flow resulting from new corporate tax loopholes was used "to increase dividends, expand cash reserves, fund mergers or acquisitions, raise executive pay, or increase advertising budgets."[68]

This was only one of the failures of the conservative economic program in the 1980s. But most economists at policy-planning organizations welcomed the reduction in the inflation rate and the restrictive monetary policy of the Federal Reserve Board under Paul A. Volcker, and were unwilling to make any sharp breaks with the Reagan program. On the other hand, as early as 1982 mounting budget deficits were troubling business leaders, and the Business Roundtable, the Chamber of Commerce, and the National Association of Manufacturers called for a slowdown in military spending increases and some modest tax increases.[69] But the Heritage Foundation drew a line against any significant tax hikes or retreat from the Reagan military buildup. A Heritage team offered a plan for slashing over $100 billion from the fiscal 1985 budget through devolving many government functions to state and local levels or to the private sector, acting on the Grace Commission recommendations for eliminating waste and mismanagement, and sharply cutting back on entitlement programs.[70]

While conservative policy organizations supported a continuation of the basic directions of the Reagan revolution, the corporate moderates at the Brookings Institution have continued to move rightward, working within a lean set of assumptions summarized by economics writer Robert Kuttner as follows:

> Markets usually work; public planning cannot improve outcomes; full employment breeds unacceptable inflation; trade unions are more a problem than a solution; too much equality harms efficiency; no serious structural problems afflict American industry; and above all, the only serious economic problem in the 1980s is macroeconomic imbalance—loose budgets and tight money.[71]

In 1984 Brookings analysts presented an austere economic document whose concern for balancing the budget resembled Republican nostrums, though Walter Mondale embraced similar concerns in his campaign.[72] Brookings economists like Robert

Z. Lawrence and Charles Schultze have denied that U.S. industry faces any serious decline, arguing that alleged "deindustrialization" is simply part of normal market adjustments, and have been sharply critical of proposals for a national industry plan.

In the 1980s, economic policy debate was confined largely to "the supply-side right and the austerity-minded center," as Kuttner puts it.[73] The economic crisis of the 1970s had the effect of reshuffling the policy-planning network. The establishment liberalism of the Brookings Institution, which seemed so viable in the 1960s, was thrown on the defensive when confronted by problems to which its framework did not apply. From the political center, the Trilateral Commission outlined a more far-reaching program of crisis management through state planning, austerity policies, rationalized industrial policies and labor relations, and international economic coordination. But the Carter administration was not able to deliver on the Trilateralist agenda, and this opened the door to the market-policy advocates whose voices the elite mobilization of the 1970s amplified.

While free-market policy-planners are in ascendance, other elite approaches have been developed and are awaiting political support in the event of a late 1980s slump. An Industrial Policy Study Group led by Felix Rohatyn, Irving Shapiro, and Lane Kirkland has called for new government institutions to undergird an industrial policy.[74] But the substance of both centrist and conservative economic programs is that resources will be transferred to capitalists, workers will bear the brunt of economic "recovery," and political processes, to which we turn, will be increasingly removed from democratic pressures.

6

Politics, Ideology, and the Erosion of Liberalism

BY 1980, pressing issues in the United States were framed by terms of discourse that were increasingly economic in character. Underlying both domestic political impasse and declining U.S. power abroad, it was argued, was the laggard and uneven performance of the American economy. From left to right, programs for economic renewal were offered, compatible or in contention with the direction the Reagan administration had set. Policy-planning organizations, including the five analyzed in this book, stepped up their efforts to affect outcomes.

Social and Political Sources of Crisis

Despite the economistic nature of the policy discussion, which is laden with competing claims about the relationship between taxation, investment, productivity, growth, and employment, it is essential to consider the social and political dimensions of economic policy-planning if the crisis is to be fully understood. Implicitly or explicitly, transformations in political institutions, social structure, and cultural values enter into the explanation of the decline of liberal democratic capitalism put forth by the leading policy-planning organizations. In turn, many of their leading thinkers acknowledge that broad changes in the social and political fabric of American life must accompany programs for capitalist revitalization. In the last chapter I drew on the concept of an institutional structure of capitalist accumulation to suggest linkages between economic policy, political institutions, and social arrangements. Here I shall explore in greater detail how the American Enterprise Institute, the Brookings Institution, the Heritage Foundation, the Institute for Contemporary Studies, and the Trilateral Commission conceptualize the relationship between the crisis of the capitalist economy and the disarray pervading the polity and culture of the liberal democratic social order.

Some of these connections have already been outlined in the analysis of specific areas of substantive policy. We saw that the theorists of interdependence at the Brookings Institution and the Trilateral Commission viewed parochial, nationalist political forces as a barrier to achieving international economic coordination. Conservative analysts sponsored by the Institute for Contemporary Studies replied by blaming the rise of a noninterventionist, "globalist" foreign policy outlook for the unchecked expansion of Soviet power and the persistent annoyance of unreasonable Third World demands. The national security hawks also viewed with alarm the spread of the "Vietnam syndrome" in the populace. When combined with pro–welfare state sentiments, this "loss of will" blocked policies for rearmament. To varying degrees, all five policy-planning organizations promoted the argument that the economic crisis of the 1970s was complicated and was partially caused, by the "overloading" of popular expectations on the state. The American Enterprise Institute, in particular, made the social and cultural roots of political and economic malfunctioning a specific object of inquiry and policy prescription. Much of the work of all the policy-planning institutions is marked by concern over the dwindling legitimacy and authority of the state as it faces choices of unprecedented difficulty. In drawing attention to these complex linkages, policy-planning organizations were both shaping and reflecting wider elite thinking in the United States, thereby confirming the interpretation that the postwar political economy was in a crucial transitional period in which basic restructuring was on the agenda.

As a register of ruling-class analysis and as a point of comparison with the five policy-planning organizations examined here, the 1980 special issue of *Business Week* on "Reindustrialization" is a particularly insightful and frank document. As I have noted, its concern for restoring international competitiveness through a conscious industrial policy and its emphasis on neocorporatist relations between government, business, and labor run parallel with the Trilateralist agenda and are anathema to conservative free-market proponents. But its wider appeal to capitalists lies in its arguments for increased subsidies and incentives to business, reduced taxes and regulations, and a redirection of funds from consumption to investment. For our present purposes, what is notable is how restoring economic growth becomes the touchstone to which all government policies must conform, entailing a transformed liberal democratic public sphere.

If the U.S. economy is to undergo the "fundamental change" necessary to prevent an "irreversible slide," it will "require a total reprogramming of the way in which Americans think about their economy," the editors of *Business Week* maintain.[1] Keynesian-based macroeconomic policy sees a shortfall of demand as the cause of economic stagnation and ignores the problems of supply and production, while social policy and U.S. labor are more concerned with redistributing wealth than creating it. By the mid-1970s a "psychology of affluence" had developed in the United States, resting on beliefs in equality and entitlement, an adversarial posture toward government, and a weakening of the traditional work ethic. Unfortunately, from the perspective of *Business Week* those foreboding changes took hold just at the time when the postwar economic expansion began to falter, and they stand in the way of the recognition of "new realities," most centrally "that limitless growth can no longer be taken for granted: It must be worked for."[2]

If the U.S. economy is to avoid sinking, all sectors of American society must subordinate their competing claims to the goal of economic revitalization: "Special groups must recognize that their own unique goals cannot be satisfied if the U.S. cannot compete in world markets. The drawing of a social contract must take precedence over the aspirations of the poor, the minorities, and the environmentalists."[3] In effect, American society is to be rigorously functionalized to the end of restored economic growth, so that an environment is created in which business profits can be made, since corporate well-being is the precondition of any social advancement. While citizens will be invited to join in a new "consensus," their participation will consist largely of after-the-fact acclamation, for the *Business Week* team makes it clear that reindustrialization "depends on whether the business, bureaucratic, and political elites can get together to provide the leadership."[4] As early as 1974, *Business Week* had understood that this program might prove unappealing:

> It will be a hard pill for many Americans to swallow, the idea of doing with less so that big business can have more. . . . Nothing that this nation, or any other nation, has done in modern economic history compares in difficulty with the selling job that must now be done to make people accept the new reality."[5]

Programs for reindustrialization raise the question of whether liberal democracy and capitalism can thrive together in a period of crisis, or whether the former will have to give way before the imperatives of renewed accumulation. This question cuts across other issues that policy-planning organizations have been led to as the economic and political crisis deepened after 1973: the relationship between economic strategies and the role of the state, the realignment of political forces, the decreasing legitimacy of established institutions, and the disruption of social norms around which motivations supportive of liberal democratic capitalism form. Because it bluntly confronts these matters, and because its argument anticipates many neoconservative themes, I shall discuss Samuel Huntington's contribution to the Trilateral Commission's work on *The Crisis of Democracy*, then outline the tentative and unsystematic attempts of Brookings Institution policy analysts to come to terms with the issues raised by Huntington.

Huntington: The Democratic Distemper

The Crisis of Democracy is concerned with the "governability of democracies," a phrase that recalls the "problem of order" with which Western political philosophy has been preoccupied since Hobbes. Huntington has long been involved with questions of order and political stability, and it is appropriate that he quotes Madison's *Federalist Paper* number 51 in his Trilateral Commission article. Like Madison, Huntington analyzes the sources of discontent in the polity, the better to contain and defuse challenges to state authority.

Huntington makes it clear that the reality of political power in modern capitalist societies departs from its liberal democratic appearance. In Chapter 4 I noted his discussion of the private establishment, which constitutes the effective ruling bloc in the United States: "For twenty years after World War II presidents operated with the cooperation of a series of informal governing coalitions." President Truman, for example, drawing on "the existing sources of power in the country," brought "a substantial number of nonpartisan soldiers, Republican bankers, and Wall St. lawyers into his administration."[6] This elite governing coalition must be distinguished from the electoral coalition, which has served its purpose once a president is elected: "The day after his election the size of his majority is almost, if not entirely, irrelevant to his ability to govern the country. . . . What counts then is his ability to mobilize support from the leaders of the key institutions in society and government."[7] By the mid-1970s these patterns of rule had been disrupted to such an extent that the authors of *The Crisis of Democracy* noted the recurring images of "the disintegration of civil order, the breakdown of social discipline, the debility of leaders, and the alienation of citizens."[8] What caused this malaise?

For Huntington it was the democratic "surge" of the 1960s, a period of "creedal passion," that led to the erosion of governmental authority and the distrust of business. A spirit of equality contributed to the democratic challenge: "People no longer felt the same compulsion to obey those whom they had previously considered superior to themselves in age, rank, status, expertise, character, or talents."[9] Newly politicized groups such as women, blacks, students, and ecologists, pressed their demands on the state, even while expressing little confidence that the government could serve the public interest. Far from invigorating the political system, increased participation has led to paralysis at a time when economic crises and international challenges were looming.

As Peter Steinfels has argued, the empirical data that Huntington presents does not conclusively support a link between declining confidence in government and the loosely defined democratic surge. Moreover, Huntington downplays the causal significance of specific issues, such as the Vietnam War, race relations, the Watergate affair, and stagflation, which at one point he admits may have spurred increased polarization and participation and reduced support for established institutions.[10] Setting up an opposition between "democracy" and "governability," Huntington is led to call for "a greater degree of moderation in democracy."[11] To achieve a subdued public sphere that is more compatible with the state's managerial functions, citizens must lower their voices and expectations. Recommendations by the Trilateralists aim at fortifying authority. Power in Congress should be centralized, the presidency strengthened, and the political parties reinvigorated. More broadly, the Trilateralists are worried about the growing influence of "value-oriented intellectuals" who derogate leadership, challenge authority, and unmask established institutions, and whose behavior "constitutes a challenge to democratic government which is, potentially at least, as serious as those posed in the past by the aristocratic cliques, fascist movements, and communist parties."[12] This contemporary "treason of the intellectuals" should be combatted with measures to "restore an appropriate balance between the press, the government, and other institutions in society" and to "relate educational planning to economic and political goals."[13] It is no accident that business leaders concerned with public disenchantment with the corporate system in the mid-1970s saw the media and the universities as the most egregious purveyors of negative ideas.[14]

Within the Trilateral Commission, *The Crisis of Democracy* aroused much debate, with some members believing that it was overly pessimistic about the conflict between governability and democracy. But it was taken seriously as a signpost in the evolution of American liberalism away from the optimism of the first two postwar decades. It also explored connections between the crisis of the economy and the waning of legitimacy in a way that would be filled out by policy analysts at the AEI, where Huntington himself became an adjunct scholar in 1979. Reconstructing social and political processes to mesh with the reality of interdependence was a foundational objective of the Trilateral Commission, and to the extent that popular activities and expectations impeded progress toward this goal, democracy should be limited. Though stated in a more restrained and indirect manner, a similar conclusion about the political dimensions of the crisis was reached by Brookings Institution thinkers.

Technocratic Liberalism

As we have seen, the predominant outlook on economic crisis at the Brookings Institution reveals an awareness that problems are structural in nature, while still suggesting remedies of a technical and pragmatic sort. In part this contradiction is rooted in the period when the Brookings economic analysis became most influential. For a time in the 1960s, basic defects in the system's functioning appeared to have been eradicated, with those that remained amenable to fine-tuning policies based on technical knowledge of the economy. Habits of thought formed in a period oriented to short-term, piecemeal adjustment are not conducive to reflection on the underlying determinants of the system as a whole. Furthermore, because the Brookings Institution's studies are based on empiricist, data-grounded methods, they are less likely to develop explanations in which more diffuse social and cultural forces are intrinsically related to concrete political and economic problems.

These quandaries are plainly evident in several works by top scholars at Brookings about the problems of political management. In the expanded 1976 *Setting National Priorities*, a retreat from Keynesian economics and Great Society social policy was accompanied by calls for more realistic limits on what government can accomplish. Problems of government efficacy are seen as largely organizational. Graham Allison and Peter Szanton called for a more precise delineation of the roles of Congress and the executive branch and enlarging the discretion of the President in economic affairs.[15] They recommended centralization of the White House staff and creation of an executive committee of the cabinet, "Ex-Cab," composed of the secretaries of state, treasury, and defense, which would act as the chief forum for major policy decisions.[16] These and other organizational changes were aimed at cutting through the morass of the policy-making process so that the state could act more effectively as a manager in domestic and international arenas. But the government would also be more shielded from constituency interests, leading critics to argue that the Brookings authors "share the Nixon quest for a neo-Hamiltonian presidency, one capable of making policy without the direct intervention of domestic constraints."[17] What the Brookings Institution wanted to avoid was a situation in which "public controversy about policy measures is more likely to be couched in simplistic, irrelevant ideological terms than to be a debate about realistic and useful alternatives."[18] These words of Henry Owen and Charles Schultze hint at the fear of public sphere politicization shared by Huntington and other liberals, who provide a large role for technical and managerial elites in their plans for fending off social chaos.

It was the hope of the Brookings Institution that the Carter administration, untainted by Vietnam or Watergate, could restore public support by improving the workings of government. But in the fall of 1980 the leading Brookings Institution scholar of political institutions, James L. Sundquist, wrote, "Public confidence in our leaders and our institutions has fallen to appalling levels."[19] While he argues that the political system, not just the personalities of leaders, is responsible for the crisis, Sundquist's proposed reforms amount to managerial rearranging of existing governmental institutions. Technocratic liberalism, represented by the Brookings Institution, seeks to reduce entropy and fragmentation in political processes by centralizing power and reducing pressure points on which organized interests can push. Thus Sundquist calls for restoring presidential leadership, especially in foreign policy and through elimination of the legislative veto, developing "central integrative mechanisms" in Congress, and creating a corps of professional government managers to replace the "waves of transient amateurs brought in by each new administration."[20]

Sundquist's regard for expertise is clear from his discussion of political parties, which he thinks must be roused from their state of torpor. What objectives could parties adopt that would increase historically low voter participation? Sundquist recognizes that ideological and programmatic identifications can form the basis of political parties, as in Western Europe, but he consigns this scenario in America to the distant future, if at all: "If the political world currently lacks clear and overwhelming public policy issues of the kind that brought parties into being in the past, that is beyond the control of anyone."[21] Some on the liberal left argue for transforming the Democratic Party into a social democratic vehicle by stressing class issues and breaking with all-inclusive centrist coalitions. The popular mobilization involved in this strategy would clash with Sundquist's proposed reform of the method of presidential selection. Hoping to ensure that there will be candidates with "appropriate experience" who are not "unacceptable to the party establishment," Sundquist suggests limiting the number of primaries and increasing the number of convention seats held by party leaders.[22] Thus, while Sundquist views public disaffection as a serious problem, many of his proposals would further insulate political processes from citizen purview.

Charles Schultze's *Public Use of Private Interest*, discussed in Chapter 5, also reveals a commitment to technical solutions to problems in political performance and legitimacy. As we have seen, Schultze wants to eliminate the clumsy "command-and-control" mode of government activity at a time when "there is a growing need for collective influence over individual and business behavior that was once the domain of purely private decisions."[23] His answer is to base government regulation on marketlike incentives to help bring private interests in line with public purposes. Schultze admits that it is a "rebuttable presumption" that the private market is the most desirable mode of carrying out economic and social arrangements, but he also believes that capitalism rests on a realistic appraisal of human nature:

> Market-like arrangements not only minimize the need for coercion as a means of organizing society; they also reduce the need for compassion, patriotism, brotherly love, and cultural solidarity as motivating forces behind social improvement.... Harnessing the "base" motives of material self-interest to promote the common good is perhaps the most important social convention mankind has achieved.[24]

For Schultze, capitalist relations are not themselves coercive, and the historically constituted relationship between the state and the economy is not the source of the problems to which state regulations are directed. Instead he sees a productive economy of individual units that occasionally create side-effects ("market failures") to which government must respond.

But in the end, Schultze admits that questions of ends and values in the political process remain and that social intervention by government will continue to be a source of conflict: "There is no instrumental solution to the dilemma."[25] In the era of economic expansion, mainstream liberalism, embodied by the Brookings Institution, held that growth itself would undercut conflicts, generating sufficient funds for private investment and public programs. In the more constrained circumstances Schultze and his Brookings colleagues are working in, where economic choices resemble a zero-sum game, technocratic solutions are a precarious reply to problems of legitimation. In his own words, Schultze ends "rather lamely." Rooted in a tradition determined by liberal individualism, classical welfare economics, and empiricist social science, Schultze is unable to ground normative claims in a developed concept of the public interest or justice. His call for "a steady maturing of both the electorate and political leaders" has a hollow ring.[26]

That liberal democracy might stand in the way of the "hard choices" necessary to manage systemic crises was a point shared by many Trilateral Commission and Brookings Institution thinkers. Citing the influence of Schultze's book, Arthur Okun reflected the skeptical outlook underlying center-liberal policy-planning in the late 1970s: "I myself am in a much more sober mood toward what you can get by throwing money at problems, although I was never all that optimistic about the prospects of turning a five-year-old ghetto kid into a model of equal opportunity."[27] It is perhaps not surprising that contradictions of the capitalist accumulation process and the structural relation between the state and the economy maintain a low profile in the accounts of political and legitimation problems given by these policy analysts. Before exploring the more vigorous efforts of the American Enterprise Institute, the Institute for Contemporary Studies, and the Heritage Foundation to reshape the polity along conservative lines, I shall outline the elements of an interpretive framework that includes a structural explanation of political-economic relationships.

Systemic and Social Crisis

Policy-planning organizations help translate class interests into state action by defining and promoting lines of policy that ensure the stability and reproduction of a system shaped by capitalist social relations. While anchored in economic conditions, this process has political and cultural dimensions that are no less important to the achievement of hegemony over the definition of problems and the standards by which they will be evaluated and resolved. The major policy institutions in the United States bring together representatives of business, politics, law, the media, "technical intellectuals" from academia, and civic organizations, and these constitute a historically specific ruling bloc. Neither the maintenance of hegemony nor the reproduction of capitalist relations is a self-contained infrastructural process.

According to some accounts, the decline of liberal democratic capitalism is to be explained by contradictions within the capitalist accumulation process, which lead to an economic crisis that affects political, social, and cultural spheres. In contrast, a nonderivative approach tries to show how political and social processes enter into conjunctural economic crises with their own weight.[28] From this perspective we can then integrate the political, social, and ideological analysis of policy-planning organizations, which differ among themselves in their concern for noneconomic issues, into their general concept of crisis.

Jürgen Habermas and James O'Connor have attempted to develop a crisis theory in which the specificity of liberal democratic capitalism is addressed. In *Legitimation Crisis*, Habermas attempts to develop a theory that integrates "systemic" and "social" levels of analysis and to apply a concept of their relationship to the crisis of advanced capitalism.[29] The "systemic" level refers to the relationship of a society to "external" nature and the material reproduction of its conditions of existence, and to the crises that occur when the steering mechanisms that guide this process are disrupted, impairing material production and the objective structure of social integration. The "social" level refers to the "internal" integration of a society and the shared normative structures that shape personal identity and enable communication to take place. In a crisis of social integration, institutions that secure identity disintegrate, publicly-sanctioned norms fail to orient action, and interpersonal relationships become anomic. According to Habermas, contemporary capitalist societies exhibit crisis tendencies in the economic, political, and sociocultural systems.

Late capitalism differs markedly from its nineteenth-century predecessor. The growing concentration of capital, the increased organization of markets, and the escalating intervention of the state into the economy signal the end of laissez-faire liberal capitalism. The relationship between the state and the economy is such that crises cannot be predicted on the basis of investigating the laws of motion of the economy, independently conceived. While economic crises may occur, the market-supplementing and market-replacing functions of the modern capitalist state tend to displace crises into the political and sociocultural realms.

In the political sphere, the state's administrative system employs a variety of fiscal and regulatory policies to correct and supplant market mechanisms within the limits set by private investment prerogatives. While this steering system has gained a limited planning capacity, output problems develop in the form of inflationary pressures and a permanent crisis of public finance. In addition, bureaucratic planning meets crises only reactively, the implemented policies are not fully coordinated, and client influences are still a significant force in policy formation. The expanded role of the state in the capitalist economy increases the state's need for legitimation, since the liberal ideology of fair exchange is no longer effective. The distribution of social wealth, once seen as a natural outcome of an impersonal market, is now revealed as the result of quasi-political decisions. From a Habermasian perspective, the political crises to which the Brookings Institution and the Trilateral Commission offer managerial solutions are rooted in the structurally delimited relationship between the formally democratic state and an economic system based on the priorities of private capital.

This arrangement depends on an ideology of civic privatism grounded in family life and on an orientation to leisure, consumption, and career. But the spread of administrative rationality into these once-private areas threatens the normative structures they sustain, undercuts taken-for-granted meanings, and politicizes new regions of social life that had previously helped supply legitimacy to the state. Social changes attendant on capitalist modernization undermine the ability of the sociocultural sphere to produce motivations among citizens supportive of bourgeois civilization. To cite one of his examples, Habermas argues that the growth of a large state-supported population, the spread of areas of concrete rather than abstract labor, and the expansion of aesthetic and leisure pursuits help to weaken exchange-value dispositions in the public.[30] Even if Habermas incorrectly identifies certain crisis tendencies, the erosion of motivations he points toward forms a part of the crisis that policy-planning organizations increasingly address, though they understand its origins in a much different way. As we have seen, and will explore further, the AEI attributes the breakdown of integrative norms to the pernicious influence of the New Class. In response to such disparagement of authority and the weakening of "exchange orientation," the AEI has initiated projects to strengthen the "mediating structures" that produce goals and values that sustain, rather than undermine, the bourgeois order.

While James O'Connor does not explore cultural or common-normative dimensions of modern societies, he, like Habermas, sees the capitalist state as implicated in the economic crisis by virtue of the accumulation and legitimation functions it performs.[31] The state must both assist the process of capitalist accumulation through social expenditures and incur social expenses for policies, such as welfare, that maintain citizen allegiance and relative social harmony. But as the contradictory development of late-capitalist political economies compels the state increasingly to underwrite both functions, a structural gap between expenditures and revenues is created, leading to a fiscal crisis. In the Trilateral Commission's *Crisis of Democracy*, Samuel Huntington twists O'Connor's argument to support the view that democratic politics is the cause of political overloading and impasse.[32] This is a telling revision, for Huntington has no analysis of the imperatives that the capitalist economy places on state resources, and he misses O'Connor's point that many of the demands the state must respond to as its legitimation function are themselves reactions to uneven capitalist development. However, these lacunae are not merely Huntington's; they pervade the analyses of the policy-planning organizations.

More recently O'Connor has emphasized that the main contemporary problem for capitalism is not "system integration" but rather "social integration" and "social rationality," arguing that it is "the permanent presence of the organized and unorganized working class which has become the crucial barrier to capitalist accumulation."[33] A variety of economic-crisis ideologies have arisen to legitimate austerity policies, which aim at boosting profits through productivity-enhancing programs. But O'Connor also stresses that "it is less and less true that everyday life . . . stands outside of the process of accumulation. Further, social reproduction means more than control of labor power; it also means control of needs, symbols, ideologies."[34]

The holistic, noneconomistic analyses of Habermas and O'Connor enable us to see how the state, class relations, and culture are involved in the crisis of the political economy. After 1973 these linkages were scrutinized with growing urgency by conservative policy-planning organizations. First we describe the AEI's active development of an ideology of democratic capitalism promoting "social integration" in accordance with the goals of corporate economics, then discuss the efforts of the ICS to build an agenda for the reordering of political and governmental processes, and finally characterize the Heritage Foundation's vision of a "conservative revolution."

The Public Philosophy of the AEI

While the AEI continued to pursue its traditional studies of the economy and governmental policies, it also entered the terrain of the "war of ideas" in the 1970s. Fearing a drift of public opinion toward anticapitalist or at least anticorporate views, the AEI set out quite consciously to do battle with the "adversary culture" and to turn the norms shaping public policy away from egalitarianism and toward the kind of liberty that capitalism flourishes on. This task was multifaceted, drawing on expanded AEI resources to fund study projects and publications, attract eminent scholars, and conduct various forms of opinion-shaping outreach, in much the same way that economic policy was targeted for an overhaul of its basic premises. Following an overview of the key tenets of AEI ideology, we shall describe how these tenets are applied by the AEI in the areas of "corporate theology," the project on mediating structures, and the study of political processes.

Decisive to the intellectual credibility that the once-fringe AEI won in the 1970s was its success in bringing the neoconservative current into its ongoing projects. Leading intellectuals who affiliated with the AEI included Irving Kristol, Seymour Martin Lipset, Robert Nisbet, Ben Wattenberg, Michael Novak, Peter Berger, Nathan Glazer, Richard Scammon, James Q. Wilson, and Jeane Kirkpatrick. Participants in AEI activities include many of the editors and regular contributors to *Commentary* and *The Public Interest*, which are regarded as the most prominent neoconservative journals. While their voices would have been heard anyway, the AEI provided these scholars and writers with amplification and access to practically oriented political and business elites, whose search for legitimation in the 1970s intertwined with the swelling ideological offensive of the AEI.

Recurrent motifs in the AEI's public philosophy reflect the neoconservative world-view. As explained by Peter Steinfels, these include the belief that a crisis of authority has beset the West as governing institutions lose legitimacy and ruling elites lose confidence, thereby threatening the stability of liberal civilization. Governing elites and capitalist institutions bear little responsibility for the crisis. Instead, neoconservatives blame the disorder in values and morals on the rising influence of an antiauthority "adversary culture," which has been animated by a loosely defined New Class, based in the "knowledge industry" and liberal professions. Reformist, egalitarian demands have been sponsored by this class, which stands to gain from expanded social policies because its members are well entrenched in the state sector and in the occupations it works with. For the neoconservatives, these excessive demands must be rejected and authority reasserted. The New Class and its adversary culture must be tamed, not by widening democracy but by fortifying the Establishment.[35] What the AEI has specialized in, on the one hand, is alleging that New Class policies and attitudes have had a negative impact on the performance of the economy and, on the other hand, arguing that only a sound capitalist system can assure the survival of the civilized culture and orderly polity that neoconservatives hold dear. In other words, the American Enterprise Institute has brought together economic and cultural conservatives in the political battle against the common foe who threatens them.

A central thrust of the AEI's assault on liberalism is a sharp critique of egalitarian social policies and income redistribution. At a joint AEI–Hoover Institution conference on the latter theme, Irving Kristol supported a meritocratic principle of reward: "I think status differentials of character, ability, and talent, that they are deserved, and that we should have as many of them as possible."[36] Kristol's attack on liberal policies for greater equality, represented at the conference by Arthur Okun and Henry Aaron of the Brookings Institution, rests on three central claims, First, he denies that income distribution is a serious problem in the United States, the levels of inequality having been vastly exaggerated. Second, Kristol claims that antipoverty programs have often intensified the very problems they address. Speaking of the "welfare population," which has "sunk to various depths of social pathology," Kristol argues, "It is not at all implausible to think that, had we been less generous in our welfare program, these people would now be better off."[37] Third, Kristol implies that egalitarians are modern Jacobins in reformist clothing: "The passion for equality, then, is always dangerous to liberty because it is a passion for power: the power to impose one's ideal of justice-as-equality on other people."[38]

In the same forum, an even more sweeping indictment of the ideology of equality was delivered by the social philosopher Robert Nisbet, a member of the AEI's Council of Academic Advisers. Pondering why liberty and authority are both declining, Nisbet finds the answer in "the extraordinary power that equality has come to have on the intellectual and increasingly on the political person."[39] While ordinary citizens share a distrust of the social consequences of equality with Nisbet, who sees it as a code word for social revolution, the intellectual "clerisy" embraces equality with religious fervor. Unfortunately, these attitudes find their way into public policy by virtue of the influence intellectuals have on the media and government bureaucrats. If this trend continues, the United States will find that "the final line between freedom and collectivist servitude has been crossed."[40] While Nisbet's language is extreme, the implication that a counterintelligentsia must be formed to struggle against the adversary culture is a staple of AEI neo-conservatism.

While countering what it considers to be irresponsible criticism of American society, the AEI has established a Project on Democratic Capitalism to promote a positive view of the economic system. It is significant that this project not only rests on arguments about the material advantages of a market economy, but also emphasizes the moral–cultural component of democratic capitalism. Long the target of criticism from adversary intellectuals, the AEI views the culture of capitalism as the seat of freedom of ideas, tolerance, social concern, and the search for talent in all classes. An affirming view of capitalism's relation to freedom was upheld by those AEI scholars who contributed to the symposium of twenty-six intellectuals on the theme of "Capitalism, Socialism, and Democracy" in a 1978 issue of *Commentary*. The decision of the AEI to reprint this work was undoubtedly due to agreement with the premises of the *Commentary* statement, which begins:

> The idea that there may be an inescapable connection between capitalism and democracy has recently begun to seem plausible to a number of intellectuals who would once have regarded such a view not only as wrong but even as politically dangerous. So, too, with the idea that there may be something intrinsic to socialism which exposes it ineluctably to the "totalitarian temptation."[41]

In short, what the AEI has helped to develop is a more attractive argument for capitalism, which is depicted not as a Hobbesian jungle or a barren plain of mechanistic rationality, but as a precondition for achievement of the finest liberal ideas.

One of the most intriguing aspects of the AEI's work in the realm of ideas is the Project on Religion, Philosophy, and Public Policy, headed by the prolific Michael Novak. Novak's attempt to locate a theological grounding for corporate capitalism takes place amid a worldwide explosion in the political salience of religion. In the Middle East, Iran, India, and Latin America the connections between religious movements and sociopolitical conflict are painfully clear. But in advanced industrial countries, the secularization of culture has largely removed the weight of religious influence on the state. However, as Walter Dean Burnham has pointed out, the United States stands apart from this pattern.[42] Statistical analyses have shown that the variation from society to society in the percentage of the population for whom religious belief is an anchor of existential identity can be explained largely by the level of material development. But in the United States there is a much greater affirmation of religiosity than one would predict from its advanced-development status. Arguing that secularization has been an essential precondition for the emergence of leftist parties in Europe, Burnham speculates that the legacy of dissenting and evangelical Protestantism in America has helped displace social conflicts onto the terrain of religious morality.[43]

During the 1980 election, a wave of religious politics was evident in the activities of the Moral Majority and other fundamentalist groups, and in the declarations by candidates Carter, Reagan, and Anderson of their "born-again" beliefs. From a different slant, the National Conference of Catholic Bishops soon took up the question of nuclear warfare with the intent to guide their 50 million parishioners. Amid the tangle of religion and social questions, the AEI's goal was to define a dominant perspective in which the values and structure of the American political economy are spiritually anointed and the religious left is discredited.

In *Toward a Theology of the Corporation*, Michael Novak maintains that theologians have been woefully ignorant of economics and have subjected the corporation to unfair and naive criticism. Against the critics of possessive individualism, Novak asserts, "The corporation is an expression of the social nature of humans."[44] This social character is one of seven "signs of grace" which Novak finds in the corporation, another being that the independence of the corporation from the state "mirrors God's presence."[45] These appreciative views, held by rank-and-file Christians, differ from the negative outlook of the World Council of Churches, the National Council of Churches, and the Roman Catholic Church's Peace and Justice Commission, which are controlled "by a special class of Christians with its own understandable bias" against capitalism.[46] Similarly, Irving Kristol laments "the surrender of the churches . . . to the spirit of modernity at the very moment when modernity itself is undergoing a kind of spiritual collapse."[47] Even in spiritual institutions, the new class spreads its influence.

As part of its fight to define the norms of social integration, the AEI has joined in the struggle over religion and politics in a practical way. Several AEI theologians, including Novak and Lutheran pastor Richard Neuhaus, are leading figures in the Institute on Religion and Democracy (IRD). Funded by conservative foundations and drawing much of its leadership from the neoconservative Coalition for a Democratic Majority and the Committee for the Free World, the IRD, founded in 1981, has attacked church support for Third World liberation movements and involvement in domestic social activism. Its first major media exposure came on a PBS program hosted by AEI Senior Fellow Ben Wattenberg, which criticized actions of the National Council of Churches.[48]

Another AEI spinoff is the Institute for Educational Affairs (IEA), conceived of in 1978 by Irving Kristol and William Simon as a bridge between academia and business. With corporate and foundation backing, the IEA enters the war of ideas against the adversary culture by dispensing funds to educational projects that uphold the business system.[49] The IEA has teamed with the AEI to sponsor *This World*, a new journal on religion and economics whose purpose is "to restate, in contemporary terms, the moral values that undergird our society; to assert their relevance to the political, economic, and cultural issues of our time; and, by the force of superior logic, to uphold them against self-serving and uninformed assaults."[50] Michael Novak is a co-editor. Novak has been an outspoken critic of the Catholic Bishops' pastoral letter on war and peace and has been actively attempting to steer the bishops' ongoing study of economic justice toward pro-business conclusions.

Closely related to the studies on religion and public policy is the AEI's project on "mediating structures," which began in 1977 under the direction of Richard Neuhaus and sociologist Peter Berger. In *To Empower People*, Berger and Neuhaus note the gap between the desire for government services and suspicion of government itself. They argue that the state should increasingly deliver services through "mediating structures," defined as those institutions standing between the individual in his private life and the large institutions of public life.[51] Against the encroachment of professionalism, Berger and Neuhaus defend neighborhood, family, church, and voluntary associations as sources of meaning that help to legitimate the larger political order. It is interesting that a later study of mediating structures edited by Michael Novak includes an essay by Richard B. Madden, who became chairman of the AEI board of trustees, which claims that the corporation is also a key mediating structure that must be nurtured, because in pursuing profit it achieves valuable social ends.[52]

This line of inquiry led the AEI to establish a Center for the Study of Private Initiative in 1981. Its purpose was to investigate ways the private sector can help solve problems and provide services in the areas of health care, education, child welfare, youth unemployment, housing, crime prevention, and economic development. Tax, administrative, and regulatory policies that impede self-help efforts were to be studied, with policy options to be forwarded to President Reagan.[53] For the AEI, unleashing the private sector is part of the solution to social problems, one that not incidentally reduces popular expectations.

Still other AEI projects have set out to shape thinking about traditional political institutions and legal processes. In 1979 the AEI launched a Congress Project and "A Decade of Study of the Constitution." Already in motion was its legal policy studies project, which stresses the importance of market economic concepts entering into legal processes. Robert Bork, chair of the Legal Policy Studies Advisery Council and a member of the AEI Council of Academic Advisers, was appointed to a federal appeals court position by Ronald Reagan. Supreme Court Justice Antonin Scalia was also involved in AEI legal projects.

This survey of the parameters of the AEI's ideology of liberal democratic capitalism shows how economic, political, and social lines of inquiry were merged into a coherent conservative position and concretized in policy proposals, which were then channeled through the many lines of access to public influence established by the AEI. This stepped-up approach to conservative policy-planning met the needs of capitalists, who were in search of system-legitimating arguments in the 1970s, as increasing criticism of business provoked anxiety about public opinion. Referring to a key AEI concept, David Vogel states: "The popularity of the new-class doctrine among businessmen is easily explained. It reassured business executives that their interests and those of the public were indeed identical: whatever tensions had developed between business and the American people were the artificial creation of an elitist minority."[54]

The public philosophy of the American Enterprise Institute might be described as ruling-class Gramscianism. Antonio Gramsci, the Italian Marxist, argued that class rule in modern capitalist societies rests not only on state coercion and the compulsion of economic relationships, but also on the hegemony of a system of values, beliefs, and morality supportive of the existing order. Dominated classes internalize these conceptions, which are generated within an array of noneconomic institutions in civil society. Social revolution involves breaking with the ideological hegemony and creating a new culture and a new view of humanity and society that can win the active support of masses of people.

Believing that policy questions are affected by the ideological currency of the times, the AEI has initiated projects aimed at securing active support for capitalism as an economic, political, and moral–cultural way of life. Its theorists understand that political orientations are shaped in a variety of mediating institutions, where the ideas of the New Class must be confronted. Coexisting with the AEI's cost–benefit analysis is a nontechnocratic strategy of restoring legitimacy, rekindling motivations, and achieving social integration through the control of needs, symbols, and ideologies. In this way, the AEI has responded to the Trilateralist imperative of controlling the democratic distemper and bolstering state authority.

Habermas has concisely criticized the analytic weaknesses of AEI-style neoconservatism. This school of thought, Habermas argues, attributes troubling symptoms such as hedonism, narcissism, the lack of social identification, the lack of obedience, and the withdrawal from competition for status and achievement to developments in the realm of culture, specifically the influence of the modernist intellectuals of the New Class.[55] For Habermas, these cultural discontents are themselves reactions to "a form of modernization guided by standards of economic and administrative rationality. But neoconservative doctrines turn our attention precisely away from such societal processes: they project the causes, which they do not bring to light, onto the plane of a subversive culture and its advocates."[56] This is not merely an intellectual error; if the AEI thinkers questioned these standards of rationality, their allegiance to the democratic capitalist political economy would be challenged.

Along with recasting the bonds of politics and culture, conservative policy-planning organizations also seek to control the "steering mechanisms" of government institutions and the substance of public policy. The Institute for Contemporary Studies developed an agenda for the Reagan presidency while designing measures to bring the media, the universities, and the black movement into the conservative orbit. In the last decade the Heritage Foundation has translated the aspirations of the New Right and other conservatives into a far-reaching set of policy proposals.

A Conservative Agenda for the 1980s

In a 1978 study of the American political system for the AEI, Anthony King noted the recent constraints placed on the Presidency, the dispersion of power in Congress, the decline of political parties, and the rise of "issue networks" that resemble our concept of policy currents. "The ideas of the New Deal are no longer the ideas around which American politics is organized," King wrote. "American politics have become, to a high degree, atomized."[57] King was describing what political analysts have called the "dealignment" of American politics—the exhaustion of the political coalitions that structured electoral choices and policy agendas in the past. Symptoms of this condition include the fact that just over half the eligible electorate voted in recent presidential elections, the drop in party identification, and the growth of independent voters. Historically, a "critical election"—such as those in 1896 and 1932—has realigned the electorate and brought a new governing coalition into power. Were the 1980 and 1984 elections of Ronald Reagan realigning elections that will lead to the dominance of a conservative Republican coalition for the remaining years of the twentieth century? Walter Dean Burnham notes that Reagan's 28 percent share of the eligible voters in 1980 was slightly less than the share Wendell Willkie received in 1940 in his crushing defeat by Franklin D. Roosevelt.[58] Still, the drift away from Democratic Party loyalties on the part of large numbers of its traditional constituents provided an opening for the Republicans. Seymour Martin Lipset concluded an ICS study of *Party Coalitions in the 1980s* by writing that political fortunes "will continue to depend on larger, often uncontrollable events, the state of the business cycle, international developments, as well as on the competency of the president and other leaders."[59] Lipset, an ICS academic adviser, wondered whether the weak-government system consciously designed by the 18th-century founders could deal effectively with contemporary problems. A goal of the ICS was to provide ideas for competent presidential leadership that would cut through intergovernmental obstacles to confront problems with conservative policy responses.

At the beginning of Reagan's first term, the ICS published *Politics and the Oval Office* as a guide for the presidency. The premise of the thirteen essays in the volume is that, while the crisis of confidence in government is real and effective leadership faces many obstacles, the President can govern and is not condemned to ceaseless frustration. Each chapter outlines institutional and political constraints that the President will confront and suggests measures to improve working relations in order to raise the likelihood of successful executive leadership.[60] The ICS circulated drafts of the book to the Reagan transition team before the inauguration.

A memorandum to President Reagan was written by the editor, Arnold J. Meltsner, an ICS adviser and a longtime Democrat who voted for Reagan. Meltsner advised the President to make a list of three or four major objectives to work toward over his term and to link these to a theme that embodied a conception of the future. While using the executive bureaucracy to achieve his goals, the President should maintain his personal standing and have nongovernmental scapegoats, such as international conditions, ready to blame when things go wrong. Bolstering and maintaining public trust in presidential efficacy would be essential. Reagan reportedly was impressed by Meltsner's memorandum.

A discussion of "The Imperial Media" by Robert M. Entman reinforces Meltsner's suggestion that the President keep some distance from the media. Entman describes the growth of an adversarial relationship between the presidency and the media in the 1970s and suggests ways that media obstruction can be circumvented. These include reducing reporters' expectations of access to officials, discouraging mingling between the press and the White House staff, and in general lowering reliance on media events to build public support. In conclusion, Entman states, "Pumping up approval ratings through the media is feasible mainly in connection with foreign policy initiatives and crises."[61]

The role of the media was examined in another ICS study in 1981, *What's News: The Media in American Society*, edited by veteran journalist Elie Abel.[62] Many of the essays give noncontroversial analyses of the history and economic structure of the media, the rapid growth of electronic media, and first-amendment questions. The content of news reporting does come in for criticism, however. Edward Jay Epstein and William A. Henry III explain how the news media are biased toward presentation of immediate events rather than background explanation, and to a quest for clear-cut conflicts and dramatic or narrative unity.[63] Extending these observations, Michael Jay Robinson argues that the media increasingly accentuate the negative in their coverage of political personalities and issues, leading the voting public to the view that the only available choices are "between fools or scoundrels."[64] According to *Wall Street Journal* editor Robert Bartley, the media similarly tend to distort economic news, stereotyping business leaders as motivated solely by greed, and failing to explain the the role of profit in the economic system.[65] While the ICS authors do not argue that the media form a domain of the adversary culture, the overall perspective is that news reporting needs to be more responsible and less critical of established political and economic processes.

Another milieu in which views critical of business have sprung up is the American university system. But the increased costs of university compliance with federal regulations in the 1970s led the ICS to promote the notion that academia is part of the private sector, subject to many of the same unreasonable governmental intrusions as business. The result was a study of *Bureaucrats and Brainpower* that stressed the similar situation of universities and business with respect to government regulation and suggested that "this commonality of interest may be the most important insight to be drawn from this book."[66]

Affirmative-action programs, access rights for the handicapped, restrictions on animal and human subjects in research, and the inroads of OSHA and the NLRB into the university are singled out for criticism. Paul Seabury sees the source of overregulation in the motives of bureaucrats: "The regulators now wish the university to be a laboratory of social change."[67] Calls by conservative intellectuals to reverse the politicization of the universities coincided with expanded corporate subsidization of research on campuses in the late 1970s and the endowment of "Chairs of Free Enterprise" to counter negative views of business. Faced with falling enrollment, budget constraints, and burdensome regulations, many administrators welcomed improved corporate ties to academia.[68]

A final area in which the ICS was involved in strategic issue development and the offensive against liberalism was its Black Alternatives Conference in December 1980. The conference was organized on behalf of the ICS by Thomas Sowell, probably the leading black conservative intellectual in the United States, who referred to the gathering as "a historic opportunity."[69] About a hundred black leaders from around the nation attended the well-publicized two-day meeting, whose purpose was "to start a dialogue stressing the stake in the market system held by blacks and other minorities, and showing how government intervention in the market—in education housing, transportation, and other areas—have systematically denied opportunities to blacks and shut them out."[70] The perspective that the real source of black progress is to be found in capitalist economic growth was underscored by the presence of Milton Friedman, Michael J. Boskin, and other free-market advocates at the conference, and by the remark of black television personality Tony Brown: "You can sit next to all of the white people in the world if you have an American Express or another credit card."[71] Signifying the political importance of a movement of black conservatism was the participation of Edwin Meese, an ICS director and then head of Ronald Reagan's transition team, in the conference.

Among other things, conservative think tanks are trying to defeat liberalism as an intellectual and cultural force. No group has pursued this objective more systematically than the Heritage Foundation, ferreting out liberalism wherever its perfidious presence is detected. Thus a scan of the Heritage journal *Policy Review* reveals attacks on antinuclear energy groups,

National Public Radio, George Kennan, the Union of Concerned Scientists, feminists, and the National Writer's Union, to name but a few. Perhaps more important, the Heritage Foundation has pressed the Reagan administration to either eliminate or strictly control those government agencies said to be under liberal ideological domination, among them the Environmental Protection Agency, the National Endowment for the Humanities, and the Legal Services Corporation. The Heritage Foundation has also been one of the main forces in raising "internal security" issues in recent years. *Mandate for Leadership*, prepared in 1980, called for a vast expansion of U.S. intelligence services and pointed to "organized internal groups that could become internal security problems," specifically naming the Institute for Policy Studies, the North American Congress on Latin America, and the Campaign for Economic Democracy, along with "some anti-defense and anti-nuclear lobbies."[72] These sentiments fed into a number of media attacks on such groups in 1980–1981 and into the concern with "terror networks" and "Soviet disinformation" orchestrated by an internal security network that include, according to John Judis, "the conservative Right, the agents and supporters of right-wing dictatorships, former intelligence officers ousted in the 1975–1978 cleanup, and intellectuals and journalists from conservative think tanks and publications."[73]

More recently, the Heritage Foundation has presented an agenda for "continuing the conservative revolution" that would substantially alter government and implement at least part of the New Right's platform. Among the proposals are further reductions in social spending, the institution of "workfare" for entitlement recipients and a "sub-minimum wage" for young people, tuition tax credits for families with children in private schools, opposition to abortion, and tolerance of organized school prayer.[74] Many of these measures would increase the role of government in citizens' lives, but it is important to see that free enterprise is not the key issue for many conservatives, who instead are chiefly concerned with traditional morality and social relations.

Democracy and the Limits of Policy-Planning

The critique of liberal social policies, the campaign for pro-business economics, and the fashioning of conservative ideologies by the American Enterprise Institute, the Heritage Foundation, and the Institute for Contemporary Studies were, within the rationality of existing class relations, appropriate strategies in response to systemic crises. The postwar accords could not be sustained in the 1970s. As Samuel Bowles and Herbert Gintis argue, liberal democratic capitalism combines the social relations of capitalist production, vesting rights in property, and the social relations of liberal democracy, vesting rights in persons.[75] By the 1970s the institutional structure of postwar capitalist accumulation in the United States was increasingly incapable of sustaining profitable growth. The political and distributional gains made by the working class were one source of the crisis and stood as a barrier to its resolution through raising profitability. To the extent that liberal democracy opened the state to popular pressures and funded programs that increased the social wage, it came into conflict with accumulation imperatives when the economy faltered. In various ways, and with differing degrees of awareness, the social and political perspectives of all five policy-planning organizations were marked by the growing contradiction between liberal democracy and capitalism.

As we have seen, the boldest elite plans for reconstructing the political economy in the mid-1970s were initially made within the centrist, managerial camp. These moves led many on the left to believe that the capitalist class was rapidly formulating a strategy for managing the crisis through state regimentation of the economy and the imposition of austerity in concert with the corporate-banking sector. But free-market proponents reacted to these steps swiftly and sharply, moving to defeat preemptively any enlargement of economic planning by the state. Moreover, this position appeared to conform to the dominant view among capitalists. The political mobilization of business was one of the most striking developments in American politics in the late 1970s, but it did not issue in a call for a rationalized state capitalism or corporatist arrangements. Whether registered in the direct lobbying of the Business Roundtable, the creation of scores of political action committees, or the growing sponsorship of probusiness policy-planning organizations like the AEI and the ICS, the effect of the capitalist offensive was to pull the center to the right. By 1980 there was general agreement among political and economic elites that defense spending should rise and domestic government policy should be tailored to provide incentives for private sector accumulation. Proposals for planning, industrial policy, and a new international economic order were relegated to the margins of policy debate, even though many elite managerialists continued to view them as in the long-term interest of the stability of liberal democratic capitalism.

Policy-planning organizations have played an important role in this process of political and ideological reconstruction over the last decade, reflecting broader elite thinking on major issues while refining it into a coherent, long-range perspective. Policy institutions actively sought to define problems, shape public opinion, and set the policy agenda through briefing government officials, bringing their findings to the attention of the media, and providing a forum where members of different power centers (business, politics, law, academia, and so on) could seek common positions on important policy questions. But while policy-planning organizations can influence the perception of problems and provide justification for policy, can they supply the kind of rationality and data-based analysis that will enable state managers to master the technical aspects of the administration of capitalist political economies? This is an important question. If the answer is yes, it suggests that capitalism can master its own environment and secure its conditions of existence, undercutting much of the ground of radical critique.

Historian Gabriel Kolko has criticized the notion of an integrative capitalist rationality, which he believes descends from the work of Max Weber through Herbert Marcuse's social theory to the "corporate liberalism" school of American history.[76] Kolko states, "The notion that capitalism's desire to find the most rational, efficient methods of operation inevitably leads to such techniques being discovered and then successfully implemented in the world of practical affairs has therefore become a tenet of radical as well as conservative faith."[77] Kolko demonstrates that expertise based on research and intelligence has never had the impact on economic or foreign policy that its promoters claim, that empirically grounded forecasts have usually been proved wrong, and that "the state budget mechanism, the ultimate political form capitalism has for integration, is not much different from the jungle [Herbert] Hoover described half a century earlier."[78]

My analysis of policy-planning organizations, in the context of political and economic crisis from 1973 to 1985, suggests that elites react to and are undercut by ongoing developments more than they master them, that they are deeply divided among themselves, and that the policy-oriented research they produce is strongly colored by already-arrived-at ideological and conceptual premises. Given these limitations on managing the crisis, Kolko's comments on the relationship between political knowledge and political action are pertinent:

> The functioning of the state's intelligence mechanisms is constrained by a larger structural environment and by the inherent irrationality which foredooms the entire effort to base action on informed insight. Even when the insight is exact, and ignorance is not greater than knowledge, political and social limits often place decisive constraints on the application of "rationality" in the historical process. For the problems are not simply matters of a general consensus, but touch upon questions of the struggle between elites in the division of material gains or control of policy and power. The political imperatives of power interests basically define the nature of "relevant" truth in American society.[79]

Although Kolko would probably not deny that policy-planning organizations have consequential political impacts, his argument suggests that these efforts are inherently incapable of producing a rationalized capitalist system. Contradictions, and the limitations on their resolution, still define capitalist societies, despite the increased role of policy-planning organizations.

While technocratic policy-planning may be incapable of efficiently guiding state policies of crisis management, it does imply that problems confronting the polity are not amenable to resolution through democracy. As we have seen, all the policy-planning organizations see democracy as posing dangers to system maintenance, whether stated openly, as with Huntington, or more indirectly, as with the AEI's displaced critique of the New Class. None calls for the revitalization of American politics through increased citizen participation in public debate and policy formation. While policy-planning organizations cannot ensure the stable rule of the interests they represent, they can and have helped direct debate away from capitalism and toward the alleged excesses of democratic aspirations as a source of crisis.

This reflects the values of "order" and "stability" that set limits on the range of imaginable outcomes. When it flourished, liberal democratic capitalism in postwar America offered hopes of increased prosperity while diverting attention from the structure of power in society and the imperatives driving the economy. As the crisis of the 1970s unfolded, elites saw the expansion of liberal democracy as endangering the social order and the economic system they presided over. In differing ways, this contradiction established the terms in which the policy-planners of the center and the right approached the task of rescuing a system in decline.

Notes

Chapter 1

1. B. Drummond Ayres Jr., "Conservative Researchers Expect New Prominence," *New York Times*, 17 November 1980, p. D-12.

2. David Schribman, "Group Goes from Exile to Influence," *New York Times*, 23 November 1981, p. A-20.

3. Gregg Easterbrook, "Ideas Move Nations," *Atlantic Monthly*, January 1986, p. 70.

4. "Carter's Brain Trusts," *Time*, 20 December 1976, p. 19. On Carter's ties to the Trilateral Commission, see Laurence H. Shoup, *The Carter Presidency and Beyond: Power and Politics in the 1980s* (Palo Alto, Calif.: Ramparts Press, 1980).

5. Thomas R. Dye, "Oligarchic Tendencies in National Policy-Making: The Role of Private Policy-Planning Organizations," *Journal of Politics* 40 (May 1978): 309.

6. Kenneth M. Dolbeare and Murray J. Edelman develop this approach in *American Politics: Policies, Power, and Change*, 5th ed., (Lexington, Mass.: D. C. Heath, 1985).

7. Leonard Silk and Mark Silk, *The American Establishment* (New York: Avon Books, 1981).

8. Ibid., p. 19.

9. David Rockefeller, "The Trilateral Commission Explained," *Saturday Evening Post*, October 1980, p. 84.

10. Philip H. Burch Jr., "The American Establishment: Its Historical Development and Major Economic Components," in *Research in Political Economy*, vol. 6, ed. Paul Zarembka (Greenwich, Conn.: JAI Press, 1983), p. 84.

NOTES TO CHAPTER 1

11   Irvine Alpert and Ann Markusen, "The Professional Production of Policy, Ideology, and Plans: Brookings and Resources for the Future," *The Insurgent Sociologist* 9, nos. 2–3 (Fall 1979–Winter 1980): 94.

12   Thomas R. Dye, *Who's Running America? The Conservative Years*, 4th ed. (Englewood Cliffs, N.J.: Prentice-Hall, 1986); G. William Domhoff, *The Powers That Be: Processes of Ruling-Class Domination in America* (New York: Vintage Books, 1978).

13   Dye, *Who's Running America?* p. 243.

14   Ibid., p. 189.

15   Ibid., chap. 9, esp. pp. 244–48.

16   Ibid., p. 246.

17   Ibid., p. 261.

18   Domhoff, *The Powers That Be*, p. 10.

19   Ibid., p. 62.

20   James Weinstein, *The Corporate Ideal in the Liberal State* (Boston: Beacon Press, 1968); David Eakins, "The Development of Corporate Liberal Policy Research in the United States" (Ph.D. diss., University of Wisconsin, 1966).

21   Laurence H. Shoup and William Minter, *Imperial Brain Trust: The Council on Foreign Relations and United States Foreign Policy* (New York: Monthly Review Press, 1977).

22   David Eakins, "Business Planners and America's Postwar Expansion," in *Corporations and the Cold War*, ed. David Horowitz (New York: Monthly Review Press, 1969); Robert Collins, *The Business Response to Keynes, 1929–1964* (New York: Columbia University Press, 1981); Kim McQuaid, *Big Business and Presidential Power: From FDR to Reagan* (New York: William Morrow, 1982).

NOTES TO CHAPTER 1

23 David Eakins, "Policy-Planning for the Establishment," in *A New History of Leviathan*, ed. Ronald Radosh and Murray Rothbard (New York: E. P. Dutton, 1972).

24 Silk and Silk, *The American Establishment*, p. 226.

25 Fred Block, "Beyond Corporate Liberalism," *Social Problems* 24 (February 1977): 352–61.

26 Theda Skocpol, "Political Response to Capitalist Crisis: Neo-Marxist Theories of the State and the Case of the New Deal," *Politics and Society* 10, no. 2 (1980): 155–201.

27 These arguments are from a review by Domhoff in *Social Policy*, Winter 1983, pp. 53–59.

28 Michael Klare, *Beyond the Vietnam Syndrome: U.S. Interventionism in the 1980s* (Washington, D.C.: Institute for Policy Studies, 1981), pp. 5–10.

29 Ibid., p. 6.

30 Paul Joseph, *Cracks in the Empire: State Politics in the Vietnam War* (Boston: South End Press, 1981).

31 Ibid., pp. 51–52.

32 Ibid., p. 52.

33 Unless otherwise indicated, all information on the Brookings Institution is drawn from Silk and Silk, *The American Establishment*, chap. 5; and Charles B. Saunders, *The Brookings Institution: A Fifty-Year History* (Washington, D.C.: The Brookings Institution, 1966). For a more recent look, see Donald T. Critchlow, *The Brookings Institution, 1916–1952: Expertise and the Public Interest in a Democratic Society* (DeKalb: Northern Illinois University Press, 1985).

34 Silk and Silk, *The American Establishment*, p. 165.

35 *The Brookings Bulletin,* Fall–Winter 1976, p. 1.

36 For data on the elite backgrounds of Brookings trustees, see Dye, "Oligarchic Tendencies in National Policy-Making," pp. 318–22.

37 In this section I draw on the wealth of facts in *Trilateralism: The Trilateral Commission and Elite Planning for World Management,* ed. Holly Sklar (Boston: South End Press, 1980).

38 Kenneth M. Dolbeare, "The Trilateral Commission Takeover of the U.S. Government: What It Means" (Amherst: University of Massachusetts, 1977, Mimeographed), p. 5.

39 For the links among these groups, see Shoup, *The Carter Presidency and Beyond,* passim.

40 *The Trilateral Commission: Questions and Answers* (New York: The Trilateral Commission, 1980).

41 See Carter's remarks in *Trialogue,* no. 13 (Winter 1976–1977), p. 12.

42 Craig Karpel, "The Real President," *Penthouse,* December 1977, p. 166.

43 Peter H. Stone, "Conservative Brain Trust," *New York Times Magazine,* 10 May 1981, pp. 18ff. This is an excellent source on the AEI, which reproduced and distributed Stone's article.

44 Philip H. Burch Jr., *Elites in American History: The New Deal to the Carter Administration* (New York: Holmes & Meier, 1980), p. 309.

45 John S. Saloma III, *Ominous Politics: The New Conservative Labyrinth* (New York: Hill & Wang, 1984), p. 67.

46 Stone, "Conservative Brain Trust."

47 Quoted in ibid.

48 Quoted in Silk and Silk, *The American Establishment,* p. 182.

49 Robert D. Hershey Jr., "Shifts at Enterprise Institute," *New York Times*, 27 June 1986, p. D-1; *National Journal*, 30 November 1985, p. 2739.

50 In addition to the Heritage Foundation's own publications, see Saloma, *Ominous Politics*, pp. 14–19; Morton Kondracke, "The Heritage Model," *New Republic*, 20 December 1980, pp. 10–14; Dom Bonafede, "Issue-Oriented Heritage Foundation Hitches Its Wagon to Reagan's Star," *National Journal*, 20 March 1982, pp. 502–7; James Rosenthal, "Heritage Hype," *New Republic*, 2 September 1985, pp. 14–16.

51 This is the finding of J. Craig Jenkins and Teri Shumate, "Cowboy Capitalists and the Rise of the 'New Right': An Analysis of Contributors to Conservative Policy Formation Organizations," *Social Problems 33*, no. 2 (December 1985): 130–45.

52 Quoted in Arthur Gavshon, "The Power and Influence Behind America's Right," *Manchester Guardian Weekly*, 1 December 1985, p. 9.

53 Basic information on the ICS is available in an article by Douglas Foster, "When ICS Speaks, Reagan Listens," originally in *San Francisco Magazine*, June 1981, pp. 53–60, reprinted under the same title by the ICS. Also, see Saloma, *Ominous Politics*, pp. 12–14, and the ICS newsletter, *The Letter*, various issues.

54 Quoted in Foster, "When ICS Speaks."

Chapter 2

1 I take this term from Samuel Bowles and Herbert Gintis, "The Crisis of Liberal Democratic Capitalism: The Case of the United States," *Politics and Society* 11, no. 1 (1982): 51–93.

2 Edward S. Greenberg, *Capitalism and the American Political Ideal* (Armonk, N.Y.: M. E. Sharpe, 1985), p. 48. On the concept of capitalist democracy, see Joshua Cohen and Joel Rogers, *On Democracy* (New York: Penguin Books, 1983), chap. 3.

NOTES TO CHAPTER 2

3 One of the clearest accounts of the postwar political economy is in Cohen and Rogers, *On Democracy*, chap. 4.

4 Thomas D. Willett, "Major Challenges to the International Economic System," in *Challenges to a Liberal International Economic Order*, ed. Ryan C. Amacher, Gottfried Haberler, and Thomas D. Willett (Washington, D.C.: American Enterprise Institute, 1979), pp. 17–18.

5 Fred L. Block, *The Origins of International Economic Disorder* (Berkeley and Los Angeles: University of California Press, 1977), chap. 3.

6 Joan Edelman Spero, *The Politics of International Economic Relations*, 2d ed. (New York: St. Martin's Press, 1981), p. 37.

7 Motoo Kaji, Richard N. Cooper, and Claudio Segre, "Towards a Renovated International System," in *Trilateral Commission Task Force Reports, 1–7* (New York: New York University Press, 1977), pp. 3–4.

8 W. Elliot Brownlee, *Dynamics of Ascent: A History of the American Economy*, 2d ed. (New York: Alfred A. Knopf, 1979), p. 469.

9 From the statement of purpose, "The Industrialized Democratic Regions in a Changing International System."

10 Stephen D. Krasner, "United States Commercial and Monetary Policy: Unravelling the Paradox of External Strength and Internal Weakness," in *Between Power and Plenty: Foreign Economic Policies of Advanced Industrial States*, ed. Peter J. Katzenstein (Madison: University of Wisconsin Press, 1978), p. 75.

11 Melvyn P. Leffler, "The American Conception of National Security and the Beginnings of the Cold War, 1945–48," *American Historical Review* 89 (April 1984): 379.

12 Ibid., p. 349.

13 Gabriel Kolko, *Main Currents in Modern American History* (New York: Pantheon Books, 1984), p. 318.

NOTES TO CHAPTER 2

14 Quoted in Fred Block, "Economic Instability and Military Strength: The Paradoxes of the 1950 Rearmament Decision," *Politics and Society* 10, no. 1 (1980): 47

15 Krasner, "United States Commercial and Monetary Policy," pp. 67, 79.

16 See Cohen and Rogers, *On Democracy*, pp. 101–6.

17 Jeff Frieden, "The Trilateral Commission: Economics and Politics in the 1970s," in *Trilateralism: The Trilateral Commission and Elite Planning for World Management*, ed. Holly Sklar (Boston: South End Press, 1980), p. 65.

18 Ibid., p. 66.

19 Data from Thomas Weisskopf, "The Current Economic Crisis in Historical Perspective," *Socialist Review*, no. 57 (May–June 1981), pp. 9–10.

20 Cohen and Rogers, *On Democracy*, p. 96.

21 Weisskopf, "The Current Economic Crisis," p. 13.

22 Both Weisskopf and Cohen and Rogers give detailed accounts of the postwar economy using this basic framework.

23 Walter Dean Burnham, "The Ascendency of the Right," *Dissent*, Fall 1983, p. 437.

24 James T. Campen and Arthur MacEwen, "Crisis, Contradictions, and Conservative Controversies in Contemporary U.S. Capitalism," *Review of Radical Political Economics* 14 (Fall 1982): 3, 5.

25 Cohen and Rogers, *On Democracy*, p. 94.

26 Robert M. Collins, *The Business Response to Keynes, 1929–1964* (New York: Columbia University Press, 1981), chap. 7; Kim McQuaid, *Big Business and Presidential Power: From FDR to Reagan* (New York: William Morrow, 1982), chap. 6.

NOTES TO CHAPTER 2

27 Cohen and Rogers, *On Democracy*, p. 92.

28 Campen and MacEwen, "Crisis, Contradictions, and Conservative Controversies," p. 5.

29 Weisskopf, "The Current Economic Crisis," p. 17.

30 Campen and MacEwen, "Crisis, Contradictions, and Conservative Controversies," p. 5.

31 Godfrey Hodgson, *America in Our Time* (Garden City, N.Y.: Doubleday, 1976), p. 76.

32 Quoted in Leonard Silk and Mark Silk, *The American Establishment* (New York: Avon Books, 1981), p. 181.

33 Quoted in Hodgson, *America In Our Time*, p. 225.

34 For a good brief discussion, see Krasner, "United States Commercial and Monetary Policy," pp. 57–64.

35 The two major works are Grant McConnell, *Private Power and American Democracy* (New York: Vintage Books, 1966); Theodore Lowi, *The End of Liberalism* (New York: W. W. Norton, 1969).

36 Kenneth M. Dolbeare, *Democracy at Risk: The Politics of Economic Renewal* (Chatham, N.J.: Chatham House, 1984), p. 38.

37 Walter Dean Burnham, "The 1984 Election and the Future of American Politics," in *Election 84: Landslide Without a Mandate?*, ed. Ellis Sandoz and Cecil V. Crabb Jr. (New York: New American Library, 1985), p. 206.

38 Thomas Edsall, *The New Politics of Inequality* (New York: W. W. Norton, 1984), pp. 146–47, drawing on the work of David Cameron.

39 See Andrew Martin, *The Politics of Economic Policy in the United States: A Tentative View from a Comparative Perspective* (Beverly Hills, Calif.: Sage Publications, 1973), pp. 32–40.

NOTES TO CHAPTER 2

40   For a brief, pointed treatment, see Geoffrey Rips, "In Whose Interest? Big Labor's Foreign Policy," *Texas Observer*, 4 April 1986, pp. 7–10.

41   David Vogel, "The Public-Interest Movement and the American Reform Tradition," *Political Science Quarterly* 95 (Winter 1980–1981): 607–27; idem, "The Power of Business in America: a Reappraisal," *British Journal of Political Science* 13 (January 1983): 19–43.

42   Vogel, "The Power of Business in America," p. 20.

43   On Team B, see Jerry W. Sanders, *Peddlers of Crisis: The Committee on the Present Danger and the Politics of Containment* (Boston: South End Press, 1983), pp. 197–204.

44   John B. Judis, "CIA: No Big Soviet Arms Boost in '70s," *In These Times*, 7–13 December 1983, p. 3.

45   Arthur Macy Cox, "The CIA's Tragic Error," *New York Review of Books*, 6 November 1980, pp. 21–24, and a short version in the *New York Times*, 20 October 1980, p. A-19.

46   Cox, *New York Times*, 20 October 1980, p. A-19.

47   Thomas Ferguson and Joel Rogers, *Right Turn: The Decline of the Democrats and the Future of American Politics* (New York: Hill & Wang, 1986), pp. 146–54. This book, as with Ferguson and Rogers' previous work, has been enormously stimulating to me.

48   Chuck Lane, "The Manhattan Project," *New Republic*, 25 March 1985, pp. 14–15.

49   For a detailed account of business political activity, see Edsall, *The New Politics of Inequality*, chap. 3; and Vogel, "The Power of Business in America."

50   Thomas Ferguson and Joel Rogers, "The Knights of the Roundtable," *The Nation*, 15 December 1979, pp. 620–25.

51 Vogel, "The Power of Business in America," p. 33.

52 Edsall, *The New Politics of Inequality*, p. 131.

53 Ibid., pp. 151–54. Also, see Michael Goldfield, "Labor in American Politics—Its Current Weakness," *Journal of Politics* 48 (February 1986): 2–29.

54 Vogel, "The Power of Business in America," pp. 37–38.

55 Edsall, *The New Politics of Inequality*, pp. 118–19.

56 Michael Useem, *The Inner Circle: Large Corporations and the Rise of Business Political Activity in the U.S. and U.K.* (New York: Oxford University Press, 1984).

Chapter 3

1 Walter F. Mondale, "Beyond Détente: Toward International Economic Security," *Foreign Affairs*, October 1974, pp. 1–2.

2 See *The Capitalist System*, ed. Richard Edwards, Michael Reich, and Thomas Weisskopf, 2nd ed. (Englewood Cliffs, N.J.: Prentice-Hall, 1978), pp. 475–76, for data in this and the next paragraph, unless otherwise indicated.

3 John Judis, "How Reagan Is Speeding the American Empire's Decline," *In These Times*, 4–10 November 1981, p. 15.

4 Paul Sweezy and Harry Magdoff, "U.S. Foreign Policy in the 1980s," *Monthly Review*, April 1980, p. 9.

5 *The Capitalist System*, p. 481.

6 Sweezy and Magdoff, "U.S. Foreign Policy," p. 9.

NOTES TO CHAPTER 3
253

7 Jeff Frieden, "The Trilateral Commission: Economics and Politics in the 1970s," in *Trilateralism: The Trilateral Commission and Elite Planning for World Management*, ed. Holly Sklar (Boston: South End Press, 1980), p. 62.

8 For details on Nixon's appointees and supporters, see Philip H. Burch Jr., *Elites in American History: The New Deal to the Carter Administration* (New York: Holmes & Meier, 1980), pp. 231–58.

9 On the history of the Bilderberg Conference, see Peter Thompson, "Bilderberg and the West," in *Trilateralism*, pp. 157–89.

10 Craig Karpel, "The Real President," *Penthouse*, December 1977, p. 160. See also Holly Sklar, "Founding the Trilateral Commission: Chronology 1970–1977," in *Trilateralism*, pp. 76–82.

11 Zbigniew Brzezinski, "U.S. Foreign Policy: The Search for Focus," *Foreign Affairs*, July 1973, p. 717.

12 Ibid., p. 723.

13 Frieden, "The Trilateral Commission," pp. 66–67.

14 C. Fred Bergsten, "The New Economic Policy and U.S. Foreign Policy," *Foreign Affairs*, January 1972, pp. 199–200.

15 See Rockefeller's remarks in *Trialogue*, no. 13 (Winter 1976–77), p. 16.

16 C. Fred Bergsten, Robert O. Keohane, and Joseph S. Nye, "International Economics and International Politics: A Framework for Analysis," in *World Politics and International Politics*, ed. C. Fred Bergsten and Lawrence B. Krause (Washington, D.C.: The Brookings Institution, 1975), p. 5.

17 Ibid.

18 François Duchene, Kinhide Mushakoji, and Henry Owen, "The Crisis of International Cooperation," in *Trilateral Commission Task*

Force Reports, 1–7 (New York: New York University Press, 1977), p. 35.

19 Bergsten, Keohane, and Nye, "International Economics and International Politics," p. 14.

20 From the statement of purpose of the Trilateral Commission, "The Industrialized Democratic Regions in a Changing International System."

21 Quoted in Jeremiah Novak, "The Trilateral Connection," *Atlantic Monthly*, July 1977, p. 57.

22 *Reshaping the International Economic Order* (Washington, D.C.: The Brookings Institution, 1972), p. 3.

23 Richard Cooper, Karl Kaiser, and Masataka Kosaka, *Towards a Renovated International System* (New York: The Trilateral Commission, 1977), p. 37.

24 Ibid., p. 32.

25 Ibid., p. 37.

26 Ibid., p. ix.

27 Ibid.

28 Edward R. Fried and Philip H. Trezise, "The United States in the World Economy," in *Setting National Priorities: The Next Ten Years*, ed. Henry Owen and Charles L. Schultze (Washington, D.C.: The Brookings Institution, 1976), p. 167.

29 Bergsten, Keohane, and Nye, "International Economics and International Politics," p. 18.

30 Duchene, Mushakoji, and Owen, "The Crisis of International Cooperation," p. 38.

NOTES TO CHAPTER 3

31 C. Fred Bergsten, Georges Berthoin, and Kinhide Mushakoji, *The Reform of International Institutions* (New York: The Trilateral Commission, 1976), p. vi.

32 See Rockefeller's 1980 statement, "Foolish Attacks on False Issues," reprinted in *Trilateralism*, pp. xi–xii.

33 Robert W. Cox, "Ideologies and the New International Economic Order: Reflections on Some Recent Literature," *International Organization* 33 (Spring 1979): 257–302.

34 Ibid., p. 257.

35 Ibid., p. 260.

36 Ibid.

37 Ibid., p. 267.

38 Frieden, "The Trilateral Commission," p. 64.

39 Ibid., p. 70.

40 Ibid., p. 69.

41 See the editors' comments in *Challenges to a Liberal International Economic Order*, ed. Ryan C. Amacher, Gottfried Haberler, and Thomas D. Willett (Washington, D.C.: American Enterprise Institute, 1979), pp. 1–2.

42 H. Monroe Browne, then president of the ICS, in the "Preface" to *Tariffs, Quotas, and Trade: The Politics of Protectionism* (San Francisco: Institute for Contemporary Studies, 1979), p. xii.

43 Guido Colonna di Paliano, Philip H. Trezise, and Nobuhiko Ushiba, "Directions for World Trade in the 1970s," in *Task Force Reports, 1–7*, p. 79.

44 Ibid.

NOTES TO CHAPTER 3

45 Richard N. Cooper, "Prolegomena to the Choice of an International Monetary System," in *World Politics and International Economics*, p. 63.

46 Cooper, Kaji, and Segré, "Towards a Renovated World Monetary System," in *Task Force Reports, 1–7*, pp. 5–6.

47 Ibid., p. 18.

48 Cooper, Kaiser, and Kosaka, *Towards a Renovated International System*, pp. 45–49.

49 Colonna di Paliano, Trezise, and Ushiba, "Directions for World Trade in the 1970s," p. 96.

50 Ibid., p. 97.

51 Fried and Trezise, "The United States in the World Economy," p. 180.

52 Ralph C. Bryant and Lawrence B. Krause, "World Economic Interdependence," *Setting National Priorities: Agenda for the 1980s*, ed. Joseph A. Peckman (Washington, D.C.: The Brookings Institution, 1980), p. 87.

53 Marina v. N. Whitman, "International Interdependence and the U.S. Economy," in *Contemporary Economic Problems*, ed. William Fellner (Washington, D.C.: American Enterprise Institute, 1976), p. 186.

54 Herbert Stein, "International Coordination of Domestic Economic Policies," AEI *Economist*, June 1978, p. 5.

55 Gottfried Haberler, "The Present Economic Malaise," in *Contemporary Economic Problems*, ed. William Fellner (Washington, D.C.: American Enterprise Institute, 1979), p. 280.

56 Gottfried Haberler, "Reflections on the U.S. Trade Deficit and the Floating Dollar," in *Contemporary Economic Problems*, ed. William

Fellner (Washington, D.C.: American Enterprise Institute, 1978), p. 233.

57 John T. Cuddington and Ronald I. McKinnon, "Free Trade versus Protectionism: A Perspective," in *Tariffs, Quotas, and Trade*, pp. 3–23; idem, "The United States and the World Economy," in *The Economy in the 1980s: A Program for Growth and Stability*, ed. Michael J. Boskin (San Francisco: Institute for Contemporary Studies, 1980), pp. 161–93.

58 C. Fred Bergsten, "The Threat from the Third World," *Foreign Policy*, no. 11 (Summer 1973), p. 105.

59 Ibid.

60 Richard N. Gardner, Saburo Okito, and B. J. Udink, "A Turning Point in North–South Economic Relations," in *Task Force Reports, 1–7*, p. 59.

61 Christopher J. Makins, "Is Reform an Illusion," *Trialogue*, no. 8 (Fall 1975), p. 2.

62 Carl E. Beigie, Wolfgang Hager, and Sueo Sekiguchi, *Seeking a New Accommodation in World Commodity Markets* (New York: The Trilateral Commission, 1976), p. 4.

63 Preface by H. Monroe Browne to *The Third World: Premises of U.S. Policy*, ed. W. Scott Thompson (San Francisco: Institute for Contemporary Studies, 1978), p. ix.

64 Peter T. Bauer and Basil Yamey, "The Third World and the West: An Economic Perspective," in ibid., pp. 99–121.

65 From an AEI forum discussion summarized in *Challenges to a Liberal International Economic Order*, p. 484.

66 Thomas D. Willett, "Major Challenges to the International System," in *Third World*, ed. Thompson, p. 31.

NOTES TO CHAPTER 3

67 Harry Magdoff, "The Limits of International Reform," *Monthly Review*, May 1978, pp. 1–11.

68 John C. Campbell, Guy de Carmoy, and Shinichi Kondo, "Energy: The Imperative for a Trilateral Approach"; idem, "Energy: A Strategy for International Action"; Richard N. Gardner, Saburo Okita, and B. J. Udink, "OPEC, the Trilateral World, and the Developing Countries: New Arrangements for Cooperation, 1976–1980," all in *Task Force Reports, 1–7*; John C. Campbell, Keichi Oshima, and Hans W. Maull, *Energy: Managing the Transition* (New York: The Trilateral Commission, 1978).

69 "Energy: The Imperative for a Trilateral Approach," p. 117.

70 "Energy: A Strategy for International Action," p. 145.

71 See Ball's remarks in *Trialogue*, no. 6 (Winter 1974–1975), pp. 6–9.

72 "Energy: A Strategy for International Action," p. 147.

73 Ibid., p. 146.

74 Ibid.

75 *Toward Peace in the Middle East* (Washington, D.C.: The Brookings Institution, 1975).

76 Richard Erb, "International Raw Materials Developments: Oil and Metals," in *Contemporary Economic Problems*, 1976 volume, esp. pp. 341–43.

77 See the comments by Nick Thimmesch after the death of William Baroody in *AEI Memorandum*, July–August 1980, p. 7.

78 "Energy: The Imperative for a Trilateral Approach," p. 110.

79 Richard J. Sweeney, "Energy, the OPEC Surplus, and the Future of the Dollar," in *Tariffs, Quotas, and Trade*, passim.

NOTES TO CHAPTER 3

80 For example, see Henry S. Rowen, "The Threatened Jugular: Oil Supply of the West," in *National Security in the 1980s: From Weakness to Strength*, ed. W. Scott Thompson (San Francisco: Institute for Contemporary Studies, 1980).

81 Barnaby J. Feder, "Foreign Stake in U.S. Stirs Social and Political Doubts," *New York Times*, 29 December 1985, p. A-1.

82 "The Third World Threat to the West's Recovery," *Business Week*, 7 February 1983, p. 48.

83 For an example of an ODC perspective, written by the group's vice-president, see Richard E. Feinberg, *The Intemperate Zone: The Third World Challenge to U.S. Foreign Policy* (New York: W. W. Norton, 1983).

84 The ideas discussed here can be found in Nobuhiko Ushiba, Graham Allison, and Thierry de Montbrial, *Sharing International Responsibilities Among the Trilateral Countries* (New York: The Trilateral Commission, 1983); Takeshi Watanabe, Jacques Lesourne, and Robert S. McNamara, *Facilitating Development in a Changing Third World: Finance, Trade, Aid* (New York: The Trilateral Commission, 1983); and David Owen, Zbigniew Brzezinski, and Saburo Okita, *Democracy Must Work: A Trilateral Agenda for the Decade* (New York: New York University Press, 1984). For discussion, see Holly Sklar, "Trilateralism: Renovated for the 1980s," *NACLA Report on the Americas*, September–October 1984, pp. 12–14.

85 *Mandate for Leadership: Policy Management in a Conservative Administration*, ed. Charles L. Heatherly (Washington, D.C.: The Heritage Foundation, 1981), pp. 669–87. These proposals are from a chapter on the Treasury Department by Norman Ture, a supply-side economist who served in the Reagan administration as a Treasury Department under secretary for tax and economic affairs.

Chapter 4

1. Richard H. Ullman, "Trilateralism: 'Partnership' for What?" *Foreign Affairs*, October 1976, p. 11.

2. Quoted in Fred Halliday, *The Making of the Second Cold War* (London: Verso, 1983), p. 15.

3. *Vital Speeches of the Day*, 15 June 1977, pp. 354–56.

4. *New York Times*, 24 January 1980, p. A-12.

5. Michel J. Crozier, Samuel P. Huntington, and Joji Watanuki, *The Crisis of Democracy: Report on the Governability of Democracies to the Trilateral Commission* (New York: New York University Press, 1975), p. 92.

6. Jerry W. Sanders, *Empire at Bay: Containment Strategies and American Politics at the Crossroads* (New York: World Policy Institute, 1983), p. 3.

7. For an analysis of how the Vietnam War opened up divisions among national security managers, see Paul Joseph, *Cracks in the Empire: State Politics in the Vietnam War* (Boston: South End Press, 1981).

8. Sanders, *Empire at Bay*, p. 1. See also Sanders' *Peddlers of Crisis: The Committee on the Present Danger and the Politics of Containment* (Boston: South End Press, 1983).

9. In *The Making of the Second Cold War*, Halliday discusses the specific role of the nuclear arms race in the East–West relationship and in international politics generally.

10. Kermit Gordon, "Foreword," in *The Next Phase in Foreign Policy*, ed. Henry Owen (Washington, D.C.: The Brookings Institution, 1973), p. vii.

11. Henry Owen, "Introduction," in ibid., p. 3.

NOTES TO CHAPTER 4

12   Ibid., p. 1.

13   Ibid., p. 8.

14   Seyom Brown, *New Forces in World Politics* (Washington, D.C.: The Brookings Institution, 1974), pp. 3, 2.

15   Henry Owen, "Conclusions," *The Next Phase in Foreign Policy*, p. 330.

16   The term "creative pluralism" is used by Peter T. Knight and John N. Plank, "U.S. Policy Toward Latin America," in *The Next Phase in Foreign Policy*, p. 108.

17   *Toward Peace in the Middle East* (Washington, D.C.: The Brookings Institution, 1975). Brzezinski was a co-author.

18   Ibid., p. 6.

19   Brown, *New Forces in World Politics*, pp. 186–90.

20   Zbigniew Brzezinski, "U.S.–Soviet Relations," in *The Next Phase in Foreign Policy*, p. 131.

21   Brown, *New Forces in World Politics*, p. 7.

22   For analysis of Nixon's and Kissinger's foreign policy, see Halliday, *The Making of the Second Cold War*, pp. 204–14; Sanders, *Peddlers of Crisis*, chap. 5; Bruce Cumings, "Chinatown: Foreign Policy and Elite Realignment," in *The Hidden Election: Politics and Economics in the 1980 Presidential Campaign*, ed. Thomas Ferguson and Joel Rogers (New York: Pantheon Books, 1981), pp. 196–231.

23   Halliday, *The Making of the Second Cold War*, p. 207.

24   Zbigniew Brzezinski, "U.S. Foreign Policy: The Search for Focus," *Foreign Affairs*, July 1973, pp. 708–27.

25 See Sanders, *Peddlers of Crisis*, chaps. 5 and 6, for a detailed account of this resurgence of Cold War liberalism.

26 Robert J. Pranger, ed., *Détente and Defense* (Washington, D.C.: American Enterprise Institute, 1976); *Defending America: Toward a New Role in the Post-Détente World* (New York: Basic Books, 1977), edited and co-published by the ICS.

27 Sanders, *Peddlers of Crisis*, p. 152.

28 Brzezinski, "U.S. Foreign Policy: The Search for Focus," and Stanley Hoffmann, "Choices," in *Détente and Defense*, pp. 56–75 and 75–99, respectively. Hoffmann's essay originally appeared in *Foreign Policy*, no. 12 (Fall 1973), pp. 3–35.

29 Charles Burton Marshall, "National Security: Thoughts on the Intangibles," in *Defending America*, p. 82.

30 See the essays by Draper and Grossman in ibid., and see "Détente: An Evaluation by a Group of Students of Soviet and International Affairs," in *Détente and Defense*, pp. 190–215.

31 G. Warren Nutter, "Kissinger's Grand Design," *Détente and Defense*, pp. 270–71. Nutter's essay is excerpted from a study of the same title published by the AEI in 1975.

32 Eugene V. Rostow, "The Soviet Threat to Europe Through the Middle East," in *Defending America*, pp. 63–64.

33 W. Scott Thompson, "The Projection of Soviet Power," in ibid., p. 35.

34 Paul Seabury, "Beyond Détente," in ibid., p. 240.

35 Rostow, "The Soviet Threat," pp. 60, 63.

36 Marshall, "National Security," pp. 93–94.

37 Paul H. Nitze, "Nuclear Strategy: Détente and American Survival," in *Defending America*, p. 106. This essay appeared as "Deterring Our

Deterrent," in *Foreign Policy*, no. 25 (Winter 1976–1977). A companion essay entitled "Assuring Strategic Security" is in the AEI's *Détente and Defense*, pp. 376–400 (reprinted from *Foreign Affairs*, January 1976, pp. 207–32). In these essays, Nitze drew on the research of T. K. Jones, who became a deputy undersecretary of defense under Reagan and is best known for his remark that recovery from nuclear war is possible if there are "enough shovels."

38 Alan Tonelson, "Nitze's World," *Foreign Policy*, no. 35 (Summer 1979), p. 83.

39 Ibid., p. 80.

40 For an effective critique of Nitze and the related arguments of Richard Pipes, see Fred Kaplan, *Dubious Specter: A Skeptical Look at the Soviet Nuclear Threat* (Washington, D.C.: Institute for Policy Studies, 1980).

41 For a discussion of Wohlstetter's long career as a nuclear strategist, see Fred Kaplan, *The Wizards of Armageddon* (New York: Simon & Schuster, 1983).

42 Albert Wohlstetter, "Racing Forward or Ambling Back?" in *Defending America*, p. 163.

43 Jerome H. Kahan, "Strategic Armaments," in *The Next Phase in Foreign Policy*, p. 246.

44 On these issues, see the essays by Eugene Rostow, Edward Luttwak, Robert Conquest, Walter Laqueur, and Leonard Schapiro in *Defending America*.

45 For an analysis of Third World revolutions in the 1970s, see Halliday, *The Making of the Second Cold War*, chap. 4; for the events in Angola, see esp. pp. 87–88.

46 Richard Cooper, Karl Kaiser, and Masataka Kosaka, *Towards a Renovated International System* (New York: The Trilateral Commission, 1977), pp. vii–viii.

NOTES TO CHAPTER 4

47 *Setting National Priorities: The Next Ten Years*, ed. Henry Owen and Charles L. Schultze (Washington, D.C.: The Brookings Institution, 1976), pp. 6, 5, 15.

48 Barry M. Blechman, "Toward a New Consensus in U.S. Defense Policy," in ibid., pp. 127–28.

49 Ibid., p. 63.

50 Chihiro Hosoya, Henry Owen, and Andrew Shonfield, *Collaboration with Communist Countries in Managing Global Problems* (New York: The Trilateral Commission, 1977).

51 Jeremy R. Azrael, Richard Lowenthal, and Tohru Nakagawa, *An Overview of East–West Relations* (New York: The Trilateral Commission, 1978). For discussion, see Alan Wolfe, "The Trilateralist Straddle," *The Nation*, 31 December 1977, pp. 712–15.

52 Azrael, Lowenthal, and Nakagawa, *An Overview of East–West Relations*, p. 1.

53 Ibid., p. v.

54 Ibid., pp. 4, vi.

55 Ibid., p. viii.

56 Ibid., pp. 39–40.

57 Ibid., p. vii.

58 On Carter's foreign policy team, see Cumings, "Chinatown," pp. 206–18; John Judis, "The Carter Doctrine," *The Progressive*, March 1980, pp. 35–38.

59 On PRM-10, see Sanders, *Peddlers of Crisis*, pp. 244–47.

60 The domestic setting of foreign policy debate is covered well in ibid., while Halliday, *The Making of the Second Cold War*, analyzes the broader international context in the 1970s.

NOTES TO CHAPTER 4

61 These neoconservative themes can be found in the writings of Norman Podhoretz and others around *Commentary*.

62 Sanders, *Empire at Bay*, p. 7.

63 On the political economy of détente, see Thomas Ferguson and Joel Rogers, "The Empire Strikes Back," *The Nation*, 1 November 1980, pp. 436–40.

64 Sanders, *Peddlers of Crisis*, p. 179.

65 Quoted in Laurence H. Shoup, *The Carter Presidency and Beyond: Power and Politics in the 1980s* (Palo Alto, Calif.: Ramparts Press, 1980), p. 147.

66 Robert R. Bowie, "Outlook for the 1980s," *Trialogue*, no. 22 (Winter 1980), p. 3.

67 Brzezinski interview, *Trialogue*, no. 25 (Winter 1980–1981), pp. 17–18.

68 Data from Joe Stork, "U.S. Targets Persian Gulf for Intervention," MERIP *Reports*, no. 85 (February 1980), p. 3.

69 Quoted in Shoup, *The Carter Presidency*, p. 118.

70 Jan Austin, "U.S. Seeks New Mideast Alliance," *International Bulletin*, 12 March 1979, p. 1.

71 On the RDF, see Michael Klare, *Beyond the "Vietnam Syndrome": U.S. Interventionism in the 1980s* (Washington, D.C.: Institute for Policy Studies, 1981), chap. 5.

72 Richard Burt, "How U.S. Strategy Toward Persian Gulf Region Evolved," *New York Times*, 25 January 1980, p. A-6.

73 Quotations from Brown in this paragraph are taken from Klare, *Beyond the Vietnam Syndrome*, chap. 2.

NOTES TO CHAPTER 4

74 From a speech that Brown delivered before the Council on Foreign Relations in New York on 6 March 1980. Reprinted in MERIP Reports, no. 90 (September 1980), pp. 20–23.

75 *Setting National Priorities: Agenda for the 1980s*, ed. Joseph A. Pechman (Washington, D.C.: The Brookings Institution, 1980), p. 17.

76 Ibid., p. 18.

77 On the AEI's growth, see Peter H. Stone, "Conservative Brain Trust," *New York Times Magazine*, 10 May 1981, pp. 18 ff.

78 Sanders, *Peddlers of Crisis*, p. 218.

79 *AEI Defense Review* 2, no. 2 (1978): 44.

80 *AEI Foreign Policy and Defense Review* 1, no. 4 (1979): 53.

81 Ibid., 2, no. 2 (1980): 62.

82 Herbert Stein, "National Security and the Economy," *AEI Economist*, January 1980, p. 4.

83 Andrew J. Goodpaster and Samuel P. Huntington, *Civil–Military Relations* (Washington, D.C.: American Enterprise Institute, 1977).

84 *Grand Strategy for the 1980s*, ed. Bruce Palmer Jr. (Washington, D.C.: American Enterprise Institute, 1978); see pp. 14–16 for Taylor's proposals.

85 Jeane J. Kirkpatrick, *Dictatorships and Double Standards: Rationalism and Reason in Politics* (New York: Simon & Schuster, 1982; co-published with the AEI).

86 Jeane J. Kirkpatrick, "A Respect for History," *AEI Foreign Policy and Defense Review* 3, no. 6 (1982): 7.

87 Ibid.

NOTES TO CHAPTER 4

88 Roger W. Fontaine, in *Liberation South, Liberation North*, ed. Michael Novak (Washington, D.C.: American Enterprise Institute, 1981), p. 95.

89 Quoted in Stone, "Conservative Brain Trust."

90 H. Monroe Browne, "Preface," in *National Security in the 1980s: From Weakness to Strength*, ed. W. Scott Thompson (San Francisco: Institute for Contemporary Studies, 1980), p. x.

91 See the ICS newsletter for July–August–September 1980 for information about the media campaign.

92 W. Scott Thompson, "Introduction," in *National Security in the 1980s*, p. 4.

93 Ibid., p. 13.

94 Elmo R. Zumwalt Jr., "Heritage of Weakness: An Assessment of the 1970s," in ibid., p. 18. See Kaplan, *Dubious Specter*, for an opposing view.

95 Quoted in Halliday, *The Making of the Second Cold War*, p. 49. See the similar comments of Paul Nitze in *National Security in the 1980s*, p. 455.

96 W. Scott Thompson, "Toward a Strategic Peace," in ibid., p. 473.

97 Zumwalt, "Heritage of Weakness," p. 44; Edward N. Luttwak, "On the Meaning of Strategy," in *National Security in the 1980s*, p. 272.

98 Geoffrey T. H. Kemp, "Defense Innovation and Geo-Politics: From the Persian Gulf to Outer Space," in *National Security in the 1980s*, pp. 84, 85–86.

99 Leonard Sullivan in *National Security in the 1980s*, p. 405. See Nitze's similar comments, in ibid., pp. 458–59.

100 Thompson, "Toward a Strategic Peace," p. 482.

NOTES TO CHAPTER 4

101   *Mandate for Leadership: Policy Management in a Conservative Administration*, ed. Charles H. Heatherly (Washington, D.C.: The Heritage Foundation, 1981).

102   Jeffrey B. Gayner, "The State Department," in ibid., pp. 548–49.

103   Christopher Price, "An Outpost of the Evil Empire," *New Stateman*, 13 December 1985, pp. 17–18.

104   *Mandate for Leadership*, p. 570.

105   For an account by a supporter, see Charles Krauthammer, "The Reagan Doctrine," *Time*, 1 April 1985, pp. 54–55.

106   *Mandate for Leadership II: Continuing the Conservative Revolution*, ed. Stuart M. Butler, Michael Sanara, and W. Bruce Weinrod (Washington, D.C.: The Heritage Foundation, 1984), p. 324.

107   Richard Shultz, "Low-Intensity Conflict," in ibid., pp. 264–70. For discussion, see Michael T. Klare, "The New U.S. Strategic Doctrine," *The Nation*, 28 December 1985, pp. 697, 710–16.

108   *Beyond Containment: Alternative American Policies Toward the Soviet Union*, ed. Aaron Wildavsky (San Francisco: Institute for Contemporary Studies, 1983), p. 235.

109   James L. Payne, "Foreign Policy for an Impulsive People," in ibid., p. 217.

110   From the introduction to "The Grenada Papers," by Paul Seabury and Walter A. McDougall. See *The Letter* (ICS newsletter), Winter 1985, p. 4.

111   Patrick Glynn, "The Moral Case for the Arms Buildup," in *Nuclear Arms: Ethics, Strategy, Politics*, ed. R. James Woolsey (San Francisco: Institute for Contemporary Studies, 1984), pp. 23–51.

112   Dimitri Simes, quoted in Holly Sklar, *Reagan, Trilateralism, and the Neoliberals: Containment and Intervention in the 1980s* (Boston: South End Press, 1986), p. 12.

NOTES TO CHAPTER 5

113 See, e.g., Gerard C. Smith, Paolo Vittorelli, and Kiichi Saeki, *Trilateral Security: Defense and Arms Control Policies in the 1980s* (New York: The Trilateral Commission, 1983).

Chapter 5

1 *New York Times*, 6 February 1981, p. A-6.

2 *Setting National Priorities: The Next Ten Years*, ed. Henry Owen and Charles L. Schultze (Washington, D.C.: The Brookings Institution, 1976), p. 7.

3 Ibid., p. 1.

4 Ibid., p. 13.

5 Ibid.

6 Interview with Arthur Okun, *The Brookings Bulletin*, Summer 1975, p. 12; Arthur Okun, *Equality and Efficiency: The Big Tradeoff* (Washington, D.C.: The Brookings Institution, 1975).

7 George L. Perry, "Stabilization Policy and Inflation," in *Setting National Priorities: The Next Ten Years*, p. 272.

8 *The Brookings Bulletin*, Spring 1978, p. 3, summarizing *Curing Chronic Inflation*, ed. Arthur Okun and George Perry (Washington, D.C.: The Brookings Institution, 1978).

9 Charles L. Schultze, "Federal Spending: Past, Present, and Future," in *Setting National Priorities: The Next Ten Years*, pp. 358–59.

10 Michael Harrington, *Decade of Decision: The Crisis of the American System* (New York: Simon & Schuster, 1980), p. 99.

11 Charles L. Schultze, *The Public Use of Private Interest* (Washington, D.C.: The Brookings Institution, 1977), p. 5.

NOTES TO CHAPTER 5

12 Allen V. Kneese and Charles L. Schultze, *Pollution, Prices, and Public Policy* (Washington, D.C.: The Brookings Institution, 1975).

13 Quoted in Ernest Holsendolph, "The U.S. Drive for Deregulation," *New York Times*, 7 October 1980, p. D-1.

14 Alan Wolfe, *America's Impasse: The Rise and Fall of the Politics of Growth* (New York: Pantheon Books, 1981), p. 204.

15 *Setting National Priorities: Agenda for the 1980s*, ed. Joseph A. Pechman (Washington, D.C.: The Brookings Institution, 1980), pp. 2–5, 68–69.

16 Barry P. Bosworth, "Economic Policy," in ibid., p. 69.

17 Ibid.

18 Joseph A. Pechman, "Introduction and Summary," in ibid., p. 2.

19 Ibid., pp. 5, 69.

20 Michel J. Crozier, Samuel P. Huntington, and Joji Watanuki, *The Crisis of Democracy* (New York: New York University Press, 1975), p. 73.

21 Ibid., pp. 174–75.

22 Samuel P. Huntington, "The Governability of Democracy One Year Later," *Trialogue*, no. 10 (Spring 1976), p. 11.

23 Quoted in *Trilateralism: The Trilateral Commission and Elite Planning for World Management*, ed. Holly Sklar (Boston: South End Press, 1980), from a 1974 report, p. 323.

24 Quoted in ibid.

25 Both were co-authored by John C. Campbell, Guy de Carmoy, and Shinichi Kondo: "Energy: The Imperative for a Trilateral Approach" and "Energy: A Strategy for International Action," in *Trilateral Com-*

NOTES TO CHAPTER 5

mission Task Force Reports, 1–7 (New York: New York University Press, 1977).

26 "Energy: The Imperative for a Trilateral Approach," pp. 110–11.

27 Ibid., pp. 116, 121.

28 John C. Sawhill, Keichi Oshima, and Hanns W. Maull, "Energy: Managing the Transition," in *Trilateral Commission Task Force Reports, 15–19* (New York, New York University Press, 1981), p. 155.

29 *Trialogue*, no. 6 (Winter 1974–1975), p. 10.

30 Benjamin C. Roberts, Hideaki Okamoto, and George C. Lodge, "Collective Bargaining and Employee Participation in Western Europe, North America, and Japan," in *Task Force Reports, 15–19*, p. 226.

31 Ibid., p. 227.

32 Ibid., pp. 275–94.

33 John Pinder, Takashi Hosomi, and William Diebold, "Industrial Policy and the International Economy," in ibid., p. 319.

34 Ibid., p. 383.

35 Ibid., p. 384.

36 Leo Panitch, "Trade Unions and the Capitalist State," *New Left Review*, no. 125 (January–February 1981), p. 24.

37 The founding statement of the Initiative Committee is in *The Politics of Planning: A Review and Critique of Centralized Economic Planning* (San Francisco: Institute for Contemporary Studies, 1976). The quotation is from p. 350.

38 Paul Sweezy and Harry Magdoff, "The Economic Crisis in Historical Perspective," *Monthly Review*, April 1975, p. 9.

NOTES TO CHAPTER 5

39 Herbert Stein, *Economic Planning and the Improvement of Economic Policy* (Washington, D.C.: American Enterprise Institute, 1975).

40 Ibid., p. 19.

41 G. Warren Nutter, *Central Economic Planning: The Visible Hand* (Washington, D.C.: American Enterprise Institute, 1976).

42 A. Lawrence Chickering and J. Clayburn La Force Jr., "Preface," *No Time to Confuse* (San Francisco: Institute for Contemporary Studies, 1975), p. viii.

43 William H. Riker, "The Ideology of *A Time to Choose*," in ibid., pp. 154–55.

44 George W. Hilton, "*A Time to Choose* as Economic Thought," in ibid., p. 106.

45 Edward J. Mitchell, *U.S. Energy Policy: A Primer* (Washington, D.C.: American Enterprise Institute, 1974).

46 Melvin R. Laird, *Energy: A Crisis in Public Policy* (Washington, D.C.: American Enterprise Institute, 1977), p. 13.

47 David Vogel and Leonard Silk, *Ethics and Profits: The Crisis of Confidence in American Business* (New York: Simon & Schuster, 1976).

48 David Vogel, "Why Businessmen Distrust Their State: The Political Consciousness of American Corporate Executives," *British Journal of Political Science* 8 (January 1978): 50–51.

49 Walter Goodman, "Irving Kristol: Patron Saint of the New Right," *New York Times Magazine*, 6 December 1981, pp. 90 ff.

50 Quoted in Sidney Blumenthal, "The Ideology Makers," *Boston Globe Sunday Magazine*, 8 August 1982.

NOTES TO CHAPTER 5

51 Michael Novak, *The American Vision: An Essay on the Future of Democratic Capitalism* (Washington, D.C.: American Enterprise Institute, 1978).

52 Ibid., p. 41.

53 Ibid., pp. 55–60.

54 Irving Kristol, "A Regulated Society?" *Regulation*, July–August 1977, pp. 12–13.

55 Murray L. Weidenbaum, *Government-Mandated Price Increases: A Neglected Aspect of Inflation* (Washington, D.C.: American Enterprise Institute, 1975).

56 James C. Miller III and Bruce Yandle, *Benefit–Cost Analysis of Social Regulation* (Washington, D.C.: American Enterprise Institute, 1979).

57 Murray L. Weidenbaum, "What Is True Corporate Responsibility?" *Regulation*, May–June 1980, p. 31.

58 See the proposals for regulatory reform in a new administration in *Regulation*, November–December 1980.

59 Herbert Stein, "1977—On Borrowed Time," *AEI Economist*, January 1978, p. 3.

60 Herbert Stein, "Humphrey–Hawkins and the Nature of Unemployment," *AEI Economist*, March 1978, p. 5.

61 A. Lawrence Chickering, "Regulation: Hopes and Realities," in *Regulating Business: The Search for an Optimum* (San Francisco: Institute for Contemporary Studies, 1978), p. 226.

62 *Federal Tax Reform: Myths and Realities*, ed. Michael J. Boskin (San Francisco: Institute for Contemporary Studies, 1978).

NOTES TO CHAPTER 5

63 *The Economy in the 1980s: A Program for Growth and Stability*, ed. Michael J. Boskin (San Francisco: Institute for Contemporary Studies, 1980).

64 *The Letter* (ICS newsletter), January–February–March 1981, p. 2.

65 Ibid., July–August–September 1980, pp. 1–2.

66 Michael J. Boskin, "An Overview," in *The Economy in the 1980s*, pp. 421–25.

67 Ibid., p. 425.

68 Robert C. McIntyre and Dean C. Tipps, "Exploding the Investment-Incentive Myth," *Challenge*, May–June 1985, p. 51.

69 Edward Cowan, "Business Leaders Object to Deficits in Reagan Budget, *New York Times*, 4 March 1982, pp. A-1, D-15.

70 *Slashing the Deficit* (Washington, D.C.: The Heritage Foundation, 1984).

71 Robert Kuttner, "Revenge of the Democratic Nerds," *New Republic*, 22 October 1984, p. 16.

72 *Economic Choices 1984*, ed. Alice M. Rivlin (Washington, D.C.: The Brookings Institution, 1984).

73 Kuttner, "Revenge of the Democratic Nerds," p. 17.

74 Peter T. Kilborn, "Plan to Revive Industrial Vigor Urged in Study," *New York Times*, 12 January 1984, p. D-6.

Chapter 6

1 *Business Week*, 30 June 1980, p. 57.

2 Ibid., p. 84.

3   Ibid., p. 146.

4   Ibid., p. 57.

5   *Business Week*, 12 October 1974, p. 120.

6   Michel J. Crozier, Samuel P. Huntington. and Joji Watanuki, *The Crisis of Democracy* (New York: New York University Press, 1975), p. 97.

7   Ibid., p. 97.

8   Ibid., p. 2.

9   Ibid., p. 75.

10 Peter Steinfels, *The Neoconservatives: The Men Who Are Changing America's Politics* (New York: Simon & Schuster, 1979), pp. 262–69.

11 *The Crisis of Democracy*, p. 113.

12 Ibid., p. 7.

13 Ibid., pp. 181, 183.

14 See David Vogel, "Business's 'New Class' Struggle," *The Nation*, 15 December 1979, p. 625.

15 Graham Allison and Peter Szanton, "Organizing for the Decade Ahead," in *Setting National Priorities: The Next Ten Years*, ed. Henry Owen and Charles L. Schultze (Washington, D.C.: The Brookings Institution, 1976), p. 250.

16 Ibid., p. 259.

17 San Francisco Bay Area Kapitalistate Group, "*Setting National Priorities*: A Critical Review" *Kapitalistate*, no. 6 (Fall 1977), p. 201.

18 Henry Owen and Charles L. Schultze, "Introduction," in *Setting National Priorities: The Next Ten Years*, p. 12.

NOTES TO CHAPTER 6

19   James L. Sundquist, "Improving the Capacity to Govern," *The Brookings Bulletin*, Fall 1980, p. 1.

20   Ibid., p. 5.

21   Ibid., p. 2.

22   Ibid., p. 4.

23   Charles L. Schultze, *The Public Use of Private Interest* (Washington, D.C.: The Brookings Institution, 1977), p. 5.

24   Ibid., pp. 17–18, 13. For a critical discussion of Schultze, see William Connolly and Michael Best, "The Decline of Economic Virtue," *democracy*, January 1981, pp. 104–15.

25   Schultze, *Public Use of Private Interest*, p. 90.

26   Ibid.

27   Quoted in Leonard Silk and Mark Silk, *The American Establishment* (New York: Avon Books, 1981), p. 156.

28   This way of understanding crisis is developed in Samuel Bowles and Herbert Gintis, "The Crisis of Liberal Democratic Capitalism: The Case of the United States," *Politics and Society* 11, no. 1 (1982): 51–93.

29   I am summarizing the argument of Jürgen Habermas, *Legitimation Crisis* (Boston: Beacon Press, 1975).

30   Ibid., pp. 83–84.

31   James O'Connor, *The Fiscal Crisis of the State* (New York: St. Martin's Press, 1973).

32   Huntington, "The United States," in *The Crisis of Democracy*, p. 73.

NOTES TO CHAPTER 6

33 James O'Connor, "Accumulation Crisis: The Problem and Its Setting," *Contemporary Crises* 5, no. 2 (April 1981): 118.

34 Ibid., p. 122.

35 Steinfels, *The Neoconservatives*, pp. 53–69.

36 *Income Redistribution*, ed. Colin D. Campbell (Washington, D.C.: American Enterprise Institute, 1977), p. 62.

37 Irving Kristol, "Thoughts on Equality ard Egalitarianism," in ibid., p. 37.

38 Ibid., p. 42.

39 Robert Nisbet, "Where Do We Go from Here," in ibid., p. 181.

40 Ibid., p. 196.

41 *Commentary*, April 1978, p. 29.

42 Walter Dean Burnham, "The 1980 Earthquake: Realignment, Reaction, or What?" in *The Hidden Election: Politics and Economics in the 1980 Presidential Campaign*, ed. Thomas Ferguson and Joel Rogers (New York: Pantheon Books, 1981), p. 133.

43 Ibid., pp. 134–37.

44 Michael Novak, *Toward a Theology of the Corporation* (Washington, D.C.: American Enterprise Institute, 1981), p. 1.

45 Ibid., p. 38.

46 Ibid., pp. 5–6.

47 Irving Kristol, "The Spiritual Roots of Capitalism and Socialism," in *Capitalism and Socialism: A Theological Inquiry*, ed. Michael Novak (Washington, D.C.: American Enterprise Institute, 1979), p. 13.

NOTES TO CHAPTER 6

48 On the IRD, see Cynthia Brown, "The Right's Religious Red Alert," *The Nation*, 12 March 1983, pp. 289, 303–6.

49 Peter H. Stone, "The I.E.A.—Teaching the 'Right' Stuff," *The Nation*, 19 September 1981, pp. 231–35.

50 John S. Saloma III, *Ominous Politics: The New Conservative Labyrinth* (New York: Hill & Wang, 1984), p. 11.

51 Peter L. Berger and Richard John Neuhaus, *To Empower People: The Role of Mediating Structures in Public Policy* (Washington, D.C.: American Enterprise Institute, 1977), p. 2.

52 Richard B. Madden, "The Large Business Corporation as a Mediating Structure," in *Democracy and Mediating Structures: A Theological Inquiry*, ed. Michael Novak (Washington, D.C.: American Enterprise Institute, 1980).

53 *AEI Memorandum*, November–December 1981, p. 1.

54 Vogel, "Business's 'New Class' Struggle," p. 626.

55 Jürgen Habermas, "Modernity versus Postmodernity," *New German Critique*, no. 22 (Winter 1981), pp. 3–14.

56 Ibid., p. 8.

57 Anthony King, "The American Polity in the Late 1970s: Building Coalitions in the Sand," in *The New American Political System* (Washington, D.C.: American Enterprise Institute, 1978), pp. 390, 391.

58 Burnham, "The 1980 Earthquake," p. 102.

59 Seymour Martin Lipset, "The American Party System: Concluding Observations," in *Party Coalitions in the 1980s*, ed. Seymour Lipset (San Francisco: Institute for Contemporary Studies, 1981), p. 440.

60 *Politics and the Oval Office*, ed. Arnold J. Meltsner (San Francisco: Institute for Contemporary Studies, 1981).

NOTES TO CHAPTER 6
279

61 Robert M. Entman, "The Imperial Media," in ibid., p. 100.

62 *What's News: The Media in American Society*, ed. Elie Abel (San Francisco: Institute for Contemporary Studies, 1981).

63 Edward Jay Epstein, "The Selection of Reality," and William A. Henry III, "News as Entertainment: The Search for Dramatic Unity," in ibid.

64 Michael Jay Robinson, "A Statesman Is a Dead Politician: Candidate Images on Network News," in ibid., p. 186.

65 Robert L. Bartley, "The News Business and Business News," in ibid., p. 201.

66 H. Monroe Browne, "Preface," *Bureaucrats and Brainpower: Government Regulation of Universities* (San Francisco: Institute for Contemporary Studies, 1979), p. x.

67 Paul Seabury, "Epilogue—A Final Footnote," in ibid., p. 150.

68 For a detailed account of this trend, see David Dickson and David Noble, "By Force of Reason: The Politics of Science and Technology Policy," in *The Hidden Election*, ed. Ferguson and Rogers, pp. 260–312.

69 Thomas Sowell, "Politics and Opportunity: The Background," in *The Fairmont Papers: Black Alternatives Conference* (San Francisco: Institute for Contemporary Studies, 1981), p. 3.

70 *The Letter* (ICS Newsletter), January–February–March 1981, p. 1.

71 Tony Brown, "Politics, Power, and Horsetrading: The Broad Opportunities," in *The Fairmont Papers*, p. 131.

72 Samuel T. Francis, "The Intelligence Community," in *Mandate for Leadership: Policy Management in a Conservative Administration*, ed. Charles L. Heatherly (Washington, D.C.: The Heritage Foundation, 1981), p. 935.

73 See John Judis, "Setting the Stage for Repression," *The Progressive*, April 1981, p. 27.

74 For a summary analysis, see Chuck Collins, "A New Agenda from the New Right," *The Guardian* (New York), 13 February 1985, p. 3.

75 Bowles and Gintis, "The Crisis of Liberal Democratic Capitalism," p. 131.

76 Gabriel Kolko, "Intelligence and the Myth of Capitalist Rationality in the United States," *Science and Society*, Summer 1980, pp. 130–54.

77 Ibid., p. 134.

78 Ibid., p. 140.

79 Ibid., p. 153.

Index

Aaron, Henry, 223
Abel, Elie, 233
Abrams, Elliot, 159
Abshire, David, 30
Acheson, Dean, 121
Adelman, Kenneth, 154
Afghanistan, 108–9
AFL-CIO, 52, 66, 124. *See also* Unions
Allison, Graham, 211–12
Alpert, Irvine, 9
American Assembly, 14
American Council for Capital Formation, 65
American Enterprise Association, 28
American Enterprise Institute, 2, 5, 6, 65, 204, 219, 237, 241; and economic policy, 168, 187–89, 191–97; and foreign policy, 113, 125, 147–53; and international economics, 77, 85–86, 92, 97, 100–1; overview of, 27–31; public philosophy of, 220–30
American Security Council, 112
Anderson, John, 23, 225
Angola, 131–32, 160
Azreal, Jeremy, 136

Baker, James, 106
Balanced Growth and Economic Planning Act, 185, 187

Ball, George, 99
Barnett, Doak, 21
Baroody, William J., Jr., 29, 31
Baroody, William J., Sr., 28
Bartley, Robert, 234
Bauer, Peter, 97, 98, 159
Begin, Menachem, 119
Berger, Peter, 36, 148, 221, 227
Bergsten, C. Fred, 75, 78–79, 80, 94–95, 104, 137
Bilderberg Conference, 24, 74, 76
Black politics, 235
Blechman, Barry, 134–35
Block, Fred, 15
Bork, Robert, 30, 228
Boskin, Michael J., 35, 36, 198–99, 235
Bosworth, Barry, 173, 176
Bowie, Robert, 76, 142
Bowles, Samuel, 237
Bretton Woods system, 41–43, 72, 73, 88
Brookings, Robert S., 18–20
Brookings Institution, 2, 5, 6, 11, 12, 14, 24, 31, 35, 204; and economic policy, 168, 170–77, 201–2; and foreign policy, 112, 115–21, 133–35, 146–47, 161–62; and international economics, 73, 75, 76–77, 78–87, 87–91; overview of, 18–23; and technocratic liberalism, 211–15, 218

Brown, Harold, 143–46
Brown, Lewis H., 28
Brown, Seyom, 84, 115, 117, 121
Brown, Tony, 235
Browne, H. Monroe, 34, 35
Bryant, Ralph, 91
Brzezinski, Zbigniew, 26, 100, 115; foreign policy views of, 120, 123, 126, 137, 144; and formation of Trilateral Commission, 24, 74, 75, 76
Burch, Philip, 8, 28
Burnham, Walter Dean, 225, 231
Burns, Arthur, 30, 192
Burt, Richard, 154
Bush, George, 23, 30, 61, 148
Business: inner circle of, 66; political challenge to, 59; political mobilization of, 64–67, 238; resistance to planning, 189–91
Business Council, 4, 8, 12, 13, 52, 58, 74
Business Roundtable, 4, 9, 11, 13, 29, 64, 169, 193, 201
Business Week: on reindustrialization, 205–7
Butcher, Willard, C., 28, 29

Calkins, Robert, 21
Capitalism: expansion of, 70; institutional structure of, 50; and labor unions, 57; and liberal democracy, 39, 216–18, 237, 241; postwar ideology of, 54–55; reproduction of, 9; and social integration, 217–20
Carnegie Corporation, 19
Carnegie Endowment for International Peace, 6, 19, 112
Carter administration, 6, 22, 77–78, 80, 212; and economic policy, 171, 173, 175–76; and energy policy, 181; and foreign policy, 107–9, 110, 116, 132–47; 151–52, 155; and Trilateral Commission, 26, 80
Center for Strategic and International Studies, 6, 36, 113
Center for the Study of American Business, 65
Central Intelligence Agency (CIA), 61–62
Chamber of Commerce, 28, 64, 201
Chickering, A. Lawrence, 34
Citizens for Tax Justice, 200
Clifford, Clark, 147
Coalition for a Democratic Majority, 124, 148, 226
Colby, William, 147
Collins, Robert, 13
Commentary, 97, 113, 125, 151, 159, 192, 221, 265n.
Committee for East-West Accord, 140
Committee for Economic Development, 4, 8, 11, 12, 13, 52, 74
Committee for the Free World, 34, 113, 226
Committee for a Union-Free Environment, 65
Committee on the Present Danger, 6, 17, 60–62, 112, 124, 126, 137, 139, 191
Conable, Barber B., Jr., 27
Conference Board, 4, 12, 14
Conservatism: neoconservatism, 1, 30, 34, 37, 53, 230; of the New Right, 3, 32, 34, 112, 139, 236; and policy shift of elites, 2, 16, 168–69, 176, 187
Cooper, Richard, 75, 88, 92
Coors, Joseph, 32, 34
Corporate liberalism, 13–16
Corporatism, 184
Council of Economic Advisers, 55
Council on Foreign Relations, 21–

22, 44, 58, 69, 74; as key policy group, 4, 8, 11, 24, 85; and U. S. foreign policy, 12–13, 42, 112, 142, 162
Cox, Arthur Macy, 61
Cox, Robert W., 83–84
Cuddington, John T., 93

Decter, Midge, 34, 113, 124
Democracy: and capitalism, 224; Huntington on, 207–10; and policy elites, 241
Dillon, Douglas, 22
Domhoff, G. William, 9, 11–13, 15, 16
Draper, Theodore, 126
Dulles, John Foster, 121
Dye, Thomas, 7, 9–11, 15, 16

Eakins, David, 12, 13
Easterbrook, Gregg, 6
Economist (AEI), 30, 149, 195
Economy, U. S.: as capitalist democracy, 40; crisis of, 1, 4, 39, 55, 166–67, 203; growth of, 49, 54; institutional structure of, 50, 169, 204; international dimensions of, 41–42, 70–72; linkage to foreign policy, 165–66; role of state in, 50–51, 167, 217–18
Education, 234–35
Eliot, Charles W., 19
Elites: divisions among, 5, 10, 16–18, 58, 238; and foreign policy conflicts, 109–14; mobilization of, 60–67
Encounter, 125
Energy politics, 53–54, 98–102, 180–81, 188–89
Entman, Robert M., 233
Environmental Protection Agency, 53, 194
Epstein, Edward Jay, 233

Erb, Richard, 100–1
Establishment: Burch on, 8; Huntington on, 208; Silk and Silk on, 8
Ethics and Public Policy Center, 159
European Economic Community, 43, 46, 47

Fein, Bruce, 30
Feldstein, Martin, 65
Ferguson, Thomas, 62–63, 140
Feulner, Edwin, Jr., 32
Fontaine, Roger, 27, 152
Ford, Gerald, 29, 61, 123, 148, 168, 192
Ford, Henry, II, 185
Ford Foundation, 21, 35, 58, 188
Foreign Affairs, 44, 69, 75, 112, 130
Foreign Policy, 6, 75, 94, 112, 129, 130, 137
Foreign Policy: of establishment, 111–14, 162; of managerialists and militarists, 112; and Traders and Prussians, 16–17, 112; military/strategic aspects of, 44–45
Foreign Policy and Defense Review (AEI), 30, 148, 149
Frankfurter, Felix, 19
Franklin, George, 76
Fried, Edward, 91
Frieden, Jeff, 83, 84–85
Friedman, Milton, 235

Gardner, Richard, 75
Gelb, Leslie, 115, 137
General Agreement on Tariffs and Trade (GATT), 43, 47, 90, 91
German Marshall Fund, 104
Gintis, Herbert, 237
Glazer, Nathan, 148, 221
Glynn, Patrick, 161
Goldwater, Barry, 28, 123, 147
Goodpaster, General Andrew J., 150
Gordon, Kermit, 21, 115, 168

Government, U. S.: fragmented power of, 56–57, 59; legitimacy problems of, 205, 208–10; spending patterns of, 50–51
Grace Commission, 201
Gramsci, Antonio, 14–15, 229
Greenberg, Edward S., 40
Grenada, invasion of, 160–61
Grossman, Gregory, 126

Haberler, Gottfried, 92
Habermas, Jürgen, 216–20, 230
Habib, Philip, 27
Hall, Robert, 36
Harriman, Mrs. E. H., 19
Hatfield, Robert, 28
Haynes, H. J., 28
Henry, William A., III, 233
Heritage Foundation, 2, 3, 5, 30, 36, 63, 65; and domestic politics, 230, 235–37; and economic policy, 167, 199–201; and foreign policy, 113, 158–60; and international economics, 73, 77, 105; overview of, 31–34
Hodgson, Godfrey, 54
Hoffmann, Stanley, 126
Holbrooke, Richard, 137
Hoover, Herbert, 19
Hoover Institution, 5, 30, 36, 65, 113, 153
Hosoya, Chihiro, 135
Humphrey, Hubert, 124, 185
Humphrey-Hawkins Bill, 174, 185
Huntington, Samuel P., 111, 150, 190, 212; on governability and democracy, 207–10, 219, 241

Ikle, Fred, 154
Industrial policy, 183–84, 202; and reindustrialization, 205–7
Initiative Committee for National Economic Planning, 185

Institute for Contemporary Studies, 2, 3, 5, 6; and domestic politics, 204, 220, 231–35, 237; and economic policy, 167, 186–91, 197–99; and foreign policy, 113, 125, 130, 131, 153–58, 160–61; and international economics, 73, 77, 85–87, 93, 96–97; overview of, 34–37
Institute for Educational Affairs, 227
Institute for Government Research, 19, 20
Institute for International Economics, 103–4
Institute for Policy Studies, 5, 236
Institute of Economics, 19–20
Institute on Religion and Democracy, 153, 226–27
International Bank for Reconstruction and Development (World Bank), 13, 42, 81, 91, 97, 105, 106
International Monetary Fund, 12–13, 42, 47, 81, 89, 91, 105
Iran, 102, 108–9, 128, 143–44

Jackson, Henry M., 124, 126, 159
Javits, Jacob, 185
Jones, Reginald, 29
Jones, T. K., 263n.
Jones, Vincent W., 35
Johnson, D. Gale, 30
Joseph, Paul, 17–18
Journal of Contemporary Studies, 36

Kahan, Jerome, 131
Kahn, Alfred E., 175
Kampelman, Max, 124
Kemp, Geoffrey, 154, 157
Kemp, Jack, 147
Kennan, George F., 44
Kennedy, John F., 54

INDEX

Keohane, Robert O., 78–79
Keynes, John Maynard, 42
Keynesianism, 51, 168, 178, 186; and Brookings Institution, 170–77, 211
Keyserling, Leon, 124
King, Anthony, 231
Kirby, R. E., 147
Kirkland, Lane, 202
Kirkpatrick, Jeane, 27, 113, 124, 148, 221; on Carter and Reagan, 151–52
Kissinger, Henry, 74, 99, 118, 121, 123, 129
Klare, Michael T., 16–17, 112
Kneese, Allen, 175
Kolko, Gabriel, 45, 239–40
Korb, Lawrence, 27, 149–50
Krause, Lawrence, 91
Kristol, Irving, 29, 30, 63, 148, 192, 194, 198, 226, 227; on equality, 222–23
Kuttner, Robert, 201–2

Laffer Curve, 192
Laird, Melvin, 147, 148, 189
Lake, Anthony, 137
Lane, Chuck, 63
Lawrence, Robert Z., 201–2
Laxalt, Paul, 30
Lefever, Ernest, 159
Leffler, Melvyn P., 44–45
Lehrman, Lewis, 32, 34
Leontief, Wassily, 185
Lindblom, Charles, 11
Lipset, Seymour Martin, 36, 148, 221, 232
Lord, Winston, 142
Lowenthal, Richard, 136
Luce, Henry, 46
Luttwak, Edward, 36, 154, 157

McCracken, Paul, 29, 30, 31, 168, 192

McGovern, George, 124
McKinnon, Ronald I., 93
MacLaury, Bruce, 20–21
McNamara, Robert, 97, 104
McQuaid, Kim, 13
Madden, Richard B., 228
Madison, James, 208
Magdoff, Harry, 71, 186
Mandate for Leadership (Heritage Foundation), 32, 153, 158, 199–200, 236
Manhattan Institute, 63
Markusen, Ann, 9
Marshall, Charles Burton, 126, 127, 154
Marshall Plan, 44
Media, 233–34
Meese, Edwin, 32, 34–35, 235
Meltsner, Arnold, 36, 232–33
Military Spending, 45–46, 51, 61–62, 109, 146–47, 149–50, 173
Miller, James C., 27, 192, 194
Minter, William, 12
Mobil Corporation, 65
Mondale, Walter F., 22, 69–70, 106, 201
Monetary Policy (international), 41, 43, 46–47, 87–94
Moorer, Admiral Thomas, 147
Moose, Richard, 137
Moulton, Harold G., 19, 20, 21
Moynihan, Daniel Patrick, 96
Murphy, Thomas, 29, 147
Murray, Charles, 63

Nader, Ralph, 29
Nakagawa, Tohru, 136
National Association of Manufacturers, 201
National Bureau of Economic Research, 14, 65
National Civic Federation, 12, 16, 186

National Conference of Catholic Bishops, 225
National Interest, 113
National Labor Relations Act, 65
National Labor Relations Board, 234
National Planning Association, 14
National Review, 113
National Strategy Information Center, 112
Neuhaus, Richard, 226–27
New Class, 193, 194, 219, 222, 226, 229, 230
New International Economic Order (NIEO), 83, 95, 96, 98
New Republic, 113
Nisbet, Robert, 30, 221, 223–24
Niskanen, William, 192
Nitze, Paul, 61, 125, 126, 139, 147, 154; on nuclear strategy, 129–30
Nixon administration, 1, 73–74, 166, 168; foreign policy of, 115, 121–23; international economic policy of, 25, 47, 75, 82, 88
Noble Foundation, 32
North-South economic relations, 17, 81, 94–98, 103, 106
Novak, Michael, 27, 148, 192, 221, 227, 228; on capitalism and democracy, 193–94, 225–26; on foreign policy, 151, 152–53
NSC-68, 46, 129
Nuclear Weapons, 48, 61, 62–63, 122, 128–31, 142, 155–57, 161
Nutter, G. Warren, 127, 187
Nye, Joseph S., 78–79

Occupational Safety and Health Administration, 53, 194, 234
O'Connor, James, 179, 216, 219–20
Okun, Arthur, 21, 168, 170, 172, 215, 223
Olin Foundation, John M., 32, 35, 63

Olsen, Leif, 35
Organization of Petroleum Exporting Countries (OPEC), 41, 69, 88, 89, 95, 98–102, 118
Overseas Development Council, 104
Owen, Henry, 21, 22, 76, 212; on foreign policy, 115–17, 133–34, 135

Packard, David, 28, 30
Palestine Liberation Organization, 119
Panitch, Leo, 184
Penner, Rudolph, 27, 30, 192, 195
Perle, Richard, 156
Perry, George, 21, 173
Persian Gulf, 99, 102, 143–45, 156
Pew Freedom Trust, J. Howard, 32
Pipes, Richard, 61, 124
Podhoretz, Norman, 124, 198, 265n.
Policy currents, 7, 17–18
Policy formation process, 10–11, 39, 66
Policy regime, 40
Policy Review, 33, 158, 159, 235
Policy-planning organizations: perspectives on, 7–13; relation to capitalism, 9, 216; role of, 2, 3, 14, 239
Political Action Committees (PACs), 64–65
Political parties, 52, 57, 124, 212–13, 231
Pranger, Robert J., 125, 153
Presidential Directive 59, 142
Progressive era, 14, 20, 55, 186
Protectionism, 90
Public Interest, 192, 221
Public Opinion, 30
Public-interest groups, 59

Rapid Deployment Force, 144
Reader's Digest, 192

INDEX

287

Reader's Digest Association, 32
Reagan administration: and American Enterprise Institute, 27; domestic policies of, 166, 200–2, 236; foreign policies of, 107, 157, 159–62; and Heritage Foundation, 31–34; and Institute for Contemporary Studies, 34–37; international economic policies of, 86, 105–6; links to policy network, 5–6; and Trilateral Commission, 26–27
Regulation, 30, 194
Religion, 225–27
Rivlin, Alice, 195
Robinson, Michael Jay, 233
Roche, John P., 124
Rockefeller, David, 8, 23–24, 74, 76, 83
Rockefeller Foundation, 19
Rockwell, W. F., Jr., 28
Rogers, Joel, 62–63, 140
Rohatyn, Felix, 185, 202
Roosa, Robert, 22
Root, Elihu, 19
Rostow, Eugene V., 124, 125–26, 127, 131, 139
Rumsfeld, Donald H., 35

Sadat, Anwar, 119
Sanders, Jerry, 111–12
Saudi Arabia, 100–1
Scaife, Richard Mellon, 32
Scaife Foundation, 35, 63
Scalia, Antonin, 30, 228
Scammon, Richard, 221
Schlesinger, James, 126, 137
Schultze, Charles, 22, 133–34, 168, 170, 194, 202, 212; on markets and public policy, 173–75, 213–15
Seabury, Paul, 36, 128, 234

Seignious, Lieutenant General George, 147
Shakespeare, Frank, 34
Shapiro, Irving, 202
Shepard, Mark, Jr., 28
Shonfield, Andrew, 135, 182
Shoup, Laurence H., 12
Shulman, Marshall, 137
Silk, Leonard, 8–9, 14, 189–90
Silk, Mark, 8–9, 14
Simon, William, 34, 168, 192, 195, 227
Skocpol, Theda, 15
Smith Richardson Foundation, 35
Sowell, Thomas, 235
Star Wars (Strategic Defense Initiative), 33, 157, 161
Stein, Herbert, 30, 31, 92, 149–50, 168, 187, 192, 195, 196
Steiner, Gilbert, 21
Steinfels, Peter, 209, 221–22
Sullivan, Leonard, 158
Sundquist, James, 212–13
Survey, 125, 127
Sweeney, Richard, 101
Sweezy, Paul, 71, 186
Synthetic Fuels Corporation, 181
Szanton, Peter, 211–12

Taft, William Howard, 18–19
Tax policy, 50, 66, 198–99
Taylor, General Maxwell, 150–51
Team-B Report, 61–62, 139
Thompson, W. Scott, 96, 128, 154, 155, 156
Tonelson, Alan, 129
Trade policy, 43–44, 47–48, 87–94, 103
Trezise, Philip, 75, 87, 91
Trilateral Commission, 2, 3, 5, 6, 9, 17, 22, 30, 43, 44, 48, 204, 218, 219; and crisis of democracy, 207–10; and economic policies,

INDEX

Trilateral Commission (cont.)
167, 177–84; and foreign policy, 107, 120, 123, 132–47, 162; and international economy, 72, 73–76, 78–87, 87–91, 94–96, 98–100, 102; overview of, 23–27
Truman, Harry S., 208
Ture, Norman, 27, 192, 259n.
Twentieth Century Fund, 14

Ullman, Richard, 107, 139
Unions, 52, 90; and politics, 57–58, 64–65; in Trilateralist view, 182–83
United Nations, 13, 96, 100, 159

Van Cleave, William, 154
Vance, Cyrus, 137, 138
Vietnam syndrome, 128, 151
Vietnam War, 1, 41, 46, 121–22
Vogel, David, 189–90, 229
Volcker, Paul, 201

Walker, Charls E., 65
Wall Street Journal, 192, 195
Wanniski, Jude, 192

War Industries Board, 19
Warnke, Paul, 137, 138, 139, 147
Wattenberg, Ben, 30, 148, 193, 221, 227
Weidenbaum, Murray, 27, 30, 65, 192, 194–95
Weinberger, Casper, 35
Weinstein, James, 12, 13
Weisskopf, Thomas, 71
Weyrich, Paul, 32
Whitman, Marina v. N., 92
Wildavsky, Aaron, 36, 160
Willett, Thomas D., 97–98
Wilson, James Q., 30, 221
Wohlstetter, Albert, 130–31, 154
Wolfe, Alan, 175
Woodcock, Leonard, 185
Wriston, Walter, 28, 29

Yamey, Basil, 97, 98
Young, Andrew, 137, 138

Zeckhauser, Richard, 36
Zumwalt, Admiral Elmo, 154, 155, 157